THE NEW GROVE
HAYDN

THE NEW GROVE
DICTIONARY OF MUSIC AND MUSICIANS
Editor: Stanley Sadie

The Composer Biography Series

BACH FAMILY
HANDEL
HAYDN
MOZART
SCHUBERT

THE NEW GROVE

HAYDN

Jens Peter Larsen

WORK-LIST
Georg Feder

W. W. NORTON & COMPANY

NEW YORK   LONDON

First published in
The New Grove Dictionary of Music and Musicians,
edited by Stanley Sadie, 1980

First American Edition 1983

ISBN 0-393-01681-1

Printed in Hong Kong

Contents

List of illustrations

GENERAL ABBREVIATIONS

A	alto, contralto [voice]	obbl	obbligato
acc.	accompaniment	orch	orchestra
add, addl	additional	orchd	orchestrated
add, addn	addition	org	organ
ant	antiphon	ov.	overture
arr.	arrangement	perf.	performance
aut.	autumn	pr.	printed
B	bass [voice]	pubd	published
b	bass [instrument]	pubn	publication
bc	basso continuo	qnt	quintet
bn	bassoon		
cl	clarinet	R	photographic reprint
conc.	concerto	r	recto
cont	continuo	rec	recorder
db	double bass	recit	recitative
edn.	edition	repr.	reprinted
		rev.	revision
f, ff.	folio(s)	S	soprano [voice]
facs.	facsimile	str	string(s)
fl	flute	sym.	symphony
frag.	fragment	T	tenor [voice]
gui	guitar	timp	timpani
hn	horn	tpt	trumpet
hpd	harpsichord	tr	treble [instrument]
inc.	incomplete	transcr.	transcription
inst	instrument	U.	University
Jb	Jahrbuch [yearbook]	v, vv	voice(s)
kbd	keyboard	v., vv.	verse(s)
lib	libretto	v	verso
		va	viola
movt	movement	vc	cello
ob	oboe	vn	violin

BIBLIOGRAPHICAL ABBREVIATIONS

AcM	*Acta musicologica*
AMw	*Archiv für Musikwissenschaft*
AMz	*Allgemeine Musik-Zeitung*
AnM	*Anuario musical*
AnMc	*Analecta musicologica*
BMw	*Beiträge zur Musikwissenschaft*
BSIM	*Bulletin français de la Société Internationale de Musique*
FAM	*Fontes artis musicae*
GerberNL	R. Gerber: *Neues historisch-biographisches Lexikon der Tonkünstler*
GfMKB	*Gesellschaft für Musikforschung Kongressbericht*
IMSCR	*International Musicological Society Congress Report*
JAMS	*Journal of the American Musicological Society*
JbMP	*Jahrbuch der Musikbibliothek Peters*
Mf	*Die Musikforschung*
MJb	*Mozart-Jahrbuch des Zentralinstituts für Mozartforschung*
ML	*Music and Letters*
MMR	*The Monthly Musical Record*
MQ	*The Musical Quarterly*
MR	*The Music Review*
MT	*The Musical Times*
NBJb	*Neues Beethoven-Jahrbuch*
NOHM	*The New Oxford History of Music*
NRMI	*Nuova rivista musicale italiana*
ÖMz	*Österreichische Musikzeitschrift*
PRMA	*Proceedings of the Royal Musical Association*
RBM	*Revue belge de musicologie*
RdM	*Revue de musicologie*
ReM	*La revue musicale*
RISM	*Répertoire international des sources musicales*
SIMG	*Sammelbände der Internationalen Musik-Gesellschaft*
SMw	*Studien zur Musikwissenschaft*
SovM	*Sovetskaya muzïka*
ZfM	*Zeitschrift für Musik*
ZIMG	*Zeitschrift der Internationalen Musik-Gesellschaft*
ZMw	*Zeitschrift für Musikwissenschaft*

Preface

This volume is one of a series of short biographies derived from *The New Grove Dictionary of Music and Musicians* (London, 1980). In its original form, the text was written in the mid-1970s, and finalized at the end of that decade. For this reprint, the text has been re-read and modified by the original author and corrections and changes have been made. In particular, an effort has been made to bring the bibliography up to date and to incorporate the findings of recent research.

The fact that the texts of the books in this series originated as dictionary articles inevitably gives them a character somewhat different from that of books conceived as such. They are designed, first of all, to accommodate a very great deal of information in a manner that makes reference quick and easy. Their first concern is with fact rather than opinion, and this leads to a larger than usual proportion of the texts being devoted to biography than to critical discussion. The nature of a reference work gives it a particular obligation to convey received knowledge and to treat of composers' lives and works in an encyclopedic fashion, with proper acknowledgement of sources and due care to reflect different standpoints, rather than to embody imaginative or speculative writing about a composer's character or his music. It is hoped that the comprehensive work-lists and extended bibliographies, indicative of the origins of the books in a reference work, will be valuable to the reader who is eager for full and accurate reference information and who may not have ready access to *The New Grove Dictionary* or who may prefer to have it in this more compact form.

S.S.

We are grateful to the following for permission to reproduce illustrative material: Hessiche Landes- und Hochschulbibliothek, Darmstadt (fig.1); Burgenländisches Landesmuseum, Eisenstadt/ photo Forstner (fig.2); Jens Peter Larsen: from J. P. Larsen, *Drei Haydn Kataloge* (Copenhagen, 1941) (fig.3); Gesellschaft der Musikfreunde, Vienna (figs.5, 12); Österreichische Nationalbibliothek, Vienna (fig.6); British Library, London, and the Royal Philharmonic Society (fig.8); British Library, London (fig.9); Historisches Museum der Stadt Wien (figs.10, 11, 13); Staatsbibliothek Preussischer Kulturbesitz, Musikabteilung, Berlin (fig.14).

Cover: Engraving of Haydn (*c*.1792) by Luigi Schiavonetti after portrait by Ludwig Guttenbrunn

1. Early life

(i) BACKGROUND AND CHILDHOOD. Franz Joseph Haydn was born on 31 March 1732 at Rohrau, Lower Austria, a corner of the Habsburg Empire with a population of mixed ancestry – Austrian, Hungarian, Moravian, Slovak and Croatian – and attempts have been made to show him to have been variously a Czech, a Croat, a Hungarian or a gypsy. One theory in particular that received much attention was launched by Franz Kuhač in 1880 and taken up by W. H. Hadow in *A Croatian Composer* (1897), based principally on Haydn's use of Croatian folk melodies. But the matter must be regarded as settled by E. F. Schmid (1934). It may well be said that Schmid 'was even more intent to prove Haydn a German than Kuhač and Hadow had been to prove him a Slav' (Scott, *Grove 5*). But the weight of the documentary evidence that supports his case is decisive.

Haydn's great-grandfather, Kaspar Haydn, came from the village of Tadten (now Tétény, Hungary) and in about 1650 settled in Hainburg on the Danube, a few miles from Rohrau, where Haydn was to be born. His son Thomas, Haydn's grandfather, became a master wheelwright. and four of Thomas's sons took up that trade, among them Haydn's father, Mathias (*b* 31 Jan 1699; *d* 12 Sept 1763). After some years as a journeyman Mathias had settled in Rohrau by 1727. The following year he married Anna Maria Koller (*b* 10 Nov 1707; *d* 23 Feb 1754). Of their 12 children Joseph was the second, Michael – also to become a composer – was the sixth, and Johann Evangelist (*b* 23 Dec 1743; *d* 16

May 1805), a singer who in his later years was supported by Haydn, was the 11th. After the death of his
first wife Mathias Haydn remarried and had five more
children, all of whom died in childhood.

Haydn grew up in a modest home in a quiet and sober
atmosphere. His mother 'was accustomed to neatness,
industry and order, which qualities she sternly required
of her children from their tenderest years' (Dies;
Griesinger and Dies are mainly quoted in the translation
of Gotwals, 1963). His father's love of music is attested
by the accounts of Haydn's childhood (Dies):

In his youth . . . [Mathias] learnt to play the harp a little and, because he
liked to sing, to accompany himself on the harp as well as he could.
Afterwards, when he was married, he kept the habit of singing a little to
amuse himself. All the children had to join in his concerts, to learn the
songs, and to develop their singing voice.

These family concerts may have had a decisive influence
on the course of Haydn's life. Apparently there was
some ambition on the parents' part for their eldest son
to take holy orders, but (as Dies has it):

this did not come about, thanks not a little to his concerts among the
neighbours, by which he had won for himself a reputation in the whole
town and even with the schoolmaster. And thus when the talk was of
singing, all were unanimous in praise of the cartwright's son and could
not commend enough his fine voice.

Griesinger, however, reported that the decision to send
him away for a musical education was taken because
that 'would unfailingly open to him the prospect "of
becoming a clergyman" '. In any event he was sent to
school in Hainburg 'in his sixth year' (Griesinger) or
when he 'had passed the age of six' (Dies), presumably
in the spring term of 1738.

The schoolmaster in Hainburg who was to care for
the boy, Johann Mathias Franck, was distantly related to
the Haydn family by marriage. In the Franck household

Haydn sometimes received 'more thrashings than food', but he 'learnt to know all the usual instruments and to play several suitable to his age. His pleasant voice was a great recommendation for him. He was praised for his studious diligence'. It was as a choirboy that he received his most intensive musical training, and it was again his fine singing that opened the next door for him. Georg Reutter the younger, who had succeeded his father in 1738 as Kapellmeister at St Stephen's Cathedral, Vienna, was on a journey 'to find boys with good voices and ability to serve as choirboys' (Dies), and paid a visit to his friend the parish priest of Hainburg; 'the priest immediately thought of Joseph and praised his voice and his other musical abilities'. The boy was introduced and, having proved himself quick to learn, was accepted, with his father's consent, by Reutter for the cathedral choir. Reports disagree as to precisely when he moved to Vienna. In his autobiographical letter of 1776 Haydn said: '[Reutter] forthwith took me to the choir house'; according to Griesinger 'the departure from Hainburg soon followed'; Dies has a fuller and slightly different account:

Reutter gave the father the comforting promise that he would care for the boy's progress, but that he was still too young for this. He must wait until the end of his eighth year. Until then he must diligently sing the scales to cultivate a pure, firm and flexible voice.

(ii) CHOIRBOY AND FREELANCE. It seems, then, that Haydn went to Vienna about April or May 1740, having reached the age of eight on 31 March of that year. He was to remain there for 20 years, while he developed from a talented choirboy with a charming voice to a young musician and composer who had to fight his own way with little support or protection until he finally succeeded in finding a Kapellmeister's position. These

Vienna years fall into two periods each of roughly ten years, the first when he was a chorister at the cathedral and the second when he was a young freelance musician. But during the whole of this time his life centred on the performance of music, in church, at court, privately, and in all manner of entertainments. A few surviving compositions point back to these early years.

For generations the court at Vienna, the capital of a great empire, had been the centre of an important musical tradition. A series of distinguished Italian composers had worked there, and some of the emperors had been talented composers. Music had flourished at the court of Charles VI, with the Austrian J. J. Fux and the Italian Antonio Caldara as two fine representatives of the late Baroque, but that tradition came to an end just as Haydn came to Vienna. Caldara died in 1736, Fux in 1741 and Charles VI himself in 1740. His successor, Maria Theresia, faced with foreign pressure and financial stringency at home, had to reduce substantially the court's budget for music, and at the same time the successors of Fux and Caldara were musicians of lesser stature. Above all, the grand style of the Baroque was left behind. Music in the Vienna that Haydn went to in 1740 was changing, affected more by transition than tradition. In this period of decline Reutter established himself in a leading role, adding to his post as Kapellmeister of St Stephen's that of second and later first court Kapellmeister.

The choirboys boarded in the Kapellmeister's house, and Reutter received a fixed sum for their maintenance. Their education and well-being were largely his responsibility. How well Haydn was taught in the choir school is not easy to estimate. In his short autobiography he says that besides general subjects he learnt 'the art of singing, the keyboard and the violin, from very good masters'. Griesinger adds further details:

Besides the scant instruction usual at the time in Latin, in religion, in arithmetic and writing, Haydn had in the choir school very capable instructors on several instruments, and especially in singing. Among the latter were [Adam] Gegenbauer, a member of the court chorus, and an elegant tenor, [Ignaz] Finsterbusch. No instruction in music theory was undertaken in the choir school, and Haydn remembered receiving only two lessons in this from the excellent Reutter. But Reutter did encourage him to make whatever variations he liked on the motets and *Salves* that he had to sing in the church, and this practice soon led him to ideas of his own which Reutter corrected.

Dies gives a different picture:

As soon as Joseph in his newly achieved status had received as much instruction as he needed to fulfil the duties of choirboy, the instruction came to a complete standstill, due perhaps to the very pressing affairs of the Kapellmeister. . . . He did learn a little Latin. Everything else went by the board, and one might venture to say that he lost ten of the youthful years best suited for study.

It is clear that the teaching in the choir school concentrated on preparing the boys for their specific task of singing in church: the training of their voices had to come first. But apparently the young Haydn also received sufficient additional instruction to enable him, when he had to leave the choir school, to earn a modest living by giving keyboard lessons and playing the organ and violin in church services. No doubt he had little tuition in music theory or composition. As he himself once remarked, he probably learnt more from hearing music than from study.

Various stories about Haydn's life in the choir school portray him as a lively boy with a natural bent for humour and practical joking. His brother Michael, five years younger than himself, was admitted to the choir probably in 1745, and eventually took over Joseph's position as a soloist. With his voice beginning to break, Haydn's usefulness as a singer was coming to an end,

and tradition has it that Reutter used a boyish prank as a
pretext for his abrupt dismissal. Pohl is surprisingly
precise as to when this happened: 'on a humid
November evening in the year 1749'; but he cites no
authority, and again the old chronicles disagree. Griesinger says that 'Haydn was dismissed from the choir
school in his 16th year', but Haydn's autobiographical
letter says that 'until [his] 18th year' he sang 'with great
success, not only at St Stephen's but also at the court',
and adds that he had to 'eke out a wretched existence'
after that by teaching for 'fully eight years'. If this report
– the earliest of all – is correct, then Pohl was not far
wrong: Haydn may have left the choir school in 1749 or
early 1750.

According to Dies, Haydn's parents again tried to
persuade him to dedicate himself to the priesthood, 'but
Haydn remained unshakable in his purpose', though he
could expect no financial support from home. He found
a 'miserable little attic room without a stove'
(Griesinger) in the so-called Michaelerhaus (still standing, next door to St Michael's Church, opposite the
entrance to the Hofburg), and there, 'innocent of the
comforts of life, he divided his whole time among the
giving of lessons, the study of his art, and performing.
He played for money in serenades and in the orchestras,
and he was industrious in the practice of composition'.
At some time, writes Griesinger, Haydn

was first violinist for the Brothers of Mercy in the Leopoldstadt [a
suburb of Vienna], at 60 gulden a year. Here he had to be in the church
at eight o'clock in the mornings on Sundays and feast days. At ten
o'clock he played the organ in the chapel of Count Haugwitz, and at
eleven o'clock he sang at St Stephen's. He was paid 17 kreutzers for
each service. In the evenings, Haydn often went out serenading with his
musical comrades, and one of his compositions was usually played; he
recalled having composed a quintet for such an occasion in the year
1753.

Apart from passages like these there is little to indicate how Haydn earned his living, whom he met, what music he heard or performed, or how he developed as a composer. The accounts of his desperate poverty seem to refer chiefly to the time immediately after his leaving the choir school, before he had found a way of supporting himself. For the rest of his life he remembered those who helped him through this dark period, like the singer Johann Michael Spangler, who found a place for him in the single room where he lived with his wife and small child, and a lacemaker, Johann Wilhelm Buchholz, who lent him 150 gulden. In his will (dated 1804) Haydn left Buchholz's granddaughter 100 gulden, 'because her grandfather lent me 150 gulden without interest in my youth and great need, which, however, I repaid 50 years ago'.

It is not known when Haydn moved into the Michaelerhaus or when he left it. It was his home for some years, and he made invaluable contacts there. On the first floor lived the dowager Princess Esterházy, the mother of the two princes whose Kapellmeister Haydn was to be for about 30 years; presumably she was in some way involved in his appointment. The court poet Metastasio, the most famous of the day, lived on the third floor, where his friends the Martínez family also had their home. Metastasio had undertaken responsibility for the education of the talented eldest daughter, Marianna; 'Haydn gave her lessons in singing and keyboard playing and received in return free board for three years' (Griesinger). Through Metastasio Haydn met Nicola Porpora, the composer and singing teacher, who lived in Vienna for three or four years from late 1752 or 1753. Haydn was engaged as Porpora's accompanist and at times acted more or less as his valet. But Haydn acknowledged to Griesinger that he 'profited greatly with Porpora in singing, in composition, and in the Italian language'; as he put it in his autobiographical letter: 'I wrote diligently, but not quite soundly, until at last I had the privilege of learning the true fundamentals of composition from the celebrated Herr Porpora'. Haydn's contact with Porpora was no doubt a turning-point in his development as a composer, and through him he made the acquaintance of other prominent musicians: 'he sometimes had to accompany on the keyboard for Porpora at a Prince von Hildburghausen's, in the presence of Gluck, Wagenseil and other cele-brated masters, and the approval of such connoisseurs served as a special encouragement to him' (Griesinger).

Among Haydn's contacts in these years was Karl Joseph Edler von Fürnberg, on whose recommendation, according to the autobiographical letter, he was later to obtain his appointment as Kapellmeister to Count Morzin. Griesinger's description of Haydn's visits to Fürnberg's estate at Weinzierl near Ybbs is often quoted:

[Fürnberg] invited from time to time his pastor, his steward, Haydn and Albrechtsberger (a brother of the celebrated contrapuntist, who played the cello) for small musical gatherings. Fürnberg requested Haydn to compose something that could be performed by these four amateurs. Haydn, then 18 years old, took up this proposal, and so originated his first quartet which, immediately it appeared, was so acclaimed that Haydn was encouraged to work further in this form.

There are inaccuracies in this report, however; in par-ticular, there must be something wrong with the dating. If Haydn was only 18, his first quartets would have been composed about 1750, which is surely too soon. The first printed editions of his early quartets did not appear until around 1765, and those seem more mature than some of the early trios and divertimentos. And copies still survive (in Budapest) of early symphonies and other compositions formerly owned by the Fürnberg family, which apparently date back to around 1760. Haydn's Weinzierl visits and the early string quartets probably date from the end of the 1750s rather than the beginning, and constitute a sort of prelude to his engagement as Kapellmeister, first to Count Morzin and then to Prince Esterházy, which put an end to his Viennese years as a freelance musician.

Haydn's progress in the 1750s falls roughly into three stages: at first he earned a precarious living through small, casual jobs; then, around 1755, he profited by Porpora's instruction and was able to make contact with potential patrons; and by the end of the decade he had developed into a remarkable young musician, ready for a Kapellmeister's post. This progress was achieved by serious musical study, to make up for what he had not been taught at the choir school. But here again the early accounts differ. Griesinger tells of his already studying Fux's *Gradus ad Parnassum* and Mattheson's *Der vollkommene Kapellmeister* in his schooldays (though without Reutter's help), while Dies more plausibly dates his studies in music theory from after his meeting with Porpora:

Haydn ventured to walk into a bookshop and ask for a good textbook of theory. The bookseller named the writings of Carl Philipp Emanuel Bach as the newest and best. Haydn wanted to look and see for himself. He began to read, understood, found what he was seeking, paid for the book, and took it away thoroughly pleased.

The book in question must have been C. P. E. Bach's *Versuch über die wahre Art das Clavier zu spielen*, the first part of which appeared in 1753. This work, however, like Mattheson's, is mainly a textbook of musical practice, not composition, and it was certainly Fux's famous counterpoint treatise that paved the way for Haydn's learning 'the real foundations of composition' from Porpora. Just how thoroughly he studied Fux is shown by the many penetrating marginal annotations (in Latin) in his copy – unfortunately lost since World War II – though some of these must be of later date, since they refer to writings by Kirnberger from the 1770s. Also probably later is an elementary treatise on counterpoint, based on the *Gradus ad Parnassum*, which Haydn prepared for the use of his own pupils.

Three fundamental problems confront an attempt to survey Haydn's development as a composer during these early years: assembling the works in question; authenticity (numerous spurious works survive under Haydn's name); and the almost complete lack of exact chronological information. In all these respects important progress has been made in the last decades, but many problems are still unsolved and may remain so. It is tempting to try and arrange the works to demonstrate a steady line of development, but the facts are probably different. No doubt Haydn, like any typical 18th-century composer, wrote whatever was needed at a given time, rather than out of a sense of inner compulsion. The natural result of such an approach is a heterogeneous output, and any apparent advance or decline – in these early years as later – may simply reflect changing demands. There was a general tendency around this period to compose in a manner that might at the same time meet the needs of both connoisseurs and amateurs ('für Kenner und Liebhaber', as C. P. E. Bach sub-titled his six famous sets of keyboard pieces). Haydn's early compositions presumably followed the same lines as his performing activities. But information comes chiefly from the familiar early biographical sources; and only a very small number of compositions can be dated back to this period with complete certainty.

Haydn had much experience in the performance of church music when he began his independent career around 1750. His early experiments in sacred composition at the choir school are related in the early biographies. Griesinger and Dies both give accounts of his visit to the pilgrimage town of Mariazell 'soon after his departure from the choir school', taking with him 'several motets of his own composition'. It is not known whether these motets still exist, but one extant composition from the very early period, the *Missa brevis* in F, seems to be fully authenticated. Dies, writing in 1805, reported that 'Chance brought to his hands a short time ago one of his youthful compositions that he had forgotten all about'. According to Dies it had been missing since 1753; in an organ score Haydn in his old age added '1749' (a third report, giving 1742, is certainly unfounded). Presumably the mass was composed about 1750, but there are no means of knowing whether it was before or after Haydn left the choir school. Another rather primitive mass, the *Missa 'Rorate coeli desuper'* in G, came to light in 1957, but its authenticity is very doubtful (Schenk, 1960). From 1756 – the date added later by Haydn himself – there is a *Salve regina* in E, which shows a more professional style than the F major mass, perhaps indicating Porpora's influence.

One story, the account of Haydn's collaboration with the famous comic actor and manager, Kurz-Bernardon, is told in much the same way by all of Haydn's early biographers. According to Griesinger, Haydn wrote the music to Kurz-Bernardon's *Der krumme Teufel* when he was 'about 19 years old', or, according to Dies, when he was 'about 21' – in any event at the beginning of the 1750s. The music is lost, though a libretto issued for a later performance (?1758) survives. It is generally assumed that *Der krumme Teufel* was not Haydn's only work of this kind. No titles of other works of a similar nature are known but several songs from the repertory of the contemporary Viennese popular comedy (*Wiener Komödienlieder*) resemble early Haydn works of other kinds (Badura-Skoda, 1970, 1973–4).

Haydn's own words about his eight years of teaching young people, to earn his living, accord well with Griesinger's statement: 'Many of his easy keyboard sonatas, trios and so forth belong to this period, and he mostly took into account the need and the capacity of his pupils'. Carpani has a similar passage: 'His first works were small piano sonatas which he sold at a low price to the ladies he had as pupils. He also composed menuetts, allemandes and walzes'. Haydn's sonatas – insofar as they are now known – include a number of short and simple pieces that in whole or in part may date from these early years, though they cannot be traced further back than about 1765. Some more mature and expressive sonatas are said to have been influenced by C. P. E. Bach. According to Griesinger:

About this time Haydn came upon the first six sonatas of Emanuel Bach. 'I did not come away from my keyboard until I had played through them, and whoever knows me thoroughly must realize that I owe a deal to Emanuel Bach, and that I understood him and studied him diligently.'

Again, it is impossible to assign a date to this important event. Whether the works in question were really 'the first six sonatas of Emanuel Bach', the 'Prussian' Sonatas of 1742, or the second collection, the

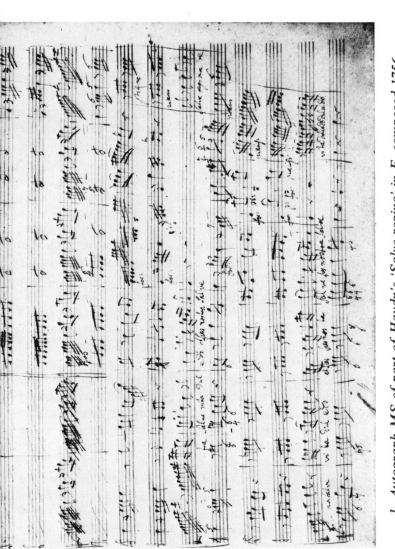

1. Autograph MS of part of Haydn's 'Salve regina' in E, composed 1756

'Württemberg' Sonatas of 1744, is uncertain, but it can scarcely have been before the early 1750s that they came into Haydn's hands. It seems reasonable to assume that they left their mark on Haydn; between his simplest sonatas and others from his early years (like H XVI:2) there are marked stylistic differences, which may reflect his encounter with such an influence. But in view of the uncertain chronology one can do no more than speculate.

Griesinger's mention of 'trios' alongside keyboard sonatas may refer to trios with keyboard, though the earliest surviving works of that category more probably date from the late 1750s or early 1760s. On the other hand some early string trios (of unverified authenticity) are such unsophisticated, simple pieces that it seems natural to refer them to the early 1750s. A hint of corroboration may be seen in Carpani's statement that the serenade said to have led to Haydn's meeting with Kurz was 'for three instruments'. Carpani adds: 'A year after *Der krumme Teufel* Haydn began his real career and started it with six trios'. String trios form one of the groups of early works prominently represented in Haydn's own 'Entwurf-Katalog' (see chapter 2), dating from around 1765 and later, together with divertimentos, serenades etc for four or more instruments. But the grouping and dating of these works too remains largely conjectural.

Towards the end of the 1750s Haydn seems to have achieved greater prominence, and, supposedly on Fürnberg's recommendation, he obtained his first real appointment, probably in 1759 (Dies says he was 'about 27 years old', Carpani has 1758). 'In the year 1759 Haydn was appointed in Vienna to be music director to Count Morzin with a salary of 200 gulden, free room, and board at the staff table ... The winter was spent in Vienna and the summer in Bohemia, in the vicinity of Pilsen' (Griesinger). He was engaged by Count Karl Joseph Franz Morzin, who lived in Vienna but spent the summer months at Lukavec. According to Pohl the count's orchestra functioned only in Lukavec, and it is often assumed that Haydn went there to take up his post. But it seems clear that he spent only the summers there and otherwise, as Griesinger says, stayed in Vienna. Among the works written for Morzin, according to Griesinger, was Haydn's First Symphony. Other compositions pointing to his contact with Czech traditions are a number of divertimentos for wind ensemble (mostly two each of oboes, horns and bassoons). Some are listed in the 'Entwurf-Katalog'; others were unknown until their discovery in Czech archives after World War II.

It is not clear how long Haydn remained in Count Morzin's service. Griesinger reports that 'the count in a short time squandered his considerable fortune' and 'had consequently to disband his orchestra; Joseph Haydn went on 19 March 1760 as Kapellmeister to Prince Nikolaus [*recte* Anton] Esterházy, whom the aforesaid symphony had pleased'. But the contract between Prince Esterházy and Haydn, which is extant, is dated 1 May 1761. The possibility that Haydn may have entered the service of Prince Esterházy some time before the official contract is perhaps supported by Carpani's story that the prince was so charmed on hearing a Haydn symphony that he immediately asked Morzin to allow him to engage Haydn, but forgot about it and had to be reminded at a later date.

In 1760 Haydn married Maria Anna Aloysia Apollonia Keller (baptized 9 Feb 1729; *d* 20 March 1800), daughter of a wigmaker ('Perückenmacher'),

*2. Joseph Haydn: portrait (c1768) by Johann Grundmann,
probably destroyed in World War II*

Johann Peter Keller. The marriage took place in St Stephen's Cathedral on 26 November; in the church register Haydn is still described as music director to Count Morzin. Griesinger and Dies both tell that Haydn had wanted to marry another sister, Josepha, but when she entered a convent he agreed, out of gratitude for Keller's kindness, to marry the elder daughter. It turned out an unsuccessful marriage. Maria Anna seems to have been totally lacking in understanding of her husband's work; Griesinger reports Haydn as saying: 'It's all the same to her if her husband is a cobbler or an artist'. All that is told of her own interests is that she was too fond of the clergy for Haydn's taste. Haydn found comfort elsewhere; as he said to Griesinger: 'My wife was unable to bear children, and I was therefore less indifferent to the charms of other women'.

Haydn's last years in Vienna, including the period with Count Morzin, saw the composition of a number of works, partly along the lines of the earliest ones but partly looking ahead. Most important among these are symphonies. Haydn seems to have been rather late in joining the new tradition of symphonic writing in Vienna, represented by such composers as Wagenseil, Holzbauer, Schlöger, M. G. Monn and, among his contemporaries, Leopold Hofmann and Ordonez. No symphony of Haydn's before 1759 can be safely dated, but he may have begun a year or two earlier, and had probably composed a number of symphonies before his move to Eisenstadt in 1761. As noted earlier, the quartets published in 1764–6 as opp.1 and 2 may belong to the late 1750s, and so may some early piano trios and concertos for harpsichord or organ, one of which (H XVIII:1) is dated 1756. In many cases, however, it is impossible to determine whether a piece was written during the last years in Vienna or the first years in Eisenstadt.

2. Esterházy Kapellmeister I: 1761-75

Haydn's appointment to the service of Paul Anton Esterházy in 1761 was the second turning-point in his career. After over a decade as a freelance musician, he was now part of a community with established traditions: he became a member of a princely court (as a 'Hausoffizier'), based at first in Eisenstadt and later for most of his time in the splendid new palace, Eszterháza. Haydn lived and worked in these surroundings until 1790 when he moved to Vienna, where, apart from his London visits of 1791–2 and 1794–5, he remained for the rest of his life, though returning to Eisenstadt for the summers.

The Esterházy family was among the richest and most influential of the Hungarian nobility. Their Kapellmeister was Gregor Joseph Werner, who had been appointed in 1728, during the regency of Prince Paul Anton's mother, the dowager Princess Octavia. A talented and well-trained musician, he was primarily a church composer, though he also wrote trio sonatas and symphonies for the small ensemble at his disposal. Prince Paul Anton was apparently planning an increase in the court activities. He had brought home from his travels a quantity of operatic music, and in the years around 1760 many new symphonies were purchased. Werner was too old and weak for a fresh start. When Haydn was appointed, the first clause in his contract concerned his relations with Werner.

He, Gregorius Werner, in consideration of his service over many years,
will remain Ober-Kapellmeister, whereas he, Joseph Heyden, as Vice-
Kapellmeister in Eisenstadt, will be subordinate to and dependent on
Gregorius Werner in choral music; on all other occasions, however,
whenever there has to be a musical performance, everything pertaining
to music will be assigned *in genere* and *specie* to him as Vice-
Kapellmeister.

That division of responsibilities stood until Werner's
death in 1766.

Haydn's contract (facsimile in Somfai, 1963–4,
pp.25ff) stipulated that he should behave and dress 'as
befits an honest house officer in a princely court', serve
as an example to the musicians subordinate to him, and
'avoid undue familiarity in eating and drinking or otherwise in his relations with them, lest he should lose the
respect due to him' etc. He was obliged to compose
music as required by the prince, and forbidden to give
away copies of such music or to compose for other
people without special permission. He was also respon-
sible for the care of the music and instruments.

The exact size or composition of the orchestra for
which Haydn had to compose is not known, but it
probably comprised 10–15 musicians, on occasion a
few more. The following years were to see a gradual
increase in its size, but even towards the end of his time
in the Esterházy service the orchestra numbered no
more than 20–25. He could however count among his
few musicians some very good men, like the fine leader
Luigi Tomasini, the cellist Anton Kraft and the excellent
horn and baryton player Karl Franz. The high standard
of his players is reflected in a number of concertos
and concerto-like pieces dating from his first Eisenstadt
years: there are concertos for violin, for horn, for harpsichord and for organ as well as the three symphonies
nos.6–8, 'Le matin', 'Le midi' and 'Le soir', on the

borderline between symphony and concerto grosso. At the time of Haydn's engagement a new theatre was built in a conservatory in the park; the way was now open for establishing an operatic tradition. But Prince Paul Anton did not live to see this carried out; he died on 18 March 1762 and was succeeded by his brother, Nikolaus (1714–90).

Prince Nikolaus Esterházy was to be Haydn's patron and employer for nearly 30 years. His musical taste and requirements inevitably became paramount in the traditions at the Esterházy court. He was never afraid of spending money on festivities. Goethe, as a boy of 15, was so impressed by the splendour of the display he sponsored at Joseph II's coronation in Frankfurt in 1764 that he described it many years later (in *Dichtung und Wahrheit*) as 'das Esterházysche Feenreich'. 'Nikolaus the Magnificent' came to be his nickname. He was a fine patron in many ways, but his personal limitations seem to have imposed certain restrictions on Haydn's artistic development.

Before he succeeded his brother, Prince Nikolaus had spent much time at Süttör (across the Neusiedlersee), where he had inherited a hunting-lodge. At first it was only a summer residence. But his predilection for the place was so strong that he rebuilt it, enlarging it into a fine palace – from 1765 called Eszterháza – and finally moving his court to it for most of the year. From about 1766–7 Eszterháza was the centre of Haydn's activities, Eisenstadt serving as a residence only for a short spell each winter, if at all.

Haydn's first years in Eisenstadt, before the court moved to Eszterháza, seem to have been mostly occupied with various sorts of instrumental music. Opera, made possible by the new theatre, was not an established part of musical life at Eisenstadt. Apart from four Italian Singspiels, of which only fragments of *La Marchesa Nespola* survive, Haydn composed only one opera in these years, *Acide*, written in 1762 and performed on the wedding of Prince Nikolaus's eldest son Anton on 11 January 1763. For the wedding celebrations Haydn also composed a cantata, *Vivan gl'illustri sposi*. Two other cantatas were written to commemorate episodes in Prince Nikolaus's life: *Al tuo arrivo felice* on his return from Frankfurt in 1764 and the lost *Dei clementi* on his recovery from an illness. Although church music was still under Werner's jurisdiction, there are a few sacred compositions by Haydn from these years, a *Te Deum* and some hymns. But most of his time was undoubtedly spent on music to be used as *Tafelmusik* or in the two weekly concerts ('academies') that seem to have been part of the routine even when the prince himself was away. 11 symphonies composed in 1763–5 survive in Haydn's autograph.

From these years, however, knowledge of Haydn's work no longer has to depend on the relatively few dated autographs and his early biographers. In 1765 a princely reprimand for negligence – a unique event in his life – prompted Haydn to put together a catalogue of his compositions, the so-called 'Entwurf-Katalog' (see fig. 3 below), which is of the utmost importance for the understanding of his early development. The reprimand caused much consternation among Haydn biographers until it became clear what lay behind it. The elderly Werner, though nominally still Ober-Kapellmeister, was increasingly having to give way to his young Vice-Kapellmeister: Haydn had taken over completely except for church music, he was much more popular as a composer and was even better paid than his nominal super-

ior. Old and sick, Werner, in October 1765, gave vent
to his bitterness in a letter to the prince (first published
by Harich, *Muszika*, ii, 1930, p.180), accusing Haydn
of slovenliness in a number of matters: singers were
allowed to miss performances, music was lost and instruments were missing. Werner's complaints unmistakably lay behind the prince's written reprimand to
Haydn shortly afterwards. A month earlier Haydn had
quarrelled with the princely administrator ('Regent'),
Rahier, over the treatment of one of his musicians, and
Rahier was no doubt happy to administer the reprimand. It is impossible to tell how justified Werner's
accusations were, but they could scarcely have been
entirely without foundation. Though this affair was probably to some extent the reaction of an older generation
against the self-assertiveness of the successful young
Vice-Kapellmeister, it seems likely that there was some
legitimate cause for complaint. For the naturally conscientious Haydn one such warning was enough.

The end of the letter to Haydn contains a sentence
unprompted by Werner's accusations but apparently
added by the prince himself: 'Finally, Kapellmeister
Haydn is urgently enjoined to apply himself to composition more diligently than heretofore, and especially to
write such pieces as can be played on the gamba'. By
'gamba' is meant the prince's favourite instrument, the
baryton. A relative of the viola d'amore, the baryton had
a number of extra strings behind the neck, which,
though primarily intended for resonance, provided a
special effect when plucked with the left thumb. It was
never very popular, and is now remembered mostly in
connection with Haydn and his prince. Haydn at once
set to work to remedy the lack of baryton compositions;
most conspicuous is the series of trios for baryton,

violin and cello, of which he wrote at least 125 over the next ten years. But Haydn must have felt that the general charge of his having neglected composition was unjust, and he rebutted it in the best possible way: by putting together a catalogue to demonstrate how active he had actually been.

This catalogue is known today, perhaps rather mis-leadingly, as the 'Entwurf-Katalog' ('draft-catalogue' – *EK*), referring to its use as one of the primary sources for the catalogue compiled in 1805 by Haydn and his copyist Johann Elssler (son of Joseph Elssler, Haydn's copyist until his death in 1782). In origin the 'Entwurf-Katalog' is not a preliminary draft; it is Haydn's own early account of his activities, including initially what he had composed until 1765 (as far as he could still re-member) and afterwards added to more or less consist-ently for a number of years, enabling the growth of his output to be followed at close quarters.

In its first stage the catalogue devoted separate sec-tions to the following groups of works: 1. symphonies; 2. divertimentos (for four or more instruments); 3. bary-ton music; 4. minuets; 5. string trios; 6. operas and secular choral music (cantatas); 7. concertos; 8. church music (hymns, *Te Deum*). This general plan is still discernible, but it is considerably overgrown by later additions, not only continuing the single groups in ac-cordance with the original layout, but in the course of time filling up all the empty spaces without regard for orderly arrangement. In particular, the plethora of new baryton trios disturbed the system but other works of the later 1760s and the 1770s, such as string quartets, piano sonatas, operas, masses etc, were also added in a rather casual manner. These additions are invaluable aids for the identification and authentication of a great

3. A page from Haydn's 'Entwurf-Katalog', begun in 1765

number of later works, but it is above all the listing of
the works before 1765 that makes the catalogue indispensable. Still, it must be recognized that the catalogue
is not comprehensive up to this date. It is primarily
concerned with works composed in Eisenstadt and with
earlier works performed in these years or in any event
still in Haydn's possession. Pieces from the 1750s no
longer owned by Haydn could easily have been forgotten or even deliberately omitted since they did not relate
to his activities as princely Kapellmeister.

The catalogue entries confirm Haydn's limited involvement with church music and cantatas during his early
years in Eisenstadt. (A few pieces are known only from
the *EK*; a few others not noted in the *EK* are known
from other sources.) But the instrumental music amply
demonstrates his intensive activity as a composer between 1761 and 1765. It is not known for exactly what
use all these works were composed. The symphonies
and concertos undoubtedly relate to the twice-weekly
'academies' and to special festivities. The same may
apply to some of the divertimentos, though others,
together with the minuets, seem to belong to the
category of music for entertainment, possibly in the
form of *Tafelmusik*. There are some works, however,
that appear to have been composed not for the
academies proper but for more intimate surroundings:
for chamber music in a small circle of performers with
or without an audience. This is certainly true of the
baryton trios, which became the prince's passion in the
following years, and it seems natural to associate the
string trios with the same kind of performance, more or
less as the forerunners of the baryton trios. Two
categories of work that receive only limited representation in the *EK* are the piano sonatas and the (early)

piano trios. The list of piano sonatas is certainly not complete, though it includes among other works seven sonatas known in no other source. Still less complete is the list of piano trios; of 10–12 pieces that may reasonably be supposed to date back to around 1765 and earlier, only one is recorded in the *EK*, and then in another version with baryton. Here other sources have to be relied upon. Surprisingly, nothing is really known about the background to Haydn's piano sonatas and trios of these early years.

In 1766 the conditions of Haydn's artistic life and development were changed decisively by two events: the death of Werner, and the moving of the princely court for the first time to Eszterháza, which was henceforth the centre of Haydn's musical activities. Werner's death must have meant two things in particular to Haydn: first, he could return to church music, in which he had been brought up but which he had had to abandon almost completely for five years; and, second, he no longer had to rub along with his older colleague, whose understanding, let alone friendship, he could never hope to win. He now had full responsibility for all musical performances at the princely court. In several respects he was very isolated, and he became still more so at Eszterháza. He was far away from any musical activities except his own performances. He had not, as in his younger years in Vienna, friends and colleagues with whom he could discuss problems. His contract told him to avoid 'undue familiarity' with his musicians and to keep them at a distance; the distance between himself and the princely family was of course still greater. Under these circumstances it is even sadder that his marriage failed to provide him with a satisfactory family life. This did not, however, stunt Haydn's spirit of

enterprise; rather, it freed him to find his own way. He
stressed this in an often-quoted reflection, reported by
Griesinger:

My prince was content with all my works, I received approval, I could,
as head of an orchestra, make experiments, observe what created an
impression, and what weakened it; thus improving, adding to, cutting
away, and running risks. I was set apart from the world, there was
nobody in my vicinity to confuse and annoy me in my course, and so I
had to become original.

The years roughly from the mid-1760s to the early
1770s saw a process of expansion in Haydn's musical
development that is unparalleled before or after. This
period has received much attention since Wyzewa
(1909) proposed the idea of some sort of 'romantic
crisis'. More recently the term 'Sturm und Drang'
('storm and stress') has gained widespread acceptance. It
is easy to see how such designations arose. A number of
works from these years stand out as remarkably strong
and expressive, far exceeding anything Haydn had written previously. Wyzewa based his case primarily on the
series of symphonies in minor keys, but there are strikingly 'passionate' works among the contemporary string
quartets and piano sonatas too. All the same, there are
reasons for feeling that neither term adequately characterizes Haydn's music of this period. The minor-key
symphonies of Wyzewa's 'romantic crisis', then thought
to date from a relatively short period around 1772, are
now known to have been spread over at least five years
(1768–72); they do not represent a short burst of passion, but are intermingled with works of quite different
character. As for 'Sturm und Drang', the literary
movement from which the term was borrowed came into
being only some years after the supposed storm in
Haydn's music had abated. Even if taken to signify only

a general parallel in mood with the intensity of the 'Sturm und Drang' in literature, the term does not seem to fit Haydn.

Both designations are simply too narrow. They leave out of the picture the large majority of Haydn's works from these years and promote a few – though certainly some of the most impressive ones – to an exaggeratedly dominant position. What characterizes this period in Haydn's development is above all its richness and many-sidedness. His works from these years comprise a great variety of musical forms and genres; several of them were more or less new to him, and even those that were not were given a fresh start. He tackled entirely new problems of form, style and expression. The three most prominent Classical instrumental forms, the symphony, the string quartet and the piano sonata, came out of this process of maturing more or less reborn and reshaped. Essential features of Haydn's complex development in these years are seen in six different types of work: church music, opera, symphony, baryton music, string quartet and piano sonata.

It was undoubtedly with happy feelings that Haydn again took up composing for the church. As many as three masses may date from the years around 1766–70. The *Stabat mater* was composed in 1767 and the substantial choral cantata *Applausus* in 1768; in 1771 followed the G minor *Salve regina*, and in 1772 the *Missa Sancti Nicolai* (H XXII:6). There is some doubt about the chronology of the masses. Until recently the *Missa in honorem BVM* ('Great Organ Mass', H XXII:4) was confidently assigned to 1766, on the assumption that a lost autograph of the Kyrie carried that date. But the recently discovered autograph of a Kyrie of 1766 has turned out to be that of the *Missa Cellensis*

('Cecilia Mass', H XXII:5), formerly supposed to be somewhat later. The *EK* lists the 'Great Organ Mass' twice, once following the (lost) D minor *Missa 'Sunt bona mixta malis'* (H XXII:2) and once preceding the 'Nicolai Mass', whereas the 'Cecilia Mass' is found together with the *Stabat mater*. It seems reasonable to suppose that all four masses belong to the years 1766–72. The *Stabat mater* won European fame only in the 1780s, but in a letter of 1768 Haydn mentioned having composed it the year before. The *Applausus* cantata, dated 1768, was composed not for the princely liturgy but for the jubilee of a prelate in the monastery of Zwettl. Haydn's letter giving directions for the cantata's performance is of great value for the information it provides on various matters of interpretation; at the same time it testifies to his assurance as a composer of church music, though he had seriously returned to sacred composition only a couple of years before. One need look no further than this group of works to find the many-sidedness referred to earlier – the late Baroque traditions still discernible in the 'cantata' manner of the 'Cecilia Mass', the almost archaic ring of a *Missa 'Sunt bona mixta malis'*, the fine expressive tendencies in the 'Great Organ Mass' and the more lighthearted style of the 'Nicolai Mass', the solid choral style in *Applausus* and the fine synthesis of old and new in the *Stabat mater*.

After the solitary *Acide* of 1762 it was not until 1766 that Haydn composed another opera. From this year dates *La canterina*, the first of a series of lighter operas, followed by *Lo speziale* (1768) and *Le pescatrici* (1769). In 1766 the court had moved to Eszterháza, but the opera house was not yet ready. *La canterina* was performed in Pressburg (now Bratislava), at that time the principal city of Hungary, in the presence of the imperial family in Lent 1767. *Lo speziale* opened the new opera house at Eszterháza on 5 August 1768, Princess Maria's name day, and *Le pescatrici* was performed there on 16 September 1770, when there was a wedding in the princely family. These operas are less varied than the church music. All three belong to the *opera buffa* or *dramma giocoso* type, far from any 'Sturm und Drang' tendencies.

In the operas Haydn was not yet free to set his own course; but the symphonies of these years bear the strong imprint of his originality, again with the emphasis on stylistic diversity. Besides the symphonies in minor keys (nos.26, 39, 49, 44, 45 and 52) there are several others of widely differing character (e.g. nos.35, 38, 59, 41, 42 and 43), all apparently dating from between 1767–8 and 1772. Some of them may still have been written primarily to entertain, but in the more 'passionate' symphonies the music is largely of an expressive character, a quality hitherto more typical of vocal music. These works were essentially different from the traditional type of symphony, not only more expressive but also richer in artistry. In the score of Symphony no.42 (1771) Haydn crossed out a few bars and added the comment: 'This was for far too learned ears'. This remark may echo a certain reserve on the part of the audience towards Haydn's bold originality – a reserve that perhaps eventually grew to the point of more direct opposition, until it affected his approach to the symphony.

Through all these years there was a constant stream of baryton music, especially trios, whose small scale and lightness present an almost bewildering contrast to the finest of the symphonies. Yet there is no real conflict here. The baryton trios might be called functional pieces, limited in their demands on the musician and the listener; but taken on their own terms they reveal a remarkable amount of fine detail in melody, texture and interplay of instruments. Haydn's musicianship, indeed his genius, is perhaps felt particularly strongly in these bagatelles, not least in the way he achieved such variety of form and expression in so many pieces with such circumscribed possibilities.

The four categories of church music, opera, symphonies and baryton compositions seem to cover Haydn's obligations as a court composer. But there are two groups of works that stand apart: the string quartets and the piano sonatas. Since the early quartets (opp.1 and 2, as they were later known), which presumably date from the time before Eisenstadt, Haydn had apparently composed no string quartets. (The so-called op.3 quartets, which include the one with the famous serenade, no.5, are now thought to be spurious; at least some of them seem to be by Roman Hofstetter.) And when he planned the *EK* he did not set aside a separate section for string quartets, but included them within the general category of divertimentos for various combinations. Apparently in 1765 he did not see the string quartet as a distinct form. But his additions to the *EK* include, in three different places, the three sets of quartets known (after the printed editions) as op.9, op.17 and op.20. The first set seems to have been entered between 1768 and 1770; op.17 and op.20 are dated 1771 and 1772 in the autographs. These 18 works are so radically different from the baryton trios that it seems unlikely that they could have been composed for Prince Esterházy. They may have been written for some other amateur, or perhaps for one of the Austrian monasteries. They were probably not composed for a publisher, although they appeared in several editions within a year or two of their composition; Haydn's contacts with publishers apparently began rather later. What prompted Haydn to compose within so short a time these quartets – milestones in the development of the genre – remains an open question.

Little more is known about the keyboard sonatas. After the mainly sonatina-like works of the 1750s, intended for teaching use, there are 14 sonatas listed in the *EK* of which seven are otherwise unknown. Among the extant sonatas are H XVI:45 (1766), 19 (1767) and 46 (1767–70, according to its position in the *EK*). Between these and the early sonatas there is a similar stylistic distance to that between the quartets of about 1770 and the early ones. It is not known for whom these sonatas were written. They are not easy sonatinas but demanding pieces, with traces of the Baroque concerto in their breeding. Like the contemporary quartets they are pioneer works, fine examples of Haydn's originality and independence of fashion.

Viewed as a whole, not merely in the light of a small number of selected compositions, this period in Haydn's life stands out not as a crisis but as the crucial breakthrough in his development. At the same time his approach was two-sided: he could change between an 'expressive' style and a 'functional' style without difficulty, and without compromising his artistic integrity. The 18th century, unlike the 19th, found no contradiction between the two.

From about 1772 various features suggest that Haydn may have felt a need, which would be understandable, to slow down after his years of intense exploration. This applies both to the number of works composed and, more conspicuously, to their character.

Symphonies in minor keys, so characteristic of his more expressive style, stop; there are no more quartets for about ten years. Two series of piano sonatas – H XVI:21–6 and 27–32 – seem to appeal more to the 'Liebhaber' than to the 'Kenner'. There may have been other forces behind this change of style, however. Nos.21–6 were printed in 1774 with a dedication to Prince Nikolaus, and his name is also associated with the G major Mass of 1772, which is conspicuously lighter in style than the preceding masses. A reaction on the prince's part may have been the main cause of Haydn's moderating his progressive tendencies. For a long time Haydn had kept the prince happy with a stream of baryton trios; but this apparently came to an end in about 1772–3, and that may have brought the symphony into prominence. It has been suggested that the change of style in the symphonies may have been in the interests of salability; but while such concessions might well be made in piano sonatas or piano trios one would scarcely expect to find them in symphonies or quartets. Furthermore, there is little evidence of Haydn's having composed directly for publishers until about 1780. One particular reason for this slowing down in instrumental music was Haydn's increased pursuit of opera and other dramatic music, which in due time was to test his capacities to a high degree.

During these years around 1770, years of unprecedented expansion, Haydn's whole existence was centred on his composing. Outside his work his life was mostly rather uneventful. In 1768 there was a great fire in Eisenstadt and Haydn's house was burnt down; he must have been in Eszterháza at the time, but probably some of his earlier works were lost. In or around 1770 he was apparently ill. A famous episode from these years, later recounted by Haydn, is the story of the 'Farewell' Symphony (1772), according to which the progressive reduction of the orchestra in the extra finale, until only the conductor and two violinists were left, persuaded the prince against further prolonging his stay in Eszterháza, and thus allowing the musicians to return to their families in Eisenstadt.

In this period Haydn had only limited contact with the wider currents of European musical life. He can have had little opportunity to visit the nearby cities of Vienna or Pressburg. Griesinger, generally reliable, is misleading when he says that 'Haydn spent these 30 years for the most part at Eisenstadt in Hungary with his prince, and only in winter came for two or three months to Vienna'. In fact, from 1766 or 1767 Haydn spent most of his time in Eszterháza and went only to Eisenstadt for the winter months. These 30 years may be divided into three periods: 1761–6, when he was mainly in Eisenstadt; 1767–78, when he was often in Eszterháza for between nine and ten months each year and spent only two or three months in Eisenstadt; and 1779–90, when he had given up his house in Eisenstadt and could either go to Vienna or stay in Eszterháza between the end of one opera season and the beginning of the next. Naturally he could visit Vienna only with the prince's consent; probably he often found some reason for a trip there, such as looking for music for Eszterháza. Apparently the musicians did not normally go to Vienna to perform in the Esterházy family's town residence. A letter survives, written just before the death of Prince Paul Anton (March 1762), in which Haydn asked a musician to come to Vienna to take part in chamber music there until the prince's return to Eisenstadt; but from the time of Prince Nikolaus no similar documents seem to exist.

Little is known about Haydn's relations with
Viennese musicians and musical life during these years
apart from isolated episodes which are exceptional and
are remembered for that reason. In March 1768 Haydn
asked for permission to go to Vienna with two singers
and the cellist Weigl to perform his *Stabat mater* in the
Church of the Brothers of Mercy at the request of
Hasse; this was not of course an 'official' performance
but a private one arranged by Haydn himself. Two years
later, on 22 March 1770, Haydn's opera *Lo speziale*
was performed in Vienna at the house of a Baron
Sumerau and the following day in a concert 'in the
presence of many persons of rank'. This time the
Esterházy orchestra took part. But again the indications
are of a private arrangement rather than some sort of
princely command performance. A performance of the
Stabat mater took place on 29 March 1771 in the
Maria Treu Church in the Josephstadt suburb. After
these three performances there is no information about
Haydn's relations with Vienna until 1774–5. A surviving letter refers to his having been in the city in March
1774 but says nothing further.

Haydn and his orchestra would have had to play in
Pressburg, rather than Vienna, and then only on special
occasions. Haydn directed a dance orchestra there once
in 1772, and appeared with his orchestra in the presence
of the Empress Maria Theresia in the mid-1770s. After
the completion of Eszterháza, however, the prince
preferred to present his musicians on their home
ground. There were a number of splendid feasts. The
visit of the French ambassador in June 1772 was celebrated with three or four days of festivity. In summer
1773 Haydn's new opera *L'infedeltà delusa* was per-

formed for the first time on 26 July in honour of the
dowager Princess Esterházy's name day. In September
Maria Theresia visited Eszterháza and there was a series
of concerts and entertainments. *L'infedeltà delusa* was
performed again, and besides various orchestral performances the empress heard Haydn's marionette opera
Philemon und Baucis in the special, newly built marionette theatre. Unlike most of Haydn's operas for the
marionette theatre, *Philemon und Baucis* has survived,
though apparently in a slightly altered version. Two
years later, in late August 1775, the Archduke
Ferdinand and Archduchess Beatrice, accompanied by
the imperial court, visited Eszterháza; again a new
Haydn opera was performed, *L'incontro improvviso*, on
a plot similar to that of Mozart's *Entführung*, and there
were concerts and other entertainments.

3. Esterházy Kapellmeister II: 1776-90

Up to about 1775 Haydn's main task had been to compose and direct instrumental music for the princely court, together with (from 1766) some church music, and from time to time to compose and perform an opera. But from 1776 onwards he was increasingly involved with opera – not only writing his own, but also arranging and performing a large repertory by other composers. The second half of his 30 years at Eisenstadt and Eszterháza is the time of Haydn the opera director (see Bartha and Somfai, 1960). After the completion of the Eszterháza theatre a tradition of theatrical performances was soon established. Every summer a troupe of actors was engaged, normally from the beginning of May to the end of October; in the winter they would play in a town like Pressburg or Graz. The most famous of these troupes was the one directed by Carl Wahr, which played in Eszterháza every summer from 1772 to 1777. Wahr's repertory consisted primarily of comedies, but also included *Hamlet, Macbeth, Othello* and *King Lear*. No operas or Singspiels were given; in these years Haydn's own operas were the sole representatives of musical theatre. But the contract with Wahr's predecessor, Passer, in 1770, had stated that the prince would ensure the supply of music for the rehearsals and performances. It is impossible to say how much music was required, or of what kind. Tradition has credited Haydn with music to *Hamlet, King Lear* and more; but no *Hamlet* music is known, and an overture and some incidental music to *King Lear* seem to be spurious (possibly by W. G. Stegmann). Symphony no.60, 'Il distratto', may be based on music for the play *Der Zerstreute*. These theatrical pieces probably consisted of an introductory symphony and entr'actes, played during the performance of the play in question but hardly an integral part of it. It may be that performances of this sort more or less replaced the concerts proper, the 'academies'.

From the 1776 season, the musical side was more strongly emphasized: opera was no longer confined to Haydn's works and a regular tradition was established. During the year five different operas were given, three by Dittersdorf, one by Sacchini and one by Piccinni. In the following year Haydn's *Il mondo della luna* had its first performance, together with operas by Gassmann, Paisiello and Dittersdorf. From the next year, 1778, a complete list of performances has survived, which shows how opera fitted into the schedule of theatrical performances. Instead of the Wahr company, no fewer than three troupes of actors were engaged in succession, so that the season was prolonged from six months to about 11 (24 January–22 December, with a number of gaps, especially an extended interval in the summer, 18 July–25 August). Out of 242 evenings, 184 were devoted to plays, six to academies (all between 30 January and 26 February) and 52 to opera, mostly on Thursday or Sunday evenings. In the following years opera performances occupied a still greater part. One of the busiest years was 1786 when no fewer than eight new operas were given together with nine revivals, in sum 124 or 125 performances, and all (with rehearsals) under Haydn's own direction. It is understandable that with such obligations Haydn could scarcely find time for composing.

The marionette opera was in some degree drawn into this increased activity. It has been suggested that marionette operas were performed daily, but that can scarcely have been true of any period. It was again in the 1776 season that the marionette opera repertory was much enlarged (Landon, 1962). In the previous years there had been only occasional performances, but 1776 saw a regular season, including at least six different plays, among them Haydn's own *Dido* and Pleyel's *Die Fee Urgele*, and perhaps also revivals of *Philemon und Baucis* and *Hexenschabbas* (both first given in 1773) and the première of *Das abgebrannte Haus*. This new wave of marionette operas did not last long, however: in 1777–9 only occasional performances were given, and a single opera in each of 1782 and 1783 brought this type of Eszterháza entertainment to an end. In 1777, at Empress Maria Theresia's request, the Eszterháza marionettes were taken to Schönbrunn for two performances. Landon suggests that the marionette director Pauersbach, and not Haydn, was in charge of the tour, but it seems questionable whether the Esterházy orchestra would have played in Schönbrunn without its Kapellmeister.

Haydn's contacts with Vienna were strengthened by two other engagements in the mid-1770s. In 1771 Gassmann, the imperial court Kapellmeister, had founded the Tonkünstler-Sozietät, a benevolent fund for musicians' dependants. For the society's concerts Haydn composed the oratorio *Il ritorno di Tobia* in winter 1774–5 and conducted performances on 2 and 4 April 1775, in which some of his own singers and musicians took part. A review makes it clear that Haydn's international reputation was becoming recognized in Vienna:

4. Joseph Haydn: engraving (c1792) by Luigi Schiavonetti after the second version of a portrait by Ludwig Guttenbrunn, the first version of which probably dates from c1770

His choruses, above all, were lit by a fire otherwise only to be found in
Handel; in short, the whole very large audience was delighted, and here
too Haydn was the great artist whose works are in great favour all over
Europe and in which foreigners recognize the original genius
[*Originalgenie*] of this master.

According to Dies, Haydn was invited to compose an
opera for the imperial court in Vienna, and responded
with *La vera costanza*; but allegedly it was withdrawn
because of intrigues, and Anfossi's setting was sub-
stituted. The date for the work's composition is given by
Pohl as 1776. Recent research however suggests a later
date (1777–8, according to Hoboken, 1971) and has
even questioned the story about the Viennese commission (Walter, 1976). But the tale as related by Dies is
unusually detailed and seemingly trustworthy.

That there may have been jealousy among Haydn's
colleagues of his growing reputation, and reluctance to
accept that in his isolation at Eszterháza he might have
outstripped his fellow composers in the capital, would
seem to be borne out by an episode a couple of years
later. In November 1778 Haydn wanted to join the
Tonkünstler-Sozietät. As he was not resident in Vienna
he was liable for extra dues, and, having already ren-
dered valuable service to the society with *Tobia*, he
suggested that he might instead compose something for
it. But when his admission was made conditional on a
written declaration that he would provide the society
with works as and when required, he wrote a furious
letter (4 February 1779) cancelling his membership and
demanding the return of the deposit he had already paid.
The fact that the society found it unnecessary to pursue
the matter further and the uncharacteristic indignation
of Haydn's letter suggest that personal animosity was
involved. Only 18 years later did the society make

amends by asking Haydn to become an 'Assessor Senior' for life.

In 1779, however, Haydn established another Viennese contact of the greatest importance, that with the publishing firm of Artaria. Up to this date only one printed edition authorized by Haydn himself is known, the six piano sonatas dedicated to Prince Nikolaus (H XVI:21–6), published by Kurzböck in 1774. The many early editions published in Paris, Amsterdam, London and elsewhere were probably issued without his knowledge or consent. In Austria it was usual to have music professionally copied rather than printed until Artaria established a tradition of music publishing. Artaria became Haydn's principal publisher for the next ten years, and remained an important contact still longer. This connection may have affected the new contract between Haydn and Prince Esterházy, dated 1 January 1779. The first contract of 1761 had given the prince exclusive rights over Haydn's compositions, but in the new terms there was no such provision. How far the old rule had been observed over the years is perhaps open to question; the new contract was probably more or less a formalization of what was happening in practice. Haydn increasingly availed himself of the possibilities that it opened up. His problem was not to find publishers for his works; rather it was to supply enough compositions to keep the publishers content.

Another event of 1779, this time of a personal nature, was of great importance in Haydn's life. In March the couple Luigia and Antonio Polzelli were taken into the Esterházy service, the 19-year-old Luigia as a singer and Antonio as a violinist. Both were second-rate artists, and they were formally dismissed at the end of 1780; but before their departure they were reinstated and they

remained at Eszterháza until Prince Nikolaus's death in
1790. Haydn's influence must have been behind this
reprieve, for he had formed a strong attachment to
Luigia. 'His late and slow development and unsatisfac-
tory marriage had left him with unspent reserves of
passion and protective tenderness' (Hughes); and his
friendship with Luigia continued for many years. In
1791, while Haydn was in London, her husband died
and she moved to Italy; they never met again. Haydn
wrote warmly and sympathetically to her from London:
'I esteem and love you as on the very first day', and he
gave her generous financial support and took care of her
two sons on his return to Vienna. After his wife's death
in 1800 he even signed a declaration that should he
decide to remarry he would take no other wife than
Luigia. But by then he may have been a little tired of
her; and she married again before his death.

The role played by Luigia Polzelli was not purely
personal, however. Many of Haydn's revisions and additions to other composers' operas performed at
Eszterháza were undertaken out of consideration for
her: difficult arias were made easier, and new ones
composed to replace others less suited to her voice
(Bartha and Somfai, 1960). Similar alterations were
made for other singers, but to a much more limited
degree.

Haydn's activities at Eszterháza in the 1780s continued on the same course as in the late 1770s, with a
regular theatre and opera season usually from February
to December. As director of the opera he had what
would normally count as a full-time job, and in his later
years he seems to have served primarily, or almost
exclusively, as the prince's conductor rather than composer. Until 1783 he was still active as an opera com-

poser. *La vera costanza* was produced at Eszterháza in April 1779. For the prince's name day, 6 December, a new opera was ready, *L'isola disabitata*. Shortly before, on 18 November, the opera house was destroyed by fire; yet the première went ahead, with the marionette theatre serving as opera house in the interim. Haydn's next opera, *La fedeltà premiata*, was planned for the opening of the rebuilt opera house in autumn 1780, as the printed libretto shows. But the house was not ready, and the first performance had to be postponed until 25 February 1781. In 1782, again on the prince's name day, *Orlando paladino*, 'dramma eroicomico', followed, and on 26 February 1784 the last of Haydn's operas for the Eszterháza theatre, *Armida*, a genuine *opera seria* or 'dramma eroico'.

During the 1780s a dichotomy developed between domestic and outside activities in a way unprecedented in Haydn's former years. Until about 1780 composing and performing for the Esterházy household had kept him fully occupied; from time to time he may have accepted an outside commission, but such works, like the *Applausus* cantata, seem to have been exceptions, and (as noted above) publications of his music were probably for the most part pirated editions of works composed for Eisenstadt and Eszterháza. From the early 1780s most of his works were apparently composed for publishers in Vienna, Paris or London, as Haydn's correspondence particularly with Artaria and Forster reveals. No doubt many pieces were played at Eszterháza too, but they were no longer the prince's exclusive property: Haydn could dispose of them at will. If life at Eszterháza was becoming a matter of routine in these years, Haydn's contacts with publishers and other clients from abroad gave variety – though the increasing number of commissions often led to trouble. It was the attempt to meet the heavy demand for his music that lay behind Haydn's selling the same compositions to two or three different publishers or even (as seems to have happened with one or two piano trios) borrowing the work of a fellow composer to fulfil a commission. The genres represented in Haydn's first years as a 'free' composer – piano sonatas, quartets, songs, symphonies, piano trios and others – reflect his commissions from various publishers rather than the music-making at Eszterháza.

In 1781, after a gap of about ten years, Haydn brought out another set of string quartets, known as op.33. These quartets have given rise to various reflections about a stylistic change that can scarcely be substantiated. Haydn had sold them to Artaria, but at the same time he wanted to make extra money by selling an issue of handwritten copies in advance, and sent letters inviting various distinguished patrons to subscribe, stressing that since these were his first quartets for about ten years they were written 'auf eine ganz neue, besondere Art' ('in a quite new, special manner'). This expression has been interpreted as Haydn's own emphasis on a change of style; more likely it was primarily intended as a selling point. After a ten-year interval Haydn's quartet style had indeed changed to some degree, but there is no basis for seeing this year as a turning-point in his general stylistic development. Neither did op.33 introduce a new wave of quartets. Apart from a single quartet dating from 1785, it was not until the late 1780s that he returned to the string quartet as an important part of his work.

Another type of chamber music in demand by publishers was the piano trio – or, in 18th-century terms, the sonata for piano with accompaniment for a violin and a cello, indicating its ancestry not in the Baroque trio sonata with continuo but in the solo keyboard sonata. Haydn had written keyboard trios before, most of them (according to Feder, 'Haydns frühe Klavier-trios', 1970) before or about 1760. (None is entered in the *EK* as a piano trio, as would certainly have been the case if they had been composed during Haydn's early years in Eisenstadt.) Meanwhile the genre had become fashionable in Paris and London, and several publishers were ready to bring out trios by Haydn, authorized or unauthorized. Besides Artaria, the London publisher William Forster was one of the first to publish new Haydn trios. He made contact with Haydn in 1781, through the British envoy in Vienna, and in the following years he published a great number of symphonies, trios and other works. The relationship came to an end a few years later when Haydn sold the same works to Forster and to Artaria, who in turn sold them to a second London publisher, Longman & Broderip.

Many other publishers issued Haydn's works, sometimes with his authority but mostly in pirated editions. Besides piano trios and string quartets, his symphonies were in great demand. The symphonies of these years (which were certainly performed at Eszterháza as well) were mostly published, like the trios, in sets of three. Nos.66–8, 76–8, 79–81 are such groups of three symphonies appearing in 1779 (Hummel), 1784 (Torricella and Artaria) and 1785 (Hummel) respectively. Among the publishers' favourite items are also the two collections of songs issued by Artaria in 1781 and 1784. Two well-known works, on the other hand, the Cello Concerto in D and the Piano Concerto in D, may reflect the continuing 'academies' at Eszterháza.

The Cello Concerto (1783) was composed for the fine cellist in Haydn's orchestra, Anton Kraft, who until the rediscovery of Haydn's dated autograph (Nowak, 1954), was for some time even credited with its composition. The Piano Concerto, published in three different editions in Paris, Vienna and London in 1784, though described as 'for the harpsichord or pianoforte' on all three title-pages, was undoubtedly written primarily for the piano and may well have been inspired by Mozart's activities as a concerto player and composer at just about this time. Another important composition stands out: the so-called 'Mariazell Mass' (1782), the result of a private commission and presumably intended as a votive offering at the pilgrimage church of Mariazell. Since the two fine masses of about 1766–70, the 'Cecilia Mass' and the 'Great Organ Mass', Haydn had composed only two smaller masses, the 'Nikolai Mass' (1772) and the 'Little Organ Mass' (?c1775). The 'Mariazell Mass' is again a fine, serious work, and it might have opened up a series of masses on a high level but for liturgical restrictions, which in 1783 forbade elaborate orchestral church music in favour of a simpler form of service. It was another 14 years before Haydn returned to mass composition.

Several of these works are manifestly important. But if the compositions of these years are compared with the impressive series of symphonies, quartets, keyboard sonatas and other works from about 1770, the difference is obvious. The fascinating breaking of new ground within a relatively short time-span around 1770 can be sensed in any of those groups; but in the years around 1780 the important symphonies, quartets and concertos stand out as isolated items, not as part of an overall strong creative impulse. Too much of Haydn's energy was still taken up in his duties as opera Kapellmeister and, until 1783–4, in the composing of operas. Here again he may have been confronted with the problem of differing tastes: in his last two works for the theatre he was approaching opera of a more serious kind, and he is said to have regarded *Armida* as his best opera. But apparently the prince preferred a less serious style, which might be one reason why Haydn stopped composing operas during his last seven years at Eszterháza, though he continued to conduct and arrange operas on a large scale.

It may be felt that giving up opera composition gave Haydn a stimulus for a fresh start in other fields; and at the same time he had the added encouragement of a constant demand for his music from outside. Compared with the music he wrote at the beginning of the 1780s, that of the later years of the decade shows more markedly Haydn's originality and his conscious creative progress. One of the most important commissions came from Paris when a concert enterprise, the Concert de la Loge Olympique, ordered six symphonies, probably in 1784–5. The scores are dated: two, nos.83 and 87, were composed in 1785, and three, nos.82, 84 and 86, in 1786 (it seems reasonable to suppose that the undated no.85 belongs with 83 and 87, forming a set of three symphonies from 1785 like the three of 1786). The six Paris symphonies stand out for their marked personality, comparable only with the expressive symphonies of about 1770 and the London symphonies of 1791–5. The Paris commission seems to have arrived at just the right moment for Haydn, as a challenge. His work in Eszterháza was approaching a state of humdrum routine. In the works composed for publishers, like

piano trios, sonatas or songs, he could – and did – excel
in fine craftsmanship; but such pieces allowed only
limited opportunities for novelty. The Paris symphonies,
on the other hand, are so personal and original that it is
immediately clear that Haydn was setting out again to
create something entirely his own.

A special sort of commission was that for *Die sieben
letzten Worte unseres Erlösers am Kreuze* ('The Seven
last Words of our Saviour on the Cross'), traditionally
dated 1785 but possibly written the following year
(Unverricht, 1959–63). The work was published by
Artaria in 1787 in three versions: the original version
for orchestra; a string quartet arrangement by Haydn
himself, later included in complete editions of Haydn's
quartets; and a piano reduction, not Haydn's own but
sanctioned by him ('I am pleased with the piano score,
which is very good and has been prepared with special
care'). Haydn's preface to his later vocal version tells of
this unique composition's origin. He was asked to
provide instrumental music for a special Lenten service
(clearly a three-hour Good Friday service) in Cádiz
Cathedral, in which the music was to serve as interludes
between meditations on each of the Seven Words.

Each time at the end of the sermon the orchestra would begin again. My
composition had to be in keeping with this presentation. It was not the
easiest task to compose seven Adagios in succession, each of them
lasting close on ten minutes, without tiring the listener, and I soon found
out that I could not be bound to the fixed time limit.

The first performance has been dated (Unverricht,
1959–63) to Holy Week 1787 in Cádiz, but performances are documented in Vienna and in Bonn from the
end of March 1787; this may indicate that the Cádiz
performance took place the previous year (as suggested
by Hoboken, 1957), which would mean that the work

must have been written in 1785 or early 1786.

The *Seven last Words* was again a stimulating challenge to Haydn. One of his finest talents, his constant ability to find new solutions to limiting problems (seen for example in his baryton trios and symphony minuets) was demonstrated here on a very high level. Few composers would have been able to avoid monotony. Haydn was rightly proud of the work, and it certainly helped pave the way for the final phase of his development as a symphonist.

In the late 1780s Haydn at last resumed the composition of string quartets, which had brought him his earliest European fame and in which he was still regarded as the unrivalled master. In 1783, after the appearance of op.33, Cramer's *Magazin der Musik* had published an open letter to Haydn from 'his admirers the German violinists', urging him to write new quartets. And in 1785 Mozart published his six quartets with the famous dedication to Haydn: 'Your approval above all encourages me to offer them to you and leads me to hope that you will not consider them wholly unworthy of your favour'. In the correspondence between Haydn and Artaria there is discussion about quartets in letters as early as 1784, and the one isolated quartet of 1785, op.42, was published separately in 1786. But no new series appeared until 1787, when the 'Prussian' Quartets (op.50), so called on account of their dedication to the Prussian King Friedrich Wilhelm II, were published. Two more sets of six, opp.54–5 and op.64, normally known as the 'Tost' Quartets, date from 1788–90 and were published in 1789–91. Presumably the Johann Tost who was a violinist in the Esterházy orchestra from 1783 to 1788 and visited Paris in or around 1789 is the same person as Johann Tost the wholesaler, who after marrying a rich wife in 1790 set up business in Vienna. Only the op.64 quartets were actually dedicated to Tost; the earlier set, together with two symphonies, were apparently sold to him, or perhaps given to him on commission, before he went to Paris (where he seems to have had some slightly dubious dealings over them).

Besides the two symphonies that Tost took to Paris (nos.88 and 89), there are three more from the late 1780s, nos.90–92 (1788–9). The title-page of what is probably the first edition of no.92 is headed 'Du Répertoire de la Loge Olympique', and the autographs of both nos.91 and 92 show dedications to the Count d'Ogny, one of the directors of those concerts, who once owned the autographs of the six earlier Paris symphonies. These three were undoubtedly written as a sequel to the previous set for the Concert de la Loge Olympique. In spite of that, Haydn also sold the symphonies to Prince Oettingen-Wallerstein as his exclusive property. No.92 later won fame as the work played when Haydn visited Oxford to receive the honorary DMus.

How far Haydn's obligations with the Eszterháza opera and his heavy commitments with outside commissions allowed him time to visit Vienna during the 1780s is uncertain. The accepted picture is hardly trustworthy, being based on few facts and much guesswork and generalization. That applies not least to the relationship between Haydn and Mozart. The two were clearly on cordial terms, at least from early 1785: Dies's account of Mozart's farewell before Haydn left for London, though highly romanticized, presumably originates to some degree from Haydn himself, and Haydn's distress at hearing of Mozart's death is clear in letters from England. All the same, calculations as to how much time

Haydn spent in Vienna during these years suggest that he and Mozart met less often than one might like to believe. Fully documented visits to Vienna are few, and, apart from an almost traditional visit around Christmas and New Year, appear generally to have been fairly short.

In December 1781 Haydn is said to have given music lessons in Vienna to Maria Fyodorovna of Russia, the wife of the Grand Duke Paul, later Emperor Paul II, and a concert at court on 25 December seems to have been devoted (largely or exclusively) to Haydn compositions. The op.33 quartets, published shortly afterwards, were dedicated to the Grand Duke (hence the name 'Russian' Quartets). At its winter concerts the same season (22 and 23 December) the Tonkünstler-Sozietät had planned to revive *Il ritorno di Tobia* and asked Haydn to make some revisions. Haydn was willing, but in the event, for some reason, Hasse's *S Elena al Calvario* was given instead. On 4 January 1782 he was back at Eszterháza, and of his visit a year later nothing is known beyond his signature on two documents dated Vienna, 1 January 1783.

In 1784 the performances of *Tobia* finally took place, on 28 and 30 March. Haydn had revised it and added two new choruses, one of which became well known as a separate 'motet' with a Latin text, 'Insanae et vanae curae'. But the society apparently saw no reason to try to straighten out its blunder of five years before. In December Haydn was again in Vienna, probably in time for the performances of *La fedeltà premiata* in the Kärntnertortheater on 19 and 20 December, his last performance in Eszterháza having been on 5 December. Later in the month (29 December) he applied for membership of the freemasons' Lodge 'Zur wahren

Eintracht'. For Haydn, unlike Mozart, freemasonry was apparently only a passing phase. His admission on 11 February 1785 as an entered apprentice was his first and last appearance at a lodge.

Mozart was prevented by a concert engagement from attending Haydn's initiation, and evidently they never met in masonic circles. But it seems to have been at just this time that they came to know each other well. Leopold Mozart, quoting a letter (now lost) from his son, wrote to Nannerl that the new quartets, later dedicated to Haydn, were played on 15 January 1785 to 'his dear friend Haydn and other good friends'. The following month Leopold arrived in Vienna and on 12 February, at a similar performance in Wolfgang's house, heard from Haydn the famous compliment: 'Before God and as an honest man I tell you that your son is the greatest composer known to me either in person or by name. He has taste and, what is more, the greatest knowledge of composition'. Michael Kelly in his colourful *Reminiscences* provides another (unconfirmed) account of a quartet evening at Stephen Storace's, possibly as early as summer 1784, where the quartet players were Dittersdorf, Haydn, Mozart and Vanhal. Apparently quartet playing was central to the contact between Haydn and Mozart, and the dedication of Mozart's quartets on their publication later in 1785 completes the picture. From the next four years, however, the only document attesting to their relationship is the famous letter from Haydn to Roth in Prague (December 1787), praising Mozart in the warmest terms. Not until the turn of 1789–90 is there evidence of their meeting again, when Mozart invited Puchberg to attend the rehearsals of *Così fan tutte* with Haydn. Altogether there is little information on Haydn's visits

5. *Joseph Haydn: anonymous miniature (?c1788)*

to Vienna in the late 1780s. Christian Gottlob Breitkopf met him there in December 1786, but this was apparently a short visit: his opera performances at Eszterháza lasted almost up to Christmas, and a letter testifies that he was back again by 29 December. In 1789 he must have been in the capital until mid-February (letter of 8 March), but nothing is known about what he did there.

In June 1789 Haydn received a letter that opened up a friendship of unique character in his life. Maria Anna (or Marianne) von Genzinger, the wife of Prince Nikolaus's Viennese doctor Peter von Genzinger, sent him a piano reduction she had made of an Andante from one of his symphonies; she asked for his corrections and expressed the hope of seeing him soon in Vienna. This was the beginning of a long correspondence, which provides an unparalleled insight into Haydn's personality as well as a charming picture of the young woman whose admiration caused Haydn to confess to her his inner feelings in a way not found in any of his other letters. He expressed his need of her understanding: 'I hope your Grace will not be discouraged from comforting me from time to time with your pleasing correspondence, which is so essential to me, in my solitude, to cheer my heart, often so deeply hurt'. One of the most impressive and charming letters is the oft-quoted one written from Eszterháza on 9 February 1790, after Haydn's return from Vienna, in which he looked back on his happy visits to the Genzinger home there and compared them with his isolation at Eszterháza during chilly February. Haydn had clearly met something previously unknown to him, or at least unknown to him for a long time – the warmth and sympathy of a circle of friends, the comforts and pleasure of kind and like-minded people. He had had a glimpse of a life very different from his own at Eszterháza, and it had made him look forward the more eagerly to the time when he could move to Vienna.

About two weeks after he wrote that letter, on 25 February, Princess Maria Elisabeth Esterházy died; Prince Nikolaus survived her by only a few months, dying on 28 September. His successor, Prince Anton, did not inherit his father's pleasure in music; he dismissed the orchestra, retaining only the wind band (or

6. *Part of an autograph letter (9 February 1790) from
Haydn to Maria Anna von Genzinger*

Feldmusik). Haydn and the fine leading violinist, Tomasini, were nominally to continue as before. He remained titular Kapellmeister, on full salary, but without obligations of any kind. He could now move to Vienna, where he first found a home with a friend, Johann Nepomuk Hamberger He declined the offer of a new position as Kapellmeister to Prince Anton Grassalkovics, intending to have a peaceful time in Vienna after the many years at Eszterháza.

4. London

Haydn's plans soon changed. The German-born violinist J. P. Salomon, now a concert manager in London, was on the Continent to engage soloists for his next season. While in Cologne he had heard of the death of Prince Nikolaus Esterházy, and he at once set off for Vienna to try to secure Haydn for his concerts. He went, according to Dies, without previous notice to Haydn's house, and said bluntly: 'I am Salomon from London and have come to fetch you. Tomorrow we shall conclude an agreement'.

The plan of bringing Haydn to London was not new. During the 1780s several attempts had been made to entice him to England, by the organizers of the Professional Concerts and by the publisher Bland, and more than once the London press had optimistically announced his imminent arrival (Roscoe, 1968). Salomon succeeded where previous attempts had failed. Free from princely duties, Haydn was now in a position to agree terms. For a substantial fee he was to compose an opera, six symphonies and 20 other pieces to be performed in as many concerts under his own direction. Leaving Vienna on 15 December, Haydn and Salomon travelled via Munich, Wallerstein and Bonn to Calais, and landed in England on New Year's Day 1791.

The two visits to London were landmarks in Haydn's life: first because they gave rise to a number of outstanding new works, among them the 12 London symphonies, and second because England provided him with fresh stimulation. The rich musical life, in public concerts, clubs and private circles, and the fine, large orchestras, could not but impress him. The cosmopolitan atmosphere, then accentuated by an influx of refugees from the French Revolution, was an exciting new experience. No single event impressed him more deeply than the great Handel Commemoration of 1791, at which he heard *Messiah* and *Israel in Egypt*; this was to have a decisive influence on the choral music of his final Viennese years. Not least, his success in London greatly increased his prestige at home; he returned to Vienna not as a provincial Kapellmeister but as an international celebrity – and, what is more, a Doctor of Music.

The London visits constitute the most fully documented period of Haydn's career. His own notebooks record the places he visited and the people he met, though much of their contents amounts to no more than a tourist's jottings; and he was of course hampered by the language barrier. A considerable number of letters to Marianne von Genzinger survive. And there is a rich source of information in London newspapers. From Pohl (1867) to Landon (1959), and beyond, much of this material has been published.

The main focus of Haydn's life in London was naturally Salomon's concerts, about which contemporary advertisements and reviews provide a wealth of detail. After two postponements the series began on 11 March 1791, with concerts in the Hanover Square Rooms every Friday (except 22 April) until 3 June. The second season, the following year, again took place on Fridays, between 17 February and 18 May, with an extra concert on 6 June. Each series followed a similar pattern: the concerts were in two parts, the first consisting of a symphony ('Overture') by another composer (Rosetti, Clementi, Gyrowetz and others), followed by concertos and instrumental and vocal solos, with Haydn's symphony reserved for the second part, when the latecomers had arrived. After the symphony there were further concertos and solos, and the programme ended with a 'Full piece' or 'Finale', or on occasion a symphony by another composer. Obviously, with so many concerts in each series, Haydn's 'New Grand Overture' could not always be a première. During the first season only two symphonies composed specially for London were heard. There were several repeat performances, often 'By particular Desire', and some of his earlier symphonies were still new to London. The London symphonies proper were not introduced in the order of the numbering now in use. The concert programmes are too vague for identification of the actual works performed, but with the help of the dated autographs, Haydn's notebooks and reports in the press Landon has been able to draw up a probable chronology of first performances for the 1791 and 1792 seasons, as follows: no.96, 11 March 1791; no.95, ?1791; no.93, 17 February 1792; no.98, 2 March 1792; no.94 (composed before no.98, autograph dated 1791), 23 March 1792; no.97, 3 or 4 May 1792. Other notable works first heard in Salomon's concerts were the *Storm* chorus to words by Peter Pindar, Haydn's first setting of an English text (24 February 1792), and the Sinfonia concertante in B♭ for violin, cello, oboe and bassoon (9 March 1792). The programmes also featured divertimentos and a series of notturnos, arrangements of those for two *lire organizzate* written for the King of Naples just before Haydn's departure for London, with the two *lira* parts replaced by flute and oboe.

Besides Salomon's regular series there were many other concerts that Haydn took part in or attended as a

7. *Advertisement from 'The Times' (16 May 1791) con-*
cerning Haydn's benefit concert, to be given on that day

listener. His benefit concert on 16 May 1791 (see fig.7),
for which he had been guaranteed receipts of £200,
brought in £350. At an extra concert on 30 May Haydn
conducted the *Seven last Words*, framed by two of his
symphonies. (There was another benefit for him towards
the end of the second season, on 3 May 1792, and
shortly afterwards, on 21 May, he in turn presided at
Salomon's benefit.) In May 1791 he attended the Handel
Commemoration in Westminster Abbey. From 6 to 8
July he was in Oxford, where he took part in three
concerts and received the honorary degree of Doctor of
Music.

Socially too Haydn was in demand in a way to which
he was quite unaccustomed, so that a week after his

arrival in London, on 8 January 1791, he could write to Marianne von Genzinger:

Everyone wants to know me. I had to dine out six times up to now, and if I wanted, I could have an invitation every day; but first I must consider my health, and second my work. Except for the nobility, I admit no callers till 2 o'clock in the afternoon.

Ten days later he was received at a court ball at St James's, and the next evening attended a concert given by the Prince of Wales. Between the two concert seasons he was a frequent guest at houses in London and the provinces. Only from one quarter did he meet with opposition: from the Professional Concerts, the rival concern to Salomon's concert series. It was apparently at their instigation that on 13 January 1791 a notice appeared in the press: 'Upon the arrival of Haydn, it was discovered that he no longer possessed his former powers. Pity it is that the discovery did not possess the merit of novelty'; and on 5 February: 'The nine days wonder about Haydn begins to abate. . . . The truth is, this wonderful composer is but a very poor performer; and though he may be qualified to preside at a harpsichord, we have never heard him celebrated as a leader of a Concert'.

Despite the success of Salomon's first series, the innuendos continued, and for the 1792 season the Professional Concerts engaged Haydn's former pupil Ignace Pleyel as a counter-attraction – 'so', as Haydn wrote to Marianne von Genzinger on 17 January 1792, 'a bloody harmonious war will commence between master and pupil'. But 'Pleyel behaved so modestly towards me upon his arrival that he won my affection again. . . . We shall share our laurels equally and each go home satisfied'. In the event there was room enough for both of them.

One project of the first London visit fell through: the opera *L'anima del filosofo* (*Orfeo ed Euridice*) had been part of Haydn's original contract with Salomon, and the work was finished in May 1791, but the failure of the impresario Gallini to obtain a licence for opera forced the abandonment of the production. The period between the two concert seasons, however, saw the beginning of work that was to occupy Haydn (and later Beethoven) for many years: the arrangement of folksongs, initially with violin and piano accompaniment, later with cello as well. The first collection, issued early in 1792, was done to help the publisher William Napier, who was in financial trouble, but the immediate success of the songs resulted in a series of further collections in later years (some apparently arranged with the help of pupils), most of them published by George Thomson in Edinburgh.

In summer 1791 Haydn took as a pupil Rebecca Schroeter, widow of J. S. Schroeter, the well-known pianist and composer. During the autumn and winter a close relationship developed between teacher and pupil: her letters, which Haydn copied into his notebook, perhaps before returning them, leave no doubt about her passionate feelings ('no language can express half the love and affection I feel for you'). It is not known whether Haydn's departure from London the following summer put an end to their romance, or whether they met during his return visit (when his lodgings were close to her home). However, an edition of three piano trios dedicated to her was published as op.73 after his second departure, in 1795, and she signed as a witness an agreement he made with a publisher in 1796.

Haydn left London at the end of June 1792. He travelled again through Bonn (where he certainly met Beethoven, who was to go to Vienna as his pupil),

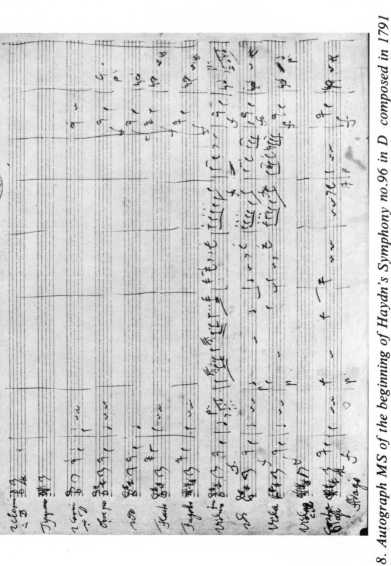

8. Autograph MS of the beginning of Haydn's Symphony no.96 in D composed in 1791

passed through Frankfurt (where he met Prince Anton, there for the coronation of Emperor Franz II) and arrived in Vienna on 24 July. His spell in Vienna between the two London visits seems to have been rather quiet. Apparently his unprecedented successes in England had made little impression in Vienna; the contrast between the interest in Haydn shown by the newspapers in London and those in Vienna is striking. He was able to work in peace, preparing for his second London visit. Symphony no.99 and the 'Apponyi' Quartets opp.71 and 74 date from this period. In November Beethoven arrived; but the two men's personalities proved incompatible. As far as is known, Haydn had earlier been a good, conscientious teacher (Pleyel is the most important of his pupils). Perhaps he was now too deeply engaged in composition; perhaps he was simply unable to follow the young titan; or he may have sensed Beethoven's genius without being able to meet him on his own terms. Beethoven moved on to teachers (like Albrechtsberger and Schenk) who could simply teach him the craft but would not tend to influence his style. In January 1793 Marianne von Genzinger died, aged only 38. Mozart had died while Haydn was in London. Luigia Polzelli had finally returned to Italy. During Haydn's stay in London, his wife had found a small house in Gumpendorf, a Viennese suburb, and had tactfully suggested that it would suit her later as a widow. Haydn bought the house in autumn 1793; he moved in four years later, remaining there until his death – from March 1800 as a widower. In autumn 1793 Haydn came to an agreement with Salomon about a second visit to London: all that is known of it is that he was again to compose six symphonies.

Haydn left Vienna on 19 January 1794, accompanied

by Johann Elssler, his copyist and assistant for about the last 20 years of his life. They stopped in Passau, where Haydn heard, probably on 21 January, his own *Seven last Words* in a choral arrangement by the local Kapellmeister Joseph Frieberth (according to Neukomm it was on his way back in 1795 that Haydn heard the arrangement); Haydn remembered this performance and after his return to Vienna made a similar version himself (first given in 1796). An episode in Wiesbaden is all that is otherwise reported about his journey to London, where he arrived later than planned, on 4 February 1794, the day after Salomon's season should have begun.

The Salomon series had been moved to Monday, the evening of the now defunct Professional Concerts. There was no longer tension between two rival enterprises, and that may account for the less complete newspaper coverage. As before, 12 concerts were given in the spring season, weekly from 10 February to 7 April and 28 April to 12 May; there were also various benefit concerts. Programmes for the single concerts were along the same lines as those of 1791–2. This was Salomon's last season: in January 1795 he advertised that the concerts would cease, primarily on account of the difficulty of obtaining 'vocal performers of the first talents from abroad' (no doubt because of the war with France). They were succeeded by a new series, the 'Opera Concerts', in which Haydn joined. These were on Mondays in 1795: 2, 16 and 23 February, 2 and 16 March, 13 and 27 April, 11 and 18 May, with Haydn's benefit concert on 4 May. His new symphonies were performed, according to Landon, as follows: no.99 (composed in 1793, in Vienna), 10 February 1794; no.101, 3 March 1794; no.100, 31 March 1794;

no.102 (composed 1794), 2 February 1795; no.103, 2 March 1795; and no.104, probably 13 April.

Haydn's contacts with English publishers were extended during his second stay in London. In 1791–2 Bland had published some piano trios and, jointly with Haydn, the cantata *Arianna a Naxos*; his edition of the second series of 'Tost' Quartets (as op.65) referred specifically to the Salomon concerts of 1791–2 ('Composed by Giuseppe Haydn and Performed under his Direction, at Mr. Salomon's Concert'). The quartets heard in the 1794 concerts, certainly from the 'Apponyi' Quartets, were published in 1795–6 by Corri, Dussek & Co., who in 1794 had published the first part of Haydn's English songs ('Dr. Haydn's VI Original Canzonettas') jointly with the composer, and in 1795 the second part on their own. Piano trios were issued by Preston and (no fewer than three series) by Longman & Broderip, partly after Haydn's return to Vienna. For some years Haydn had a special agreement with Longman & Broderip, signed in July–August 1796 between him and F. A. Hyde, 'musick seller' for Longman & Broderip (and from 1801 a partner in Clementi, Banger, Hyde, Collard & Davis); the existence of such an agreement has long been conjectured, but the actual signed contract came to light only in 1976. During Haydn's second stay in London his three last piano sonatas were written. According to a small (now lost) catalogue of his works composed in England they were intended for Therese Jansen, who in 1795 married the son of the engraver Francesco Bartolozzi; Haydn, as a friend of the Bartolozzi family, was a witness.

In spring 1795 Haydn played and conducted – and even sang – on numerous occasions for the royal family, at the Duke of York's, and above all in concerts at the Prince of Wales's at Carlton House. In April the prince married Princess Caroline of Brunswick, who was fond of music and was able to play a piano concerto 'fairly well', according to Haydn. The king and queen even tried to persuade Haydn to stay on in London, and offered him summer quarters at Windsor. But Haydn had made up his mind. He would certainly have wanted to return to Vienna in any case, but a new situation made his homecoming more urgent. In January 1794, just after Haydn's departure for London, Prince Paul Anton Esterházy had died, only four years after his father. His son, the younger Prince Nikolaus, had written as early as summer 1794 to ask Haydn to return and re-establish the orchestra. Haydn, nominally still Kapellmeister, had asked for another year's leave to be able to fulfil his obligations in London. Now he wanted to go home to take up such duties as might be required of him. He spent another couple of months in England after the end of the concert season; on 15 August he left London, and after travelling via Hamburg and Dresden arrived in Vienna probably at the end of the month.

5. Late years

Haydn's renewed activities as Kapellmeister did not prevent his settling in Vienna as planned. Eszterháza had been given up after the death of Prince Nikolaus in 1790, and the two princely residences were now Eisenstadt and Vienna. Haydn could go on living in Vienna for most of the year, spending only a few months in the summer in Eisenstadt, where he seems to have had his lodgings in the castle. His house in Vienna was not yet ready; until the early summer of 1797 he stayed in a house in the heart of old Vienna on the Neuer Markt, in the same square as the winter palace of Prince Schwarzenberg (where the first performances of his two late oratorios were to take place a few years later).

Haydn's new obligations were much lighter than his former ones. He did certainly function as Kapellmeister – at least until 1802, when Johann Fuchs was appointed Vice-Kapellmeister – but on a much more limited scale. The prince's interests centred on church music, and Haydn's most important obligation was the composition of a new mass every summer to celebrate the name day (8 September) of Princess Maria Hermenegild, for performance in Eisenstadt the following Sunday. Music at court was more as it had been in Haydn's early years in Eisenstadt than during the lavish reign of Prince Nikolaus I at Eszterháza. Haydn remained active as a composer until about 1803, and there was no falling-off in the quality of his music. Indeed, his works of these years are paralleled only by the prominent group of revolutionary symphonies, quartets and other pieces from about 1770. But more than in any earlier period it was the vocal works that took the lead. The central line of development, formerly discernible chiefly in symphonies or quartets, is now carried by the six great masses of 1796–1802; still more famous are the two late oratorios. No symphonies follow the London visits, but there were some exceptionally fine quartets.

The first years after Haydn's return from London seem to have been relatively quiet, but he attended and participated in a number of concerts. In September 1796 the first of his late masses was performed in Eisenstadt. (It was either the *Heiligmesse* or the *Paukenmesse*: both are dated 1796, and no mass is dated 1797. According to Brand and Schnerich, as opposed to Pohl, Botstiber and others, the *Paukenmesse* was the earlier, whereas the *Heiligmesse*, also begun in 1796, was finished after the *Paukenmesse* and first performed in September 1797; but there is still room for doubt.) At the beginning of 1797 he composed one of his most famous pieces, *Gott erhalte Franz den Kaiser*, which was introduced to the public in the Burgtheater on the birthday of the emperor, 12 February. The 'Emperor's Hymn', inspired by *God save the King*, was for many years Austria's national anthem.

Another work owing its inspiration to England was *Die Schöpfung* ('The Creation') begun about this time. The initial stimulus came from Haydn's experience of Handel's music in London. According to tradition he was given in London a libretto originally written for Handel, and that was the basis of the text put together for him by Gottfried van Swieten, director of the court library in Vienna, himself an amateur composer, and leader of a group of the nobility that sponsored concerts (for invited guests only) in the Schwarzenberg Palace.

Under the auspices of that society Haydn's own vocal version of the *Seven last Words* had been first performed on 26 March 1796. Van Swieten had pioneered Handel's music in Vienna: in the 1780s he had organized the famous oratorio performances in the library's great hall, in which Mozart had participated and for which Mozart's arrangements of *Messiah* and other Handel works were made. He had earlier tried to persuade Haydn to compose a work 'in the manner and spirit of Handel', and was now happy to lend his support to the projected oratorio. A close collaboration between him and Haydn resulted: van Swieten provided not only the text but also (apparently at Haydn's request) suggestions as to the details of musical treatment. Haydn even took a flat in the inner town for the winter to facilitate the collaboration. During the composition of the work Haydn became deeply involved in it, spiritually and emotionally. He feared that it might be too unusual for his Viennese audiences, but in fact it was an unprecedented success: it was first heard at two private performances in the Schwarzenberg Palace on 29 and 30 April 1798, and after its public première in Vienna the following year it was quickly taken up throughout Europe. Perhaps no other piece of great music has ever enjoyed such immediate and universal acceptance.

The success of *The Creation* naturally called for a sequel. Van Swieten and Haydn accordingly set to work on a second oratorio, *Die Jahreszeiten*, again based (though more loosely) on a model in English, James Thomson's *The Seasons*. This time their collaboration was perhaps less successful. The text of *The Seasons* is more down-to-earth, almost like the Singspiel, with an element of homespun, bourgeois morality. Haydn did not enjoy having to compose a panegyric to diligence

('O Fleiss, du edler Fleiss'), and he seems to have felt that van Swieten was overbearing in some of his musical suggestions. In spite of the conscious attempt to make *The Seasons* follow in the steps of *The Creation* the subject matter of the two works is essentially different: to paraphrase Haydn, the country folk of *The Seasons* are no match for the three archangels of *The Creation*. But the music was again of wonderful freshness and unfailing originality, though Haydn found composing the work a strain and in later years repeatedly said that the oratorio had overtaxed him. It is not, like *The Creation*, an unbroken stream of inspiration, a feeling of one great unity, but rather four relatively independent scenes of rural life, each set off against the others with masterly characterization of the varying situations. *The Seasons* was first performed privately in the Schwarzenberg Palace on 24 and 27 April and 1 May 1801, a month later publicly in Vienna, and soon, like *The Creation*, all over Europe.

In between the oratorios Haydn continued to produce his yearly mass for Eisenstadt: in 1798 the 'Nelson Mass' (headed 'Missa in angustiis' in Haydn's own catalogue but in the inventory of his estate already listed as 'Nelsonmesse'); in 1799 the *Theresienmesse*; in 1801 (there was no mass in 1800, probably on account of *The Seasons*) the *Schöpfungsmesse*; and in 1802 the *Harmoniemesse*. The greater of Haydn's two settings of the *Te Deum* dates from 1798–1800 (Becker-Glauch, 1967); according to Griesinger it was written not for Esterházy but for the Empress Consort Marie Therese. From the late 1790s there remain two collections of secular vocal works: 13 three- and four-part songs and 40–45 canons. The fine partsongs, published in 1803 in the 'Oeuvres complettes' and also separately, were 'writ-

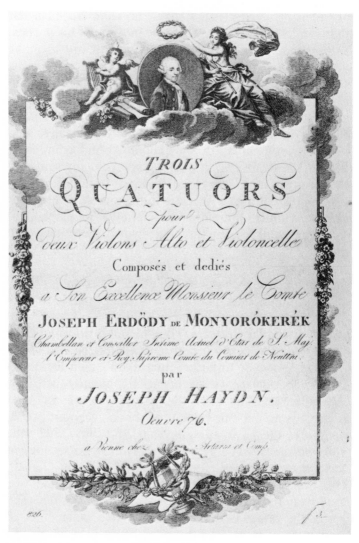

9. Title-page of the 'Erdődy' Quartets op.76, published by Artaria in 1799

ten con amore in happy hours, not commissioned', according to Haydn's words to Griesinger. The canons – their forerunners are the *Ten Commandments*, which apparently date back to Haydn's London years – are still more private. Haydn probably composed them after settling in his house in Vienna, and had them framed to decorate the walls of his study. They were not published until after his death.

The only instrumental genre that Haydn pursued into his last years as an active composer was the string quartet. The last complete set of six quartets, the 'Erdődy' Quartets (op.76), were published in 1799 but composed wholly or partly, in 1797. Two quartets that still show Haydn's special command of the medium, the 'Lobkowitz' Quartets (op.77) of 1799, appeared in 1802. One last one (op.103) was published unfinished in 1803. After that Haydn still sent arrangements of folksongs to Thomson in Edinburgh until about 1805, but it seems certain that for many of them he had recourse to assistance from Sigismund Neukomm and perhaps other pupils as well.

In his late years Haydn came to be the 'grand old man': honorary citizen of Vienna, honorary member of music societies, recipient of gold medals, and so on. Numerous visitors from home and abroad paid him visits, which pleased him, though in his last years he was often not strong enough to entertain foreign guests. Publishers sought to put together various kinds of 'collected editions', and prospective authors sought biographical material for memoirs of him. Through Griesinger, counsellor to the Saxon Legation in Vienna, the famous Leipzig publishing house of Breitkopf & Härtel secured Haydn's collaboration on – or at least his authorization of – a series of 12 volumes called with substantial exaggeration 'Oeuvres complettes' but in fact comprising only piano sonatas (and other pieces), piano trios and songs, among them the three- and four-part songs and the cantata *Arianna a Naxos*. They also started publishing Haydn's masses in score, but stopped after seven. A famous quartet edition was issued in 1802 by Pleyel, by now a publisher in Paris, including the spurious 'op.3' and the quartet version of the *Seven last Words*; a revised edition of 1806 added the unfinished op.103, thereby arriving at the canonical figure of 83 quartets which remained unchallenged until fairly recently. Even if not 'complettes', relatively comprehensive editions of Haydn's symphonies in score (something quite unusual at the time) appeared in London and Paris, a few of them in premature pocket scores.

Besides acting as a mediator for Breitkopf & Härtel, Griesinger through his many conversations with Haydn collected material for what was to become his biography of the composer. One of the most valuable sources of knowledge about Griesinger's gleanings, his letters to Breitkopf & Härtel, was lost in World War II, though extracts had been copied and have since been published. Dies visited Haydn for the express purpose of collecting biographical material; his single chapters, arranged chronologically as a series of interviews, give a clear picture of Haydn's changing state of mind about 1805, when Dies began his visits.

Associated with the gathering of material about Haydn's life is the 'Catalogue of all those compositions which I recall having made from my 18th to my 73rd year', generally referred to as the 'Haydn-Verzeichnis' (*HV*). Using the 'Entwurf-Katalog', the so-called 'Kees-Katalog' (of symphonies), volumes of the 'Oeuvres com-

10. *Performance of Haydn's 'Creation' in the great hall of the university in 1808: painting by Balthasar Wigand on a wooden casket destroyed in World War II*

plettes', the Pleyel quartet edition and others, Haydn's copyist the younger Elssler was able to put this catalogue together under Haydn's supervision (see Larsen, 1939, 1941). Though far from complete, it has greatly helped towards the realization of a comprehensive picture of Haydn's output.

On 26 December 1803 Haydn made his last public appearance as a conductor, directing the *Seven last Words*. He now no longer went to Eisenstadt but stayed in his house in Vienna, attending concerts from time to time, the last occasion being a performance of *The Creation* in the hall of the old university, with Salieri conducting, on 27 March 1808. A contemporary picture gives an impression of the event, and shows its modest scale: a small choir (with boys, not women) and a very small orchestra (see fig.10).

Haydn's last days were a sad time for Vienna. Napoleon besieged and conquered the city after a heavy bombardment on 12–13 May 1809. Haydn did not want to go to the inner town, and stayed in his house in Gumpendorf; after the capitulation of the city Napoleon ordered a guard of honour before his house. But Haydn was getting weaker, and did not regain his strength. On 31 May 1809 he died quietly at home. On 1 June, Corpus Christi, he was buried at the Hundsturm Cemetery; the following day Requiem Mass was celebrated in the Gumpendorf church. Two weeks later, on 15 June, a great memorial service was held in the Schottenkirche in the inner city, at which Mozart's Requiem was performed. 'The whole art-loving world of Vienna was present, mostly in mourning. Everything was very solemn and worthy of Haydn' (Rosenbaum diaries; see Radant, 1968). His remains are now interred in the Bergkirche in Eisenstadt.

6. Personality

For years the nickname 'Papa Haydn' has characterized the composer. Used by his own musicians and others as a tribute of affection and respect, that expression increasingly took on misleading connotations, and came to signify a benevolent but bewigged and old-fashioned classic. The recent revival of interest in Haydn's music has made plain that the traditional picture had become a caricature, and that it gave a false impression of the richness and diversity of his development as a composer. To obtain a true likeness of the man himself, however, is more difficult. Biographical material is scarce, and much of what is known about his personal life, deriving as it does from Haydn's reminiscences in later years, may be coloured by his views as an old man. There seems to have been a certain duality to his character. In his youth he was apparently lively and spirited, even when his circumstances were modest; but as a young Kapellmeister he could be blunt and self-assertive, as shown by his quarrels with Werner and Rahier and his letter to the Tonkünstler-Sozietät. But it seems as if at a relatively early stage he learnt to control his temper and to moderate his personal involvement in his dealings with people. Granted that many of the surviving letters are of a purely business nature, it is difficult to form an impression of Haydn through his correspondence in general. Only in the letters to Marianne von Genzinger did Haydn put aside his reserve and give his inner feelings free rein.

It is understandable that Haydn should have chosen

to conceal his personal feelings. His isolation, caused by his unhappy marriage, and by the limitations imposed on his social life by his position as a court official and his heavy commitments as Kapellmeister, was bound to make him self-reliant; he seems to have had no outside friends with whom he could share his troubles. But a fuller knowledge of his personal life would scarcely contribute towards a better understanding of his music. His aim was to make good music, and to express universal, not personal, human feelings; in this he was essentially a composer of the 18th century, however close he came to the dawn of the 19th.

As far as is known, Haydn had scarcely any pronounced literary insight or broader cultural understanding. His artistic sensibilities were primarily confined to music. As a court officer he acquired the social graces necessary to allow him to move easily in the circles of princes and kings, but that sort of life interested him little: 'I have associated with emperors, kings and many great people, and I have heard many flattering things from them, but I would not live in familiar relations with such persons; I prefer to be close to people of my own standing' (Griesinger). He was, however, fully aware of his own musical stature. He knew that only Mozart was his peer, and never hesitated to praise his young friend, as he did to Leopold Mozart, or to Burney: 'Friends often flatter me that I have some genius, but he stood far above me'.

In his daily life Haydn had a number of attractive characteristics. He was kind by nature; as he would say: 'Anyone can see by the looks of me that I am a good-natured sort of fellow' (see Pohl, 1875, i, 220). He was helpful and understanding to his musicians: several letters tell of his acting as guarantor for them to the prince.

He would remember for years a kindness shown to him when he was in need, as his will testifies. He was a modest and honest man in everyday life, notwithstanding his awareness of his position as a composer, and the many business arrangements that were certainly no less than shrewd. He was punctual, and liked to be blamelessly dressed. As Dies wrote:

Love of order seemed as inborn in him as industry. The former was to be observed, as also his love of cleanliness, in his person and in his entire household. He never received visits, for instance, if he were not first fully clothed. If he were surprised by a friend, he tried to get at least enough time to put on his wig.

This element of conventional respectability was only one facet of Haydn's many-sided personality. Another was a well-developed, but perhaps often subdued, sense of humour. 'A harmless roguery, or what the British call humour, was one of Haydn's outstanding characteristics' (Griesinger). 'The features joined with the look to express dignity if Haydn was inclined to be serious; otherwise in conversation he easily assumed a cheerful, smiling countenance. I never heard him laugh aloud' (Dies).

Haydn was a good Catholic all his life; he would normally begin his manuscripts with 'In nomine Domini' and end them with 'Laus Deo'. But in religious matters too he preserved a certain moderation. He would not follow the urging of his parents that he should take holy orders; but for some years he served as organist, and seems to have had good contacts with a number of monasteries, which obtained copies of his works soon after their composition. Yet he blamed his wife for bigotry: she was 'continually inviting the clergy to dinner, had many masses said, and was freer with charitable contributions than her situation warranted'

11. Joseph Haydn: bust (1801–2) by Anton Grassi

(Griesinger). His masses, sublime expressions of the Viennese Classical style, in later generations came to be regarded as over-secular in manner, but are now recognized as bearing witness to Haydn's true, unaffected devotion.

Haydn's appearance is known from various descriptions and from a great number of pictures and sculptures. He was not good-looking. He was 'something under medium size', and 'the lower half of his body was too short for the upper'. 'His features were fairly regular; his look was eloquent, fiery, but still moderate, kind, attractive'. One thing marred his complexion: 'His hawk's nose (he suffered much from a nasal polyp, which had doubtless enlarged this feature) and other features as well were heavily pock-marked' (Dies). Of the many Haydn portraits some were acknowledged as good likenesses by Haydn and his friends, but a great number even of the well-known ones are certainly misleading. From his earlier years there is a good painting (*c*1768) by Grundmann, the Esterházy court painter, showing the young and self-assertive Kapellmeister in his court uniform (fig.2). In a very different style is the picture after Guttenbrunn, in its original version probably dating from about 1770, showing the young composer at the keyboard (fig.4). The often-reproduced engraving by J. E. Mansfeld and the painting by Seehas (in two versions) from the 1780s cannot be counted among the good portraits. But there is a good miniature from about 1788 (in the Gesellschaft der Musikfreunde in Vienna; fig.5). Haydn's visits to London gave rise to various pictures, paintings and engravings. Most of these are fine testimonies to the English tradition of portraiture, but in several cases they tend to make Haydn appear too much of a country gentleman. One picture of Haydn from his stay in London, however, perhaps surpasses any other pictorial record of the composer: the drawing by George Dance (in two versions), which Haydn told Griesinger in 1799 was the best picture of himself (fig.13). From Haydn's late years in Vienna there are no good paintings, but a number of good sculptures, above all two busts by Grassi (fig.11), praised by Griesinger as well as by Carpani; there is also a death-mask.

7. Artistic development

Haydn's music has long been approached with prejudice; he has been seen merely as a benevolent paternal figure, father of the symphony, and a forerunner of Beethoven. More recently a period of 'Sturm und Drang' or romantic crisis has been seen in his development, adding a new dimension to the traditional view but explaining nothing beyond the limited period to which it should refer.

Any attempt at an unprejudiced survey of Haydn's many-sided development must first of all be based on an understanding of his position as a moving force in the evolution of music in his own day, the 18th century, and not the 19th. A few particular circumstances need to be kept in mind. First, his long creative life spanned pronounced changes in musical style, from the late Baroque through the rather colourless mid-century Viennese style to the mature Classical style and even, in his late years, a foreshadowing of 19th-century Romanticism. Second, except for a short stay in Lukavec (Bohemia) around 1760, Haydn spent the whole of his life up to 1790 in the relatively isolated part of Austria–Hungary from Vienna to Eisenstadt–Eszterháza and Pressburg, in which area he was born, received his musical training and worked as a Kapellmeister for about 30 years. Unlike Mozart, who grew up in cosmopolitan musical surroundings, with the accent on the Italian style, Haydn's roots were in the traditions of Austrian music, from Baroque church music to divertimento and Singspiel. Third, Haydn composed for an audience of connoisseurs and amateurs – 'für Kenner und Liebhaber', in C. P. E. Bach's terms – and it is part of his greatness that he was able to display his extraordinary musicianship and inventiveness not only in outstanding masterworks but also in more domestic pieces like the baryton trios.

Various attempts have been made to divide Haydn's artistic development into a number of periods, for example by decades (Geiringer, 1932) or with a more complex division into eight periods (Larsen, 1950 and 1956). In a modified form the latter arrangement may be represented as follows: Vienna (to *c*1761); Eisenstadt (1761–6); Eszterháza, years of expansion (1766–*c*1775); operatic activity (*c*1775–84); foreign commissions (1785–90); London (1791–5); Vienna (1795–1809).

(*i*) *Vienna, early years.* Because of the scarcity of information about Haydn's early years and the many uncertainties with regard to authenticity and chronology, his early development can be surveyed only tentatively. That this period should present a rather mixed impression of the young composer's work is hardly surprising. His course was determined not by his own preferences but by the commissions that came his way. His close contact with church music is reflected in the early F major *Missa brevis* (*c*1750) and the *Salve regina* in E (1756). The mass is a charming, simple piece, mostly homophonic, with two solo sopranos; the accompaniment, for two violins and bass only, is simple too, with traces of the younger Reutter's 'rauschende Violinen'. The *Salve regina* is in a more Italianate, professional style, apparently reflecting Porpora's influence. The only dated instrumental composition from these years, the Organ

(or Harpsichord) Concerto in C (1756), also points to
the traditions of church music and demonstrates that
Haydn had by that time established himself as a composer of some accomplishment – not yet as an in-
novator, but as a talented newcomer following in the
footsteps of Wagenseil and others.

A number of divertimentos probably date from the
1750s. A few of these have more than five movements, a
few others only four, but the type with five movements,
Allegro–Minuet–Adagio–Minuet–Presto   (or   similar)
stands out as Haydn's preferred pattern, found in a
number of works for wind ensemble ('Feldparthien'), in
mixed divertimentos for strings and wind, and in almost
all the early string quartets. Too little is known about
Haydn's background to reveal whether he adopted this
type from earlier practice or whether he devised it himself. The individual movements are often short, like

Ex.1 String Quartet, op.1 no.1, 1st movt

pieces from a Baroque suite, but the inventive power of many of these works amply justifies the early reputation that the first editions of the quartet divertimentos (opp.1 and 2, *c*1765) established for him. The beginning of the Quartet in B♭, now known as op.1 no.1 (ex.1) though not necessarily the earliest, shows a number of characteristic features: the unsophisticated melodic material, untouched by the fashionable operatic clichés of much contemporary chamber music, the spontaneous use of contrast between unison writing and harmony, the exploitation of changes in texture. Compared with similar music of the time it must have sounded new, fresh and original.

(*ii*) *Eisenstadt, 1761–6.* Haydn's appointment as princely Kapellmeister inevitably changed his life as a composer; the spectrum of his creative activities has been outlined above. The duality of approach evident in many aspects of 18th-century music – *opera seria* and *opera buffa*, church and chamber sonata, music 'für Kenner und Liebhaber' – is a decisive factor in Haydn's development. In his early dramatic music, of which only fragments survive, there is an obvious contrast between the one opera, *Acide*, and the almost completely lost Italian Singspiels. The cantatas belong to the 'official' established music. The instrumental music, insofar as it is known and can be assigned to this period with reasonable likelihood, shows an interesting diversity. To some extent conservative tendencies – possibly reflecting the taste of Prince Anton – come to the fore in a number of concertos for various instruments (violin, cello, violone, flute, horn, harpsichord). Formally, the tradition of the Baroque concerto is still discernible, as it is in the concertos of most of Haydn's contemporaries. The melodic style too is mostly traditional, though a new, more individual manner is occasionally found, as in the fine slow movement of the Horn Concerto in D (1762).

Only in the symphonies of this period are there enough dated compositions to allow a closer study of Haydn's development, even if the picture is somewhat blurred by a still greater number of undated ones. Some of these were probably composed just before Haydn went to Eisenstadt, but no clear line can be drawn. The early development of the symphony is characterized by the merging of a number of prototypes of different kinds. The Italian three-movement type, with its roots in the opera sinfonia but now well established by Wagenseil and others as an independent instrumental form, can be seen in some early Haydn symphonies, most of them probably composed before his move to Eisenstadt (nos.1, 4, 10, 27). There are four-movement ones too, including some especially characteristic C major symphonies with trumpets and drums that point back to the traditions of the intrada (nos.20, 32, 37). During Haydn's early years in Eisenstadt the traditional three-movement symphony was in effect superseded by two or three other types incorporating elements from the concerto, from contrapuntal forms and from the divertimento tradition. Symphonies nos.6–8 ('Le matin', 'Le midi' and 'Le soir') from Haydn's first year in Eisenstadt (1761) contain obvious concerto features; these three works, however, must be regarded as apart from the mainstream of Haydn's symphonic development. A merging of symphony and concerto is to be seen in a number of concerto-like movements (e.g. in nos.13, 24, 30, 36), and two works from about 1765 approach the true concertante symphony (31, 72). A contrapuntal approach is prominent in various symphonies of the normal four-movement pattern (3, 40, 23) and in one quite special type that points back to the church sonata by starting with a complete slow movement, with the Allegro or Presto following in second place (5 and 11, both early, and 21, 22 and 34). In other symphonies (12, 14, 28) the influence of the divertimento is marked. In the symphonies of 1761–5 Haydn explored a variety of possibilities. There are many charming pieces among these early works, but it was only in the great expansion of a few years later that he arrived at a complete synthesis of the heterogeneous elements.

In these years the symphony was the leading instrumental genre for Haydn. Apparently no quartets were needed, but some undated divertimentos for solo keyboard, for keyboard with one or two violins and cello and for two violins and bass seem to belong to this period. Unlike the five-movement divertimentos from about 1760 these are normally in three movements, the second or third movement being a minuet and trio. They are almost all in a lighter vein, noble music for entertainment.

(*iii*) *Eszterháza, 1766–75*. The so-called 'Sturm und Drang' years in Haydn's development, extending from 1766 to the early 1770s and waning towards the middle of the decade, represent one of the most interesting and significant phases of 18th-century music (though a less restrictive title for this period would be preferable). Prompted by outward circumstances – Werner's death and the move to Eszterháza – Haydn's ambition and energy accomplished within the space of a few years an impressive stylistic synthesis. This process was marked by his return to the composition of church music, opera and the string quartet, in a much wider spectrum of musical forms. But most striking is the remarkable expansion of expression and compositional technique. A new style developed, not as an established idiom, but rather as a new approach, a happy merging of apparently disparate traditions.

In three substantial contributions to sacred music, the 'Cecilia Mass', the *Stabat mater* and the (semi-sacred) *Applausus* cantata (1766, 1767, 1768) Haydn demonstrated his full mastery of church music in the grand style. The 'Cecilia Mass' is Haydn's only one in the form of the so-called 'cantata mass', consisting of a succession of more or less self-contained arias and choruses; the other two works follow a similar pattern. These pieces seem less indebted to the Viennese traditions of Haydn's boyhood than to contemporary church music, and in particular to Hasse, who was living in Vienna at this time and to whom Haydn sent a copy of his *Stabat mater*. But even if these works are fine proofs of Haydn's skill as a church composer (the *Stabat mater* won great European fame) they are relatively traditional in style. The following mass, the 'Great Organ Mass' (probably *c*1768–70), comes closer to Haydn's 'classical' style. Compared with the extrovert character of the 'Cecilia Mass', this is more intimate, with a tone-colour of its own through its use of english horns instead of oboes. Subdivision of the main liturgical units into separate movements is found to a certain extent here, too, but the feeling of coherence and continuity is much more pronounced. There are several solos, but they blend and combine with the choral sections. A number of impressive themes characterize the mass as a vocal counterpart to the quartets and symphonies from about 1770. The Benedictus has the concertante organ part that gives the work its familiar name. Contrapuntal textures lend a special character to the 'Crucifixus' and Sanctus.

Compared with his impressive achievements in church music, Haydn's operatic activities in these years seem to have unexpectedly little bearing on the decisive turn in his music. His two works from 1766 and 1768 are decidedly light operas. The parodistic slant of *La canterina* called for no serious dramatic power from the composer. *Lo speziale* had more to offer, even though Haydn's libretto omitted the *parte serie* from Goldoni's original; and Haydn created a fine *opera buffa* with neatly devised characterization and spirited ensemble finales. *Le pescatrici* (1769) sees the beginnings of a trend that was to become more marked in his later operas, namely a merging of features of the light and the serious genres. The arias are more individual in form and expression, there are some remarkable ensembles, and there is a stronger feeling of drama. The next opera, *L'infedeltà delusa* (1773), a 'burletta per musica', returns to a more whole-hearted *buffo* manner, with a happy ending contrived by the old trick of a false notary and a faked wedding contract. Here the ensembles are less impressive, though there are some characteristic arias. The opera that followed, *L'incontro improvviso* (1775), is one of Haydn's most interesting, with many fine arias and ensembles and more refined orchestration than in any of the previous stage works. This opera may be seen as profiting from the expansion in Haydn's development around 1770 rather than paving the way for it.

It is in the three genres that were to become the dominant instrumental ones of the Classical period – the symphony, the string quartet and the keyboard sonata – that Haydn's new power is most immediately felt. There are again chronological problems: of about a dozen symphonies composed probably between 1766 and 1771 only three are dated – nos.35 (1767), 49 (1768) and 41 (1770); and in the case of the sonatas there is still more uncertainty (a substantial number from this time are lost).

These new symphonies still impress for their striking sincerity and directness. In their own time they must have come as a revelation. The symphony was by this date more or less established as an elegant piece of entertainment for a noble audience: and Haydn had the courage to write symphonies that were completely different. The strong, passionate expression in some of these works is remarkable, and is reflected in popular names like 'La passione' (no.49) or 'Trauersinfonie' (no.44). Their most important stylistic features are a strong rhythmic drive (nos.26, 39, 44) and a new stressing of harmonic tension (43, 47); a special feature is the choice of minor keys (26, 49, 39, 44, 45, 52) in contrast to the symphonies before and most of those after this relatively short period. Contrapuntal procedures are occasionally found (47), but not as conspicuously as in the quartets of the same years. An important characteristic is the broadening of musical periods based on a much more individual treatment of harmonic progression, as in the opening period of the Symphony no.43 in E♭ (ex.2). This is far from the simple two-, four- or eight-bar construction typical of the *galant* style. The slow movements in these symphonies are now mostly adagios, more intense than the earlier andantes, and the finales are beginning to approach the first movements in character and importance. Besides the well-known 'passionate' symphonies in the minor there are some in major keys that are less dramatic in character but no less advanced in style, like the 'Maria Theresia' (no.48 in C).

Ex.2 Symphony no.43, 1st movt

Just after the peak of the 'Sturm und Drang' symphonies new trends become prominent. The strikingly expressive character sensed particularly in the minor-key symphonies of around 1770 yields to a spirit of elegant entertainment. Touches of humour are frequent (no.55, 'The Schoolmaster'), and there is a feeling of the *buffo* spirit if not traditional *buffo* style (ex.3). These symphonies obviously possess less emotional power but they show a wealth of fine craftsmanship. An important feature is the increasing individuality of the single movements, slow movements and finales in particular. Another decisive factor is the more refined instrumentation. It was only in about 1770 that Haydn took to using

Ex.3 Symphony no.55, 2nd movt

wind instruments in slow movements as a general rule, and in the symphonies of around 1772–5 there are exquisite examples of wind writing, like the extraordinary horn parts in the Adagio of no.51 or the singing bassoon in the trio of no.54. Quite apart from the expressive content of so many works of this period, the character of the symphony had been changed through this unparalleled development in Haydn's musical skill.

Exceptional progress was made in the field of the string quartet, too, after a gap of almost ten years, with the three sets opp.9, 17 and 20 (c1769–70, 1771 and 1772). How far they may have been inspired by external impulses is not known. Quartets with leanings towards the archaic manner of the old church sonata were apparently coming into fashion in Vienna around 1770, and the court Kapellmeister, Florian Leopold Gassmann (d 1774) composed many of that sort. The fugal finales in three of the op.20 quartets may reflect that particular tradition, but Haydn's quartets are much more

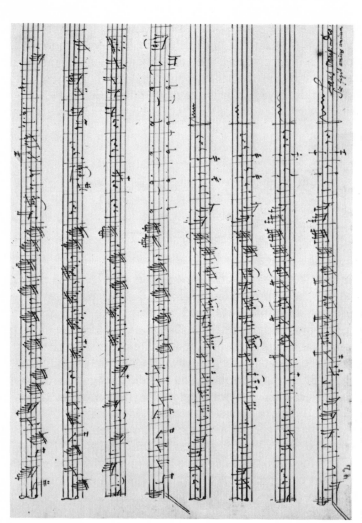

12. Autograph MS from Haydn's String Quartet in C op.20 no.2, composed 1772

individual and varied. His own work in other media – the symphony and the baryton trio – probably contributed just as much to the remarkable development in the string quartet. The long series of baryton trios required of him in the immediately preceding years may have had a dual effect: they served as exercises in a related though simpler style; and they provoked a reaction on Haydn's part against the limitations of the medium. The new quartets may be felt as a demonstration of newly realized possibilities. Here he could make the best of his symphonic experience. The indebtedness of the new quartet style to the progressive symphony is unmistakable in the more personal character of themes and motifs, the expansion of periods, the increased harmonic tension, the greater expressiveness (especially in the slow movements), the rhythmic emphasis in the quick movements and more besides. Haydn's natural feeling for true quartet texture, already evident in his early quartets, is certainly an essential factor; yet the significance of these three sets of quartets lies perhaps less in a new approach to texture than in the assimilation of symphonic trends, which open the way to the modern quartet. If these quartets had been Haydn's last compositions they would still have earned him an important position in 18th-century musical development.

In the keyboard sonata too a significant turn is found in the late 1760s. Though a number of sonatas seem to have been lost, those that survive from this period reveal a completely new type of sonata. In contrast with the earlier pieces in the divertimento tradition, these sonatas – notably H XVI:45 (1766), 19 (1767) and 46 (c1767–70) – forsake the usual minuet and introduce a serious, large-scale Andante or Adagio as second movement. Behind this change lies the unmistakable influence of the concerto. The slow movement of no.19 suggests an imitation of a cello concerto; in no.46 the layout of the Adagio even recalls the slow movement of Bach's Italian Concerto. The form and expansion of the individual movements, the thematic invention, the harmonic language and the expression of these sonatas bear witness to Haydn's unparalleled artistic growth in the years before and around 1770. This is true to an exceptional degree of the impressive C minor sonata, H XVI:20 (1771), probably one of Haydn's earliest compositions (if not the very earliest) for the piano rather than the harpsichord or clavichord, which seems almost like an early example of a 'symphonic' style in piano music.

Just as in the symphony and the string quartet, however, the great rise came to an abrupt stop. The pendulum swung back, and a reaction is felt in the sonatas that follow. The two sets op.13 (H XVI:21–6, 1773) and op.14 (H XVI:27–32, *c*1776) do not pursue the trends towards grandeur and expressiveness in the sonatas just mentioned. Yet it is obvious that Haydn had gone through a process of ripening, and the sonatas, even if less distinguished, are individual and refined. But consideration for the 'Liebhaber' element, and especially for Haydn's princely patron, had apparently become more important, as in the symphonies of just the same time.

(*iv*) *Opera, 1775–84.* The second half of Haydn's 30 years in Eisenstadt and Eszterháza was dedicated primarily to opera. But the accent was increasingly on performing works by other composers rather than writing his own: *Armida* (1783) was Haydn's last opera for Eszterháza. Until 1775 the lighter forms of *opera buffa*, Singspiel and marionette opera had been his chief concern, though serious elements had been introduced, especially in *Le pescatrici* and *L'incontro improvviso*. Still, *Il mondo della luna*, written for Eszterháza in 1777, was described by Count Zinzendorf in his diary as 'une farce pour la populace et pour les enfants'. But clearly Haydn became more and more interested in the possibilities of the serious or semi-serious opera. *La vera costanza* – composed for Vienna or Eszterháza, probably in 1777–8, but not performed until 1779, in Eszterháza – is again named a comic opera, or rather (like Mozart's *Don Giovanni*) a 'dramma giocoso per musica', but the tendency to introduce a substantial quantity of music of a serious character is more pronounced than before. The number of really expressive – and impressive – arias is remarkable, and the chain-like ensemble finales are of growing importance. *L'isola disabitata* (1779), however, may count as an *opera seria* in terms of its musical character if not of its plot. Haydn was so concerned with light opera during these years that his turn to serious opera in his later works for Eszterháza may be viewed as a sort of reaction. *L'isola disabitata* is a short and uncomplicated work, sub-titled in the libretto 'azione teatrale in due parti per musica'; Haydn himself referred to it in a letter as an 'operette'. As in *opera seria*, the development is primarily based on a series of arias of different character, but in between there is not the customary simple recitative but orchestral recitative throughout. This special feature may reflect the influence of Gluck (as suggested by Geiringer) or perhaps of Georg Benda's famous duodramas, one of which, *Medea*, had been performed in Vienna in December 1778. The next opera, *La fedeltà premiata* (1780), is again a 'dramma giocoso per musica', Haydn's last example of the type, but the 'jocose' elements are intermingled with more dramatic ones. Despite some fine features, the music is on the whole rather conventional.

As the designation 'dramma eroicomico' suggests, *Orlando paladino* (1782) is another hybrid story involving a pair of lovers, a sorceress, two Don Quixote-like 'heroes' and a sort of Leporello–Papageno servant, Pasquale. Had it been written in 1792 the subject matter would probably be seen as deriving more or less from *Die Zauberflöte*, and Haydn's music too has features to put one in mind of Mozart – the immediate juxtaposition of purely comic episodes with love-songs, the charm and sweetness of the amorous music, and Pasquale's almost Leporello-like patter. The characters are clearly defined, partly as real people and partly as caricatures, and the possibilities of the plot – which is to be taken almost as seriously as that of *Die Zauberflöte* – were fully exploited by Haydn. *Orlando paladino* was by far the best-known and most often performed of Haydn's operas in his own time, and was produced in Pressburg, Prague, Vienna, Mannheim and elsewhere.

Haydn's last opera for Eszterháza, *Armida* (1783), was again, like *Acide*, his first as Esterházy Kapellmeister, a real *opera seria*. Here the emphasis falls on the arias and the orchestral recitatives rather than the ensembles. The two principal characters, Armida and Rinaldo, dominate the action with their struggle against themselves and against each other, with Rinaldo's uncomplicated friend, Ubaldo, acting as a foil. A special feature of the setting is Armida's enchanted forest. It 'dominates the entire drama. It is the atmosphere and the dangerous weapon of Armida' (Wirth, 1951).

Why Haydn stopped composing operas is not known;

but it was probably connnected with the preference for light opera in the Eszterháza repertory. Haydn continued to perform such works but it seems that he was no longer interested in writing them. (Whether his operas may find a place in the modern repertory, now that most of them have finally been published, remains to be determined.) His operatic work during these years, both as composer and as conductor, put so much strain on him as to slow down his composing in almost every other genre. Between 1775 and 1784 only one set of quartets, two sets of piano sonatas and a number of symphonies were written. This period, in striking contrast to the previous one, does not reveal a conscious and continuous development of these forms but rather isolated works or sets of works. Related to this discontinuity is the fact that the very personal style forged during Haydn's period of marked expansion gave way to a less consistent variety of style. In perhaps no other period of his maturity are there so many works that seem to lack the distinctive stamp of Haydn's personality. In several cases there are or have been problems of authenticity, as in the (still dubious) six divertimentos or 'Feldparthien' for wind ensemble, including the St Antony Chorale used by Brahms, or the Cello Concerto in D (now proved to be authentic). The Piano Concerto in D stands out from the earlier keyboard concertos as a work approaching the modern, symphonic concerto style, related more closely to Mozart's concertos of these years than to Haydn's own previous essays in the form. In his development of the symphony a distinction may be drawn between a number of pleasant, unpretentious works of the late 1770s (nos.61, 71, 75) and the two sets of about 1782–4 (nos.76–8, 79–81), in which the quest for a new symphonic style is sensed, though more as a latent aspiration than as a true change of style. The impression is that in the time left over from his operatic activities Haydn went through a period of experimentation, not in a pioneering quest for personal solutions, as in his earlier period of expansion, but rather trying to find new ways in response to a variety of external stimuli.

To this period also belong the six quartets op.33. These have attracted particular attention on account of Haydn's description of them as having been written in 'an entirely new and special way'. Sandberger saw this remark as referring to the so-called 'thematische Arbeit', the distinctive texture of idiomatic quartet writing in which the music unfolds in dialogue between the four instruments. This may be part of the picture; but Haydn was probably referring just as much to the obvious contrast between the weighty, serious quartets of 1771–2 and the lighter, more easy-going op.33, with their use of the designation 'scherzo' instead of minuet, causing the set as a whole to be called 'Gli Scherzi'. Sandberger's interpretation has been the basis of a tendency to regard 1781 as a turning-point in the history of the quartet, and even to some extent in the development of the Viennese Classical style in general. But op.33 is actually rather isolated, and no general stylistic change can reasonably be postulated from Haydn's casual remark. Stylistic variety is again the hallmark of the six piano sonatas op.30, the first collection of Haydn's music to be issued by the Viennese publishing house of Artaria, which include some sonatas of markedly expressive character (H XVI:36 and 38, in addition to the earlier no.20 in C minor) alongside others in a more fashionable vein (nos.35, 37). A second set from these years (nos.40–42) poses a particular problem, in that a number of features might suggest that the solo sonatas, even though their publication precedes that of a string trio version, were modelled on an original for string trio or baryton trio.

An indication of Haydn's pragmatic experimentation is provided by his two collections of songs (1781, 1784). In contrast to the unambitious songs of his early years in Vienna, these lieder are based on fashionable models and sometimes even directly set out to outshine songs by a rival. Some of the songs, such as *Gegenliebe*, the tune of which Haydn also used for the slow movement of Symphony no.73, have a good deal of melodic charm, but German lyric poetry had not yet reached the point that was to give rise to the remarkable flowering of the lied in the 19th century; Schubert still seems a long way off.

Two large-scale vocal compositions reveal Haydn's greatness more clearly than most of his other works of this period: the oratorio *Il ritorno di Tobia* (originally composed and performed in 1774–5, revised and supplemented with new choruses in 1784) and the *Missa Cellensis* of 1782 (the 'Mariazell Mass'). *Tobia*, an Italian oratorio, is in a different style and tradition from the two late oratorios and consists primarily of arias in the grand manner. It is full of fine music, but the plot has insufficient interest to sustain its length, and even with the 1784 additions there are too few choruses to provide adequate variety. After the two short masses of about 1772–5, the 'Mariazell Mass' returns to the more serious tradition of the 'Great Organ Mass' and can be viewed as an early example of the grand style, to be fully developed in the late masses of the 1790s. The main impression left by this mass is one of homophonic choral declamation, rounded off by concluding fugues in the Gloria, Credo and Agnus Dei. Symphonic traditions are evident in the growing tendency to organize indi-

vidual movements in accordance with sonata-like prin-
ciples. The 'Gratias' is an extended aria, reminiscent of
the methods of the cantata mass. The Benedictus
introduces a beautiful sequential phrase that seems to
foreshadow the 'Emperor's Hymn'; in fact the entire
movement is an adaptation of an aria from *Il mondo della
luna*. Though there is no sense of incongruity, this
adaptation of a secular piece to sacred use was com-
monly held up in the 19th century as a demonstration of
Haydn's regrettable lack of propriety in the observance
of the 'true church style'.

(*v*) *Foreign commissions, c1785–90*. When Haydn's
contract of 1 January 1779 freed him from the obligation to compose exclusively for his prince, composing
for publishers and patrons of various kinds became an
important consideration in his life and a decisive factor
in what he chose to write. Apart from the occasional
substitute aria for the Eszterháza opera repertory he
composed entirely instrumental music in these years,
only on commission (mostly from publishers). His
works from this period include piano trios, string
quartets, symphonies and two specific groups of works:
the great orchestral composition *Seven last Words* and a
series of concertos and notturnos for two *lire organizzate*.

The piano trio form was taken up again after an
interval of some 15 or 20 years. Further problems of
authenticity arise here, for H XV:3 and 4 are probably
by Pleyel. The others (nos.5–10) written in 1784–5
demonstrate once again Haydn's unevenness of style at
this time. A second group (nos.11–17) followed in
1789–90, but it was only in the late trios written for
London around 1795 that Haydn went significantly

beyond the conception of the genre as music for domestic entertainment. Two piano sonatas were composed in the late 1780s, H XVI:48 for the publisher Breitkopf, in a style similar to that of the piano trios, and the more intimate no.49 (for Marianne von Genzinger), one of Haydn's finest works for piano.

The change from a period of rather casual stylistic variety to one of expansion, of purposeful individual growth and development, was caused, or at least inaugurated, primarily by two foreign commissions: the ordering of six symphonies for Paris and the quite exceptional *Seven last Words* for Spain.

The Paris symphonies are again distinctively, unmistakably the work of Haydn, yet show a remarkable diversity of form and expression. Among the typical features of these mature Classical symphonies are the increasing use of a slow introduction and the move towards thematic unity in the first movements (85); the display of a number of different types of slow movement: sonata form (83), variation (85), double variation (82), 'capriccio' (86); the generally pronounced difference in character between minuet and trio, the latter often almost in the manner of an Austrian ländler, and the merging of sonata and rondo elements in the finales, both in form and in character. Above all, however, in these symphonies every trace of stylistic vacillation has vanished. Symphonies like nos.82, 85 and 86 are among the finest expressions of Haydn's genius, and the Paris symphonies can reasonably be viewed as the beginning of Haydn's symphonic revival. They were followed by the two Tost symphonies, one of them the rightly famous no.88 with the almost chamber-music-like playfulness of its fast movements and the solemn, expressive Largo, and the three symphonies nos.90–92, again for Paris, which consolidate the developments of the preceding works in their free and characterful handling of material.

The *Seven last Words* is one of those rare works of art that stand out as unique, having no true basis of comparison with anything else. An 'Introduzione' and a final 'Terremoto' frame seven symphonic slow movements in a sonata form more fully developed than in many corresponding movements in the symphonies themselves. Of crucial importance is the impressive, at times almost declamatory, principal melodic material, especially at the opening of each movement (standing for the actual words spoken by Christ). The richness of the orchestral sonority is noteworthy, too, the orchestra here (as in the Paris symphonies) normally consisting of one flute, two each of oboes, bassoons and horns, with strings and sometimes with the addition of two trumpets and timpani. The grandeur and dignity of these movements distinguish them as truly symphonic pieces, in character if not in title.

In the late 1780s Haydn finally returned to quartet composition on a more regular basis. In op.50 (the 'Prussian' Quartets), as in the late symphonies, concentration of motivic structure is fundamental, the function of a subsidiary theme being generally taken over by a variant of the principal theme. The fine balance between unity and infinite variety is one of the most typical features of Haydn's late quartets. In contrast to the op.33 set, the op.50 set does not use the rondo type of finale; the slow movements, however, are mostly in a rondo or rondo-like form, often with characteristic elements of variation. The two series of 'Tost' Quartets (opp.54–5 and op.64) carry the Classical quartet to a peak. They reveal a Haydn free of official restraints and obligations, composing simply *con amore*, drawing on the rich treasure of idiomatic quartet style and inventive power accumulated over the past 30 years. There is no general type of quartet here, but an exquisite diversity. Whether Haydn's late quartets were influenced by Mozart is open to discussion. Occasionally there may be 'touches of Mozart's influence' (Hughes, 1966), but if one did not know of Mozart's relations with Haydn one would scarcely see anything but Haydn in these quartets.

Another notable foreign commission was the order from the King of Naples for some music for his favourite instrument, the *lira organizzata*, a variety of hurdy-gurdy, which resulted in five concertos (1786–7) and eight notturnos (*c*1790) for two *lire organizzate*. The concertos are in a more fashionable vein, but the notturnos are splendid examples of high-class music for connoisseurs and amateurs. Despite their apparent simplicity and lack of sophistication there is a lightness and grace, a mastery of form and texture and a superior handling of the instruments which place these works among Haydn's finest chamber music. His own regard for them is shown by the fact that he arranged a number of them for his London concerts, replacing the two *lire* with flute and oboe.

(*vi*) *The London period, 1791–5.* Haydn's London period was again primarily taken up with instrumental music, with a few notable exceptions: the opera *L'anima del filosofo* (or *Orfeo ed Euridice*), and two collections of songs or canzonets, to which might be added the first collection of folksong arrangements (Haydn's contribution seems to have been purely a matter of arranging, based on the melodies, not the texts). Among all the works composed in or for London in these years the 12 London symphonies (nos.93–104) stand out as his most remarkable achievement. They became more famous than his earlier symphonies, and for many years a number of them, symptomatically with popular nicknames like 'Surprise', 'Clock', 'Military' and 'Drumroll', were virtually the only ones in the general concert repertory. They hardly show any particular new facet of Haydn's symphonic style, but a few outstanding features contribute to their special character. One is the fact that these are unmistakably 'grand' symphonies, as indeed they were called in concert advertisements and published editions. This has to do partly with a broader presentation of musical ideas, and partly with sonority, a sound quality inspired by the fine orchestras and concert rooms of London. Another prominent feature is the use of themes and motifs of a basic simplicity and immediate appeal. Characteristic examples are the Andante theme in the 'Surprise' Symphony, no.94 (quoted by Haydn himself as a popular tune in *The Seasons*), the principal theme in the first movement of the 'Military' Symphony, no.100, or the Andante theme in the 'Clock' Symphony, no.101. The same trend stands behind the occasional use of folksong melodies, most prominently in the last two symphonies (nos.103, 104), though this is exceptional for Haydn.

The six so-called 'Apponyi' Quartets (opp.71 and 74), composed between the two visits to London, were certainly intended for use in the coming season's concerts, and they have a more public, less intimate character than those immediately preceding them (op.64) or those that followed (op.76). In certain aspects one may even feel the closeness of the symphony, as in some characteristic unison passages, or in the greater har-

·monic emphasis, giving rise almost to a feeling of orchestral sonority. At times there are instances of progressive harmonic and tonal practice. The slow movement of the G minor 'Rider' Quartet, op.74 no.3, is in E major, and in character it seems to approach the young Beethoven.

During his second stay in London, and possibly into the first year after his return to Vienna, Haydn composed a series of brilliant piano trios, much more impressive than the trios of about 1785. While still in the first instance 'Liebhaber' music, these late works seem to show Haydn approaching the medium with a new conviction. The trios of ten years before are in two movements, those of about 1790 in two or three; these are almost all in three. At the same time there is an expansion and stronger characterization of the individual movements. The first movements are mostly cast in extended sonata form, only occasionally in rondo or variation; the second movements generally have some sort of variation or tripartite form; and the finales, in earlier trios often rondos or stylized minuets, are in sonata form or follow a ternary scheme, perhaps with the middle section in the tonic minor and the main section returning in varied form – only two are rondos (the best-known of all the trios, H XV:25 in G with the 'Rondo all'ongarese' finale, is exceptional in having two rondos and no sonata movement). A richer harmonic vocabulary is prominent in the late trios, and the sonata movements are striking for their widely modulating development sections. Another noteworthy feature is Haydn's cantabile approach, not only in the slow movements but in the first movements as well (as in the E major Trio, H XV:28, ex.4). Altogether the late trios form an impressive final phase in Haydn's piano music.

Ex.4 Piano Trio in E, нXV: 28

In addition, together with Mozart's piano concertos,
they constitute an important step towards Beethoven,
whose piano music was inaugurated in print about this
time by the three Piano Trios op.1.

Compared with the substantial series of trios, the
three late piano sonatas, composed at about the same
time, do not form a consistent group; somehow they
seem to reflect Haydn's reaction to new currents rather
than any personal line of development. н XVI:51 in D
may betray the influence of Clementi. In no.52 in E♭,
probably the Haydn sonata most often played today, the
emphasis on a fuller and harmonically richer texture,
and the more pianistic style in general, raised the question of possible influence from Beethoven; the slow
movement is in E major, representing a remarkably
original juxtaposition of tonalities. The finest expression
of Haydn's own creative power is perhaps the first
movement of no.50 in C, less pianistic in style, but a
marvellous example of his structural mastery, develop-
ing a short and rather formal opening theme into a
varied but consistently unified piece.

Haydn's first stay in London gave rise to his last
opera, *L'anima del filosofo*. The story is the well-known
one of Orpheus and Eurydice, but as the title suggests
the aim was to give it a more sophisticated slant. In
outward form it is an *opera seria*, but in essence it is not.
The melodic character of several of the arias is closer to
the Classical style of Haydn's and Mozart's later works

than to the *seria* style of *Armida*. The chorus is important, partly playing a genuinely dramatic role and partly functioning in an oratorio-like manner, observing and commenting on the drama from outside. This is clearly different from traditional *opera seria* and from Haydn's earlier operas; his resources at Eszterháza would not have stretched to this sort of treatment. Some influence from English taste (direct or indirect, perhaps through the Handel oratorio tradition) or from Gluck may be part of the picture.

Haydn's English songs, mostly to texts by Anne Hunter (wife of the famous surgeon), are on a higher level than his two German collections. He may have had difficulty in composing to words in a language which he was far from mastering; but the character of the songs is different and the musical setting clearly more ambitious. The accompaniment is much more elaborate, the texture and harmonies more refined and the melodies themselves more expressive than in the earlier songs. This applies to most of the songs in the two published collections and also to a number of single songs from the same time, like *The Spirit's Song* and *O, tuneful voice*.

(*vii*) *Vienna, late years, 1795–1809.* A great change in Haydn's activities as a composer took place after his return to Vienna: having for more than ten years spent by far the greatest part of his time on instrumental music, he devoted his final years almost exclusively to vocal music. The long line of symphonies and piano sonatas was virtually at an end. There were a few isolated instrumental works like the fine F minor Variations for piano and the Trumpet Concerto, but otherwise only the string quartet continued for a while: the six 'Erdődy' Quartets op.76 (1797), the two 'Lobkowitz' Quartets op.77 (1799) – all he managed to finish of a projected set – and the two movements of op.103, published in 1803 after Haydn had abandoned hope of ever completing it. The op.76 set once again demonstrates Haydn's freedom and diversity. Works of a very different nature stand side by side, like the tautly argued 'Fifths' Quartet, in D minor, and the more relaxed and expansive 'Emperor' Quartet, with its fine variations on Haydn's own 'Emperor's Hymn'. The op.77 set shows Haydn's quartet style at its finest, especially no.1 in G, a model of varied and idiomatic quartet writing.

Mass composition became Haydn's principal obligation in his late years. His return to church music, after an interval of 14 years since the 'Mariazell Mass' of 1782, resulted above all in the six great masses composed betwen 1796 and 1802. Too much had happened in music in general, and in Haydn's own musical life and experience, for him simply to continue the tradition of the earlier masses. Though the six late masses naturally follow old procedures in many respects, they form a group of works of so distinctively unique a character that for once it might seem justifiable to talk of 'an entirely new and special way'. Here, as in the London symphonies, it is no longer a question of development or progress within the group. All problems of structure and technique are left behind. The individual character of each mass as a whole and of its separate parts and the wonderfully rich and inexhaustible invention are qualities that by now can be taken for granted. The ingredients of this remarkable synthesis include the symphonic mastery of the orchestral writing, the free and varied handling of the chorus (to some extent reminiscent of the diversity of Handel's choral style, which had impressed Haydn in London), and the consummate

*13. Joseph Haydn: pencil portrait (1794)
by George Dance*

classical simplicity nurtured by Haydn himself and by Mozart, especially in the music of his last months (above all *Die Zauberflöte*).

Though each of the six masses has a character of its own, all are based on a common structural pattern with only slight variations. The Kyrie is normally set as an introductory Adagio followed by an Allegro (moderato), much as in the first movements of the late symphonies; only the Kyrie of the 'Nelson Mass' (Allegro moderato) and that of the *Harmoniemesse* (Poco Adagio) are in one section. The Gloria is divided up into four or five sections, the first invariably Allegro or Vivace, and the 'Qui tollis' forming a central Adagio in a contrasting key; in three cases (H XXII:8, 10 and 12) the 'Qui tollis' is preceded by a separate 'Gratias' setting, more intimate in mood. The 'Quoniam' brings a return to Allegro or Vivace, and the last part of this section is generally a fugal treatment of the text 'In gloria Dei patris, Amen'. The Credo has a similar compound structure: Allegro (or Vivace); Adagio (no.9, Largo) at 'Et incarnatus'; Allegro (or Vivace) at 'Et resurrexit'; and a concluding Vivace (or Allegro) at 'Et vitam venturi' (usually a fugue). The Sanctus is an Adagio (no.10: Andante), normally changing to Allegro for 'Pleni sunt coeli, Osanna'. The Benedictus, surprisingly, varies from Andante (no.7) to Molto Allegro (no.12), in two cases with an independent 'Osanna' (no.9 takes up again the 'Osanna' of the Sanctus). The Agnus Dei is always divided into a slow first section (Adagio) and a quick second ('Dona nobis'), sometimes with a tendency to imitative treatment.

These contrasting sections have much in common with contrasting movements in the symphonies. The symphonic impression made by, for instance, the Kyrie from the *Missa in tempore belli* is striking (ex.5). The slow sections too have symphonic parallels, but they also share features with the concerto. The difference of

Ex.5 *Missa in tempore belli*

medium, however, naturally demands differences in formal treatment. It is the length of the texts to the Gloria and Credo that determines the division of these liturgical units into independent sections, rather than purely musical considerations. The symphonic range of the Kyrie movements is to some extent restricted through the vocal as opposed to a purely instrumental medium. But otherwise the interplay of chorus, solo ensemble and the (sparing) use of individual soloists adds greatly to the richness of the whole. Other sections are contrapuntal in character, especially the concluding fugues in many Gloria and Credo settings. Here Haydn had his roots in the traditions of the Austrian Baroque, which may have been revived in his mind by his encounter with Handel's music in London. The 'Et incarnatus' of the *Heiligmesse* and the Credo of the *Missa in angustiis*, however, are exceptional in their use of canon, by no means a typical device of the late masses.

The troubled state of Europe during the 1790s is reflected in Haydn's own titles to two of the masses: *Missa in tempore belli* (or 'Paukenmesse') and *Missa in angustiis* (or 'Nelson Mass'). Yet however strikingly individual details of these works may depict the threat of war, their ethos, like that of Haydn's other masses, is essentially one of faith and devotion. Perhaps the completest synthesis of vocal and instrumental music is found in the four masses of 1796–9. In the more fully scored last two, the *Schöpfungsmesse* and *Harmoniemesse* (1801–2), it may seem that the vocal texture had occasionally been somewhat simplified in the interest of orchestral effects and more sophisticated tonal procedures, stressing the symphonic element.

Between the great vocal works Haydn composed a number of much smaller yet fine and characteristic ones. The 'Emperor's Hymn', *Gott erhalte Franz den Kaiser*, is a wonderful synthesis of Haydn's inborn simplicity and refined artistry. The same is true of his 13 partsongs with piano accompaniment. They may have been inspired by English catches and glees, but some similar songs by Michael Haydn are dated 1795, the year before Haydn's first pieces of this sort (Mies, 1958). The texts are partly witty ('Freunde, Wasser machet stumm'), partly contemplative ('Hin ist alle meine Kraft', used by Haydn as a motto on his visiting-card in his later years), partly religious ('Du bist's, dem Ruhm und Ehre gebühret'; 'Herr! der Du mir das Leben'). Haydn's canons, though miniature compositions of a private nature, brilliantly demonstrate his remarkable inventive power within a limiting technique. The latent strength in a small piece of this kind is shown clearly by the transformation of the simple canon *Gott im Herzen*, used with striking effect as the basis for the 'Et incarnatus' of the *Heiligmesse* (1796).

Rather unexpectedly, oratorio was to be the last phase of Haydn's career – and the most brilliantly successful one, discounting not even his London triumphs. The two late oratorios have little to do with his *Tobia* of about 25 years before, and the choral version of the *Seven last Words*, dating from just before *The Creation*, is not a real oratorio but a series of impressive choruses arranged from – or rather superimposed on – the original orchestral version, which with small alterations serves as the accompaniment. It needed the inspiration of Handel's oratorios to release Haydn's mastery as an oratorio composer in *The Creation* and *The Seasons*. No doubt Handel's *Israel in Egypt* (which Haydn heard in London) provided the strongest impulse for *The Creation*. The many examples of descriptive writing in Handel's depiction of the plagues of Egypt are reflected in Haydn's fresh and charming pictures of the wonders of the creation, from the naive but always impressive 'And there was LIGHT' to the glimpses of the leaping tiger and the creeping worm. *The Creation* represents the happy union between the traditions of the Handelian oratorio, the Viennese mass, Haydn's earlier, Italian oratorio (*Tobia*) and, underlying everything, his own late symphonic style. The arias and ensembles range from the simple beauty of 'With verdure clad' to the virtuoso style of 'On mighty pens' and the great expressive duets in Part 3. The chorus is heard in massive songs of praise or combined with the soloists in lively composite numbers. The two instrumental preludes, including the superbly controlled 'Representation of Chaos', are masterly. *The Creation* is a masterwork in the special sense that it has no weak point, nothing that could be changed or omitted.

The unprecedented success of *The Creation* led to a second collaboration between Haydn and his librettist van Swieten in *The Seasons*, which, for all its fine qualities, is less consistent than *The Creation*, largely on account of its text. In *The Creation* everything seems to be an indispensable part of the whole. In contrast the four parts of *The Seasons*, though happily expressing scenes of rural life through the changing year, are not – and perhaps could not be – more than well-chosen pictures. Haydn could never have made *The Seasons* the true counterpart to *The Creation* that it was intended to be. From the beginning of the Vivace in the introduction to 'Spring' it is clear that the character is different. In the depiction of morning and noon in 'Summer' there is something of the ethereal character of *The Creation*, but otherwise the many brilliant scenes are mostly tableaux of everyday country life. Again the arias cover a wide range of expression, from Hanne's popular songs in 'Winter' to Lucas's almost dramatic description and Simon's contemplative aria in the same part. The combination of solo or ensemble with chorus is used here too, with fine effect, as in the brilliant depiction of sunrise in 'Summer' and the monumental final chorus in 'Winter'. But no less impressive are the very different hunting-chorus and drinking-chorus in 'Autumn', which seem to bring to life Brueghel's paintings of peasant conviviality.

Any attempt at a total view of Haydn presents formidable problems, for the first impression is of diversity rather than unity. The early quartets, the symphonies of around 1770, the baryton trios, *Armida*, the Cello Concerto in D, the *Seven last Words*, the 'Military' Symphony, the *Theresienmesse* have little obviously in common. Yet in Haydn's music there are strong marks

14. *Autograph sketches for Haydn's 'The Seasons',*
composed 1799–1801

of his own inner nature, of the musical surroundings in which he grew up, and of those he later encountered. Among his personal musical qualities are his originality (on which he himself remarked), his unfailing inventiveness and imagination, his integrity as a musical craftsman, his fundamental simplicity, his natural charm and his latent humour – all of them characteristics entirely consistent with what we know of Haydn as a person. His musical background confronted him with a set of problems which he tackled and to which in the course of time he found his own solutions, which in many respects came to be universally adopted. New problems continued to present themselves throughout his working life, even as late as the London visits.

During Haydn's youth the dying high Baroque style, represented in Vienna by the Fux–Caldara tradition, was giving way to a more 'modern', homophonic style, favoured by such composers as Wagenseil and Reutter. In his isolation he was able to work towards a synthesis of these antagonistic styles: into the forms of the new age – the symphony, the string quartet, the sonata – he breathed the spirit of Baroque invention, giving rise to a more unified type of sonata form. Out of the imitative counterpoint of the Baroque grew one of his most famous achievements, thematic development, brilliantly displayed especially in the middle section of a sonata movement but often latent from the opening bars. His melodic invention is richly varied. The simple melodies typical of the mid-18th century (not folksongs) always retained a hold on Haydn, particularly in such contexts as minuets and variations; but a great number of themes and motifs carry on the traditions of Baroque contrapuntal concepts. Folksong melodies proper are conspicuous in a few famous works but are of little real importance. The harmonically conceived, natural and wonderfully simple cantabile melodies in the slow movements of symphonies and quartets, in the *Seven last Words* and the late masses, are expressions of a new age – but deeply rooted in the long tradition of Haydn's development.

Recent research has paved the way for a deeper insight into Haydn's artistic life and his development, not least through the primary task of editing and publishing a great number of his works, many of which were unpublished and unknown. The completion of this task and the preparation of studies based on new, critical editions may lead to a reappraisal of some aspects of the picture of Haydn as it appears today. But it is already clear how diverse and fascinating that picture will be.

WORKS

Editions: J. *Haydns Werke*, ed. E. Mandyczewski and others, 10 vols. (Leipzig, 1907–33) [M]

J. *Haydn: Kritische Gesamtausgabe*, ed. J. P. Larsen, 4 vols. (Boston, Leipzig and Vienna, 1950–51) [L]

J. *Haydn: Werke*, ed. J. Haydn-Institut, Cologne, directed G. Feder (1962–) and J. P. Larsen (1958–61), 50 vols. (further vols. in preparation) (Munich, 1958–) [HW]

J. *Haydn: Kritische Ausgabe sämtlicher Symphonien*, i–xii, ed. H. C. R. Landon, Philharmonia series (Vienna, 1965–8) [P]

Diletto musicale, ed. H. C. R. Landon unless otherwise stated (Vienna, 1959–) [D]

(for editions of specific genres, see notes at head of relevant sections)

Catalogue: A. van Hoboken: *Joseph Haydn: Thematisch-bibliographisches Werkverzeichnis*, i: *Instrumentalwerke*, ii: *Vokalwerke*, iii: *Register, Addenda [Addl.] und Corrigenda* (Mainz, 1957–78) [H]

1. VOCAL: A. Masses. B. Miscellaneous sacred. C. Oratorios. D. Secular cantatas, choruses. E. Dramatic. F. Secular vocal with orchestra. G. Solo songs with keyboard. H. Miscellaneous vocal works with keyboard. I. Canons.

2. INSTRUMENTAL: J. Symphonies. K. Miscellaneous orchestral. L. Dances, marches for orchestra/military band. M. Concertos for string or wind instruments. N. Divertimentos etc for 4+ string and/or wind instruments. O. String quartets. P. String trios (divertimentos). Q. Baryton trios (divertimentos). R. Works for 1–2 barytons. S. Miscellaneous chamber music for 2–3 string and/or wind instruments. T. Works for 2 lire organizzate. U. Keyboard concertos/concertinos/divertimentos. V. Keyboard trios. W. Keyboard sonatas. X. Miscellaneous keyboard works. Y. Works for flute-clock.

3. FOLKSONG ARRANGEMENTS: Z. Arrangements of British folksongs.

Authentication symbols:

A – autograph, i.e. written and signed by Haydn or marked 'In nomine Domini', 'laus Deo' (or similarly) by him

C – MS copy by one of the Esterházy copyists: Anon. 11, 12, 30, 48, 63 (nos. from Bartha–Somfai)

Dies – his book on Haydn, 1810

E – MS copy by Johann Elssler

EK – entry in Haydn's *Entwurf-Katalog*, c1765–

F – MS copy by one of 3 earliest copyists of Budapest Fürnberg collection: found in various archives

Gr – Griesinger's book on Haydn, 1810, or his letters to Breitkopf & Härtel

HC – entry in non-thematic list of Haydn's music collection, 1807

HE – MS copy from Haydn's estate

HL – autograph entry in Haydn's list of librettos

HV – thematic entry in *Haydn-Verzeichnis*, 1805

H 1799–1803 – verified by Haydn in those years according to C. F. Pohl's papers, *A-Wgm* (based on lost documents in Breitkopf archives)

JE – MS copy by Joseph Elssler sr

OE – original edition, published by Haydn or authorized by him

RC – MS copy rev. Haydn

SC – MS copy signed by Haydn

Sk – sketch by Haydn

u – unsigned

1766 = composed 1766; [1766] = year of composition 1766 not documented; –1766 = composed by 1766; –?1766 = possibly composed by 1766 — signifies the absence of the work from the category concerned; i.e. not in H, not authenticated, not pubd etc

Items are numbered chronologically (as far as possible) within each category; these numbers are always shown in italics and are used for cross references between sections (e.g. E 23).

Where not specified, bn may often double the bass part.

Instrumental parts that are doubtful or are later editions (sometimes by Haydn himself) are parenthesized or given a question-mark.

Numbers in the right-hand column denote references in the text.

No.	H XXII	Title, key	Forces	Date	Authentication HV	Edition	Remarks	
1a	3	Missa 'Rorate coeli desuper', G	? 4vv, 2 vn, bc (org)	?	EK, HV	?	?lost/?identical with no.1b	11
1b	ii, 73	Mass, G		–1779	?	(London, 1957)	by G. Reutter Jr/Arbesser/Haydn	
2	1	Missa brevis, F	2 S, 4vv, 2 vn, bc (org)	?1749	SC, ?EK	L xxiii/1, 1	wind and timp pts. added Haydn (or Heidenreich), 1805	11, 86
3	5	Missa Cellensis in honorem BVM (Cäcilienmesse), C	S, A, T, B, 4vv, 2 ob, 2 bn, ? 2 hn, 2 tpt, timp, str, bc (org)	1766	EK, A (frags.)	L xxiii/1, 105	for facs. of Ky and Christe see *Haydn Yearbook*, ix (1975), 308	30, 48, 91, 103
4	2	Missa 'Sunt bona mixta malis', d	? a cappella	?c1767–9	EK	—	lost	30
5	4	Missa in honorem BVM (Missa Sancti Josephi; Grosse Orgelmesse), Eb	S, A, T, B, 4vv, 2 eng hn, 2 hn, (2 tpt, timp), 2 vn, vle, org obbl	–1774 [?c1768–9]	EK, A (frags. u)	L xxiii/1, 24	tpt and timp in authentic MS copy (JE), *H-Gk*	29, 30, 48, 91, 103
6	6	Missa Sancti Nicolai (Nikolaimesse; 6/4-Takt-Messe), G	S, A, T, B, 4vv, 2 ob, 2 hn, str, bc (org)	1772	EK, A	L xxiii/1, 270	in HV as Missa St Josephi; cf no.5	29, 30, 34, 48
7	7	Missa brevis Sancti Joannis de Deo (Kleine Orgelmesse), Bb	S, 4vv, 2 vn, b, org obbl	–1778 [?c1773–7]	EK, A	HW xxiii/2, 1	see also HW xxiii/2, 247	48
8	8	Missa Cellensis (Mariazeller Messe), C	S, A, T, B, 4vv, 2 ob, bn, 2 tpt, timp, str, bc (org)	1782	A	HW xxiii/2, 20	Benedictus uses aria from Il mondo della luna (E 17)	48, 103, 112, 114
9	10	Missa Sancti Bernardi von Offida (Heiligmesse), Bb	S, A, T, B, 4vv, 2 ob, 2 cl, 2 bn, ? 2 hn, 2 tpt, timp, str, bc (org)	1796	A, Sk	HW xxiii/2, 166	= Missa St Ofridi in EK; see also HW xxiii/2, 240, 242; cf 1 b, 44	71, 114, 115, 117
10	9	Missa in tempore belli (Kriegsmesse; Paukenmesse), C	S, A, T, B, 4vv, ?fl, 2 ob, 2 cl, 2 bn, 2 hn, 2 tpt, timp, str, bc (org)	1796	A	HW xxiii/2, 89	?1st perf. Vienna, 26 Dec 1796; see also HW xxiii/2, 237	71, *115*, 116
11	11	Missa (Nelsonmesse; Imperial Mass; Coronation Mass), d	S, A, T, B, 4vv, 3 tpt, timp, str, org obbl	10 July–31 Aug 1798	A	HW xxiii/3, 1	= Missa in angustiis in EK; perf. ?Eisenstadt, 23 Sept 1798; org pt. transcr. for ww ?by J. N. Fuchs	73, 114, 115
12	12	Missa (Theresienmesse), Bb	S, A, T, B, 4vv, 2 cl, (bn), 2 tpt, timp, str, bc (org)	1799	A	HW xxiii/3, 140		73, 114, 118

No.	H XXII	Title, key	Forces	Date	Authentication	Edition	Remarks	
13	13	Missa (Schöpfungsmesse), B♭	S, A, T, B, 4vv, 2 ob, 2 cl, 2 bn, 2 hn, 2 tpt, timp, str, bc (org)	28 July–11 Sept 1801	A	HW xxiii/4; facs. edn. (Munich, 1957)	perf. Eisenstadt, 13 Sept 1801; Gl uses song from The Creation, later replaced by Haydn (HW xxiii/4, 204)	73, 116
14	14	Missa (Harmoniemesse), B♭	S, A, T, B, 4vv, fl, 2 ob, 2 cl, 2 bn, 2 hn, 2 tpt, timp, str, bc (org)	1802	A	HW xxiii/5	perf. Eisenstadt, 8 Sept 1802	73, 114, 116

Note: over 100 spurious masses listed in Hoboken; composers of some identified by McIntyre (1982)

B: MISCELLANEOUS SACRED

No.	H	Title, key	Forces	Date	Authentication	Edition	Remarks	
1	XXIIIc:5	Lauda Sion (Hymnus/Motetto de venerabili Sacramento), i–iv, C	S, A, B, 4vv, 2 ob, 2 tpt, str, bc (org)	–1776 [?c1750]	?EK	—		
2	XXIIIb:3*	Ave regina, A	S, 4vv, 2 vn, bc (org)	–1763 [?c1750–59]	—	(Augsburg, 1970)	also with Salve regina text	
3	XXIIIb:1	Salve regina, E	S, 4vv, 2 vn, bc (org)	?1756	EK, A	—	date on autograph added later	11, *13*, 86
4	XXIIIa:4*	Quis stellae radius, motet, C	S, 4vv, ?2 tpt, ?timp, str, bc (org)	?1762	SC	—	cantata; also with other texts, incl. Quae admiranda lux; for ?secular origin, see Becker-Glauch: 'Neue Forschungen' (1970)	
5	XXIIIc:1	Te Deum, C	S, A, T, B, 4vv, 2 tpt, timp, 2 vn, bc (org)	–1765 [?1762–3]	?EK	(Vienna and Munich, 1966)	also attrib. M. Haydn	22, 24

No.	Hob.	Title	Scoring	Date		Publication	Remarks
6	XXIIIa:3	Lus aeternam, offertory motet/ hymn, G	4vv, str, bc (org)	1772 [?c1761–9]		(Leipzig, 1813)	also with text W… gnädig, with addl 2 ob, 2 tpt, timp
7	XXIIIa:2	Animae Deo gratae, offertory motet, C	2 S, T, 4vv, 2 ob, 2 tpt, timp, str/ ? 2 vn, bc (org)	–1776 [?c1761–9]	HV	—	also attrib. M. Haydn; also with text Agite properate
8	XXIIIc:4	Lauda Sion (Responsoria de venerabili [sacramento]), i–iv, Bb, d, A, Eb	S, A, T, B (?in chorus), ? 2 hn, 2 vn, bc (org)	?c1765–9	EK	(Munich, 1965) (entitled Hymnus)	MS copy as Quatuor Stationes pro Festo Corporis Christi
9	XXIIIc:3	Alleluia, G	S, A, 4vv, str, bc (org)	–1771 [?1768–9]	A	—	in MS copies always following Dictamina mea (appx B.1, 3)
10	XXIIId:3*	Herst Nachbä (Cantilena pro adventu; Pastorella), D	S, ? 2 hn, str, bc (org)	?c1768–70	EK	(Altötting, 1975)	also with other texts, incl. Jesu redemptor omnium
11	XXIIIb:2	Salve regina, g	S, A, T, B, str, org obbl	1771	EK, A	(Vienna and Munich, 1964)	1770 incorrect reading 29
12	XXIIIb:4*	Salve regina, Eb	S, A, T, ?B (?solo vv), str, bc (org)	–1773	—	(Augsburg, 1959)	?doubtful, see Landon, i (1980), 157; B in edn. ?not orig.
13	XXIIId:1	Ein' Magd, ein' Dienerin (Cantilena/Aria pro adventu), A	S, ? 2 ob, ? 2 hn, str, bc (org)	?c1770–75	EK	(London, 1957)	
14	XXIIId:2	Mutter Gottes, mir erlaube (Cantilena/Aria pro adventu), G	S, A, 2 vn, bc (org)	?c1775	?EK	—	
15	XXIIIa:1	Non nobis, Domine (Ps cxiii.9), offertory motet in stile a cappella, d	4vv, bc (org)	?	EK	(St Louis, 1960)[?1st version]; (Mainz, ?before 1840) [?2nd version]	
16	XXIIIb:1*	Libera me, Domine, d	S, A, T, B (? in chorus), 2 vn, bc (org)	?c1777–90	A (pts. u)	(Salzburg, 1969)	? only copied, ? not by Haydn

No.	H	Title, key	Forces	Date	Authentication	Edition	Remarks
17–22	ii, 181	6 English Psalms (J. Merrick, rev. W. D. Tattersall): *17* How oft, instinct with warmth divine, F (Ps xxvi. 5–8); *18* Blest be the name of Jacob's God, E♭ (Ps xxxi. 21–4); *19* Maker of all! be Thou my guard, D (Ps xli. 12–16); *20* The Lord, th' almighty Monarch, spake, C (Ps l.1–6); *21* Long life shall Israel's king behold, E♭ (Ps lxi.6–8); *22* O let me in th' accepted hour, A (Ps lxix. 13–17).	2 S, B	[1794/5]	Haydn's 3rd London notebook	(Kassel, 1978)	no.22 uses canzonetta Pleasing Pain (G 29)
23	XXIIIc:2	Te Deum, C	4vv, fl, 2 ob, 2 bn, (2 hn), 3 tpt, timp, str, bc (org)	–Oct 1800	RC	(Vienna and Munich, 1959) (with addl 3 trbn)	73

Note: Stabat mater, see Group C; The Ten Commandments, see Group I; Ave Maria, mentioned in Elssler, *Haydn's vollendete Compositionen* (MS A-Sm), not identified

Appendix **B.1**: Selected adaptations and arrangements (authorship uncertain, but Haydn's approval probable in most cases)

No.	Becker-Glauch (1970)	Title	Edition	Original version	Remarks
1	—	Audi clamorem nostrum, offertory	—	final chorus in 1st pt. of Il ritorno di Tobia (C 3)	Pohl (1882), B/m/13; also with other texts
2	B/6/c	Concertantes jugiter, offertory	HW xxvii/2, 122	aria Si obtrudat in Applausus (C 2)	
3	B/6/b-	Dictamina mea, offertory	HW xxvii/2, 68	duetto in Applausus (C 2), combined with Alleluia (B 9)	edn. without Alleluia

No.	H	Title	Edition		Remarks
4	B/8	Insanae et vanae curae (Der Sturm) offertory, motet, gradual	(Leipzig, 1809)	chorus Svanisce in un momento in Il ritorno di Tobia (C 3)	not later than 1798; authenticated by E; also with texts Des Staubes eitle Sorgen, Distraught with care and anguish
5	B/7	Maria, de reine (Aria pro adventu)	—	aria of Baucis in Philemon und Baucis (E 12)	
6	B/6/d	O Jesu, te invocamus, offertory hymn	HW xxvii/2, 170	final chorus in Applausus (C 2)	also with text Allmächt'ger, Preis dir und Ehre!
7	—	Plausus honores date, offertory motet	—	final chorus in Al tuo arrivo felice (D 4)	with orch introduction based on preceding recit
8	B/6/a	Quae res admiranda ... Christus coeli atria, offertory motet	HW xxvii/2, 4, 18	1st recit and qt in Applausus (C 2)	
9	B/3	Vicisti, heros ... Justus ut palma	—	recit and aria of Leopoldo in Marchese (E 3)	
10	HXXXIc:1	Vias tuas Domine, gradual, C, 4vv, bc	—		by unknown composer, 1576, ? ed. Haydn

Appendix B.2: Selected works attributed to Haydn

No.	H	Title, Key	Forces	Earliest reference	Edition	Remarks
1	XXIIIa:5*	Ad aras convolate, gradual, offertory, G	4vv, ? 2 ob, ? 2 trbn, str, bc (org)	1794	—	probably not authentic
2	XXIIIb:E1	Alma redemptoris mater, E	4vv, bc (org)	—	(Vienna and Graz, 1916)	probably not authentic
3	XXIIIa:8*	Ardentes Seraphini, offertory,	2 S, str, bc (org)	1765	—	doubtful
4	XXIIIb:6*	Ave regina, F	4vv, ? 2 tpt, ?timp, 2 vn, bc (org)	1782	—	doubtful
5	—	Ego virtus gratitudo, aria, C	S, 2 ob, 2 tpt, timp, str, bc (org)	1772	—	?authentic; for ?secular origin, see Becker-Glauch: 'Neue Forschungen' (1970)
6	XXIIId:G1	Ei wer hält' ihm das Ding gedenkt (Pastorella), aria, G	S, 2 vn, bc (org)	1764	(Altötting, 1975)	?authentic; ? also attrib. (J. A.) Stephan and M. Haydn
7	XXIIIc:6*	Lauda Sion (Aria de venerabili [sacramento]), F	A, 2 fl, str, bc (org)	1787	—	probably not authentic; originally without author's name

No.	H	Title, Key	Forces	Earliest reference	Edition	Remarks
8	XXIIIc:C2	Litaniae de BVM, C	S, A, T, B, 4vv, fl, ?2 ob, ?2 tpt, ?timp, 2 vn, org obbl	1776	(Vienna and Munich, 1960)	several versions; probably by J. Heyda (Hayda, Haida; c1740–1806); also attrib. M. Haydn
9	XXIIIa:C7	Magna coeli domina (Motetto de Beata), aria, C	B, ?2 tpt, ?timp, str, bc (org)	—	—	?authentic; for ?secular origin, see Becker-Glauch: 'Neue Forschungen' (1970)
10	—	Maria Jungfrau rein (Aria pro adventu), G	S, 2 vn, bc (org)	—	—	?authentic; for ?secular origin, see Becker-Glauch: 'Neue Forschungen' (1970)
11	XXIIIa:6*	Salus et gloria, offertory motet, C	4vv, 2 tpt, timp, 2 vn, bc (org)	1779	(Augsburg, 1959)	probably by L. Hofmann
12	XXIIIb:5*	Salve regina, G	S, A, 2 vn, bc (org)	1766	—	probably by J. Heyda
13	XXIIIa:7*	Super flumina Babylonis (Ps cxxxvi), motet, C	A, 4vv, 2 tpt, timp, str, bc (org)	1772	—	probably by Vanhal
		Veni tandem expectatus, see appx F.17				
14	—	Was meine matle Brust bekränket (Aria pro adventu), G	T, 2 vn, vle (org)	—	—	?authentic; MS 'Hayden' in CS–Pnm (Kuks)

Note: for chorus, D, Sit laus plena, sit sonora (text from Lauda Sion) and for recit and aria Quid hostem times, see Landon, i (1980)

117ff

C: ORATORIOS

No.	H	Title, poet	Forces	Date	Authentication	Edition	Remarks	
1	XXbis	Stabat mater, sequence/hymn	S, A, T, B, 4vv, 2 ob/eng hn, str, bc (org)	1767	EK	(Amsterdam, 1955; London, 1977)	also with texts Weint ihr Augen and Trauret Seelen; more insts added Neukomm(? or Eybler), 1803	29, 30, 36, 91

2	XXIVa:6	Applausus (Jubilaeum Virtutis Palatium), allegorical oratorio/cantata	S, A, T, 2 B, 2 ob, bn, 2 hn/ tpt, timp, str, hpd, obbl	[−4 April] 1768	EK, A	HW xxvii/2	perf. Zwettl, 17 April 1768	29, 30, 45, 91
3	XXI:1	Il ritorno di Tobia (G. Boccherini), 2 pts.	2 S, A, T, B, 4vv, 2 fl, 2 ob, 2 eng hn, 2 bn, 4 hn, 2 tpt, 2 trbn, timp, str, bc (hpd)	[1774–5]	A (pt.ii and no.13c,u), C	HW xxviii/1 (I, II)	perf. Vienna, 2, 4 April 1775; rev. and choruses Svanisce in un momento and Ah gran Dio! added 1784; both versions of acc. recits in HW; embellished versions and cadenzas in H7b, 12b dubious; rev. Neukomm with Haydn's permission, 1806; ov., cf K 9	40, 42, 53, 103, 117
4	XX/2	Die Sieben letzten Worte unseres Erlösers am Kreuze (The Seven last Words) (? J. Friebert, rev. G. van Swieten)	S, A, T, B, 4vv, 2 fl, 2 ob, 2 cl, 2 bn, dbn, 2 hn, 2 tpt, 2 trbn, timp, str	[1795–6]	A (u, partly in copyist's hand), OE	HW xxviii/2	for Haydn's orig. orch version, see K 11; uses also J. Friebert's vocal arr.; text partly uses K. W. Ramler: Der Tod Jesu; perf. Vienna, 26 March 1796	50, 51, 62, 67, 72, 78, 104, 105, 106, 117, 118, 121
5	XXI:2	Die Schöpfung (The Creation) (van Swieten, after ?Lidley (? = T. Linley (i), after Milton: Paradise Lost), 3 pts.	S, T, B, 4vv, 3 fl, 2 ob, 2 cl, 2 bn, dbn, 2 hn, 2 tpt, 3 trbn, timp, str, bc (hpd)	1796–8	OE, RC, Sk, A (dbn, trbn pts. only, u)	M 16/V	perf. Vienna, 29, 30 April 1798; several sketches in Landon, iv (1977), 357	71, 72, 73, 77, 78, 117, 118
6	XXI:3	Die Jahreszeiten (The Seasons) (van Swieten, after J. Thomson, trans. B. H. Brockes), 4 pts.	S, T, B, 4vv, 2 fl, 2 ob, 2 cl, 2 bn, dbn, 4 hn, 3 tpt, 3 trbn, timp, perc, str, bc (hpd)	1799– 1801	OE, RC, Sk	M 16/VI–VII	text incl. 2 songs by C. F. Weisse and G. A. Bürger; perf. Vienna, 24 April 1801; aria Schon eilet uses Andante from J 94; for dbn, see Landon, v (1977), 132	72, 73, 117, 118, 119

Note: Die Erlösung mentioned in HL not verified; ?identical with no.4 or to spurious arr. Der Versöhnungstod (H Anh.XXIVa:1)

D: SECULAR CANTATAS, CHORUSES

No.	H	Title, poet	Forces	Date	Authentication	Edition	Remarks	
1	XXIVa:1	Vivan gl'illustri sposi, cantata	?	-10 Jan 1763	EK	—	lost; for Anton Esterházy's wedding; in EK as Coro 1	22
2	XXIVa:2	Destatevi o miei fidi, cantata	2 S, T, 4vv, 2 ob, 2 hn, str, bc	[-?6 Dec] 1763	A, ?EK	—	for Nikolaus Esterházy's name day; ?mixed with other pieces; autograph, *PL-Kj*	
3	XXIVa:4	Qual dubbio ormai, cantata	S, 4vv, 2 ob, 2 hn, str, hpd obbl	[-?6 Dec] 1764	A, ?EK	—	for Nikolaus Esterházy's name day	
4	XXIVa:3	Da qual gioia improvvisa, cantata	S, A, 4vv, fl, 2 ob, bn, 2 hn, str, hpd obbl	?1764	A, ?EK	—	for Nikolaus Esterházy's return from Frankfurt; ?incomplete; autograph, *PL-Kj*	
5	XXIVa:5	Dei clementi, cantata	?	?	EK	—	lost; for Nikolaus Esterházy's convalescence; in EK as Coro 3	22
6	XXIVa:3	Al tuo arrivo felice, cantata	?	?1767	EK	—	lost; for Nikolaus Esterházy's return from Paris; in EK as Coro 2; in H as 1st piece of no.*4*	22
7	ii, 433	Su cantiamo, su beviamo	S, 3vv, fl, 2 ob, 2 hn, 2 tpt, timp, str	?1791	A (u)	—	adapted from final chorus of Orlando paladino (E 22)	
8a	XXIVa:8	The Storm: Hark! The wild uproar of the winds (P. Pindar), madrigal	S, A, T, B (?solo vv), 2 fl, 2 ob, 2 bn, str	[-24 Feb] 1792	A	ed. F. Szekeres, D 316 (1969)		61
8b	ii, 194	Der Sturm: Hört! Die Winde furchtbar heulen	S, A, T, B, 4vv, 2 fl, 2 ob, 2 cl, 2 bn, 2 hn, 2 tpt, 2 trbn, timp, str	-1798 [?1793]	A (pt. only, u), SC	(Leipzig, 1802)	Ger. trans. of no.*8a*; also as La tempesta with It. text	
9	XXIVa:9	Nor can I think ... Thy great endeavours (from Klareamontos: [Invocation] Neptune to the Common-wealth of England)	B, 4vv, fl, 2 ob, 2 cl, 2 bn, 2 hn, 2 tpt, timp, str	?1794	A (u)	—	aria and chorus from inc. cantata; not part of Selden's Mare clausum	
10	—	Song with orch	?	1791-5	Gr, Dies	—	lost/unidentified	
11	XXVIa:43	Gott erhalte Franz den Kaiser (L. L. Haschka), Volkslied	1v, fl, 2 ob, 2 bn, 2 hn, 2 tpt, timp, str	1797	A	(London, 1977) (see Landon, iv, 279)	for orig. version, see G *43*; perf. 12 Feb 1797	71, 116

Quis stellae radius, see B *4*

Note: most pieces of nos.*2* and *4* preserved singly

Appendix D.1: Arrangement

No.	H	Title	Forces	Date	Authentication	Edition	Remarks
1	—	God save the King	?	1791–5	Gr, Dies	—	lost

Appendix D.2: Doubtful and spurious works

No.	H	Title	Forces	Edition	Remarks
1	XXIVa:11*	Die Erwählung eines Kapellmeisters, cantata		ed. F. Szekeres, D 374 (1970)	MSS not authentic
2	Ia:D4	D'onora al piede pongansi, ov. and chorus		—	frag. without author's name; not a Haydn autograph
3	XXIVa:D2	Inimica mihi semper sydera (Applausus)		—	frag. of cantata without author's name; not a Haydn autograph

E: DRAMATIC

No.	H	Title, librettist	Forces	Date	Authentication	Edition	Remarks	
1a	XXIXb:1a	Der krumme Teufel (Singspiel, J. Kurz)	?	?1751	HL	—	lost or = no.1b; 1st known perf. Vienna, 29 May 1753	12, 14

No.	H	Title, librettist	Forces	Date	Authentication	Edition	Remarks	
1b	XXIXb:1b	Der neue krumme Teufel [Asmodeus, der krumme Teufel] (Singspiel, 2, Kurz), incl. Arlequin, der neue Abgott Ram in Amerika (pantomimic Singspiel), Il vecchio ingannato (intermezzo)	?	?*c*1758	lib	—	music lost; intermezzo ? not by Haydn	
2	XXVIII:1	Acide (festa teatrale, 1, G. B. [?G. A.] Migliavacca)	2 S, A, T, B, 2 fl, 2 ob/eng hn, 2 hn, str, bc	1762	A, EK	ov. D 39 (1959)	frag., lib extant; perf. Eisenstadt, 11 Jan 1763; ov., cf HIa:5	22, 30, 88, 100
		[2nd version]	2 S, T, 2 B with addl 2 bn	[1773]	A	—	not perf.; frag. extant; aria Tergi i vezzosi rai (Salzburg, 1964)	
3	XXX:1	Marchese (La Marchesa Nespola), comedia	?5 S, T, 2 fl, 2 ob, 2 hn, str	1763	A, EK	—	frag.; dialogues lost	22
4	XXIVb:1	? (? opera buffa; ? It. comedy)	S, B, (. . . . .), 2 eng hn, 2 hn, str, bc	?1762	A (u)	—	? = no.*5*; aria Costretta a piangere (Salzburg, 1961) and recit extant	
5	ii, 448	Il dottore (comedia)	?	?*c*1761–5	EK	—	lost	
6	ii, 448	La vedova (comedia)	?	?*c*1761–5	EK	—	lost	
7	ii, 448	Il scanarello (comedia)	?	?*c*1761–5	EK	—	lost	
8	XXVIII:2	La canterina (intermezzo in musica, 2)	3 S, T, 2 fl, 2 ob/eng hn, 2 hn, str, bc	1766	A, EK	HW xxv/2	perf. before 11 Sept (?July) 1766, Bratislava, 16 Feb 1767; lib from intermezzo in Piccinni: L'Origille, 1760, text of nos.2, 3 from Lucio Vero (Zeno), 1700; cf Q *29*	30, 92
9	XXVIII:3	Lo speziale (Der Apotheker) (dramma giocoso, 3, C. Goldoni)	2 S, 2 T, 2 fl, 2 ob, bn, 2 hn, str, bc	[1768]	A, EK	HW xxv/3	Act 3 inc.; perf. Eszterháza, aut. 1768; ov., cf K *6*	30, 31, 36, 92
10	XXVIII:4	Le pescatrici (Die Fischerinnen) (dramma giocoso, 3, Goldoni)	2 S, A, 2 T, 2 B, vv, 2 fl, 2 ob/eng hn, bn, 2 hn, str, bc	1769	A, EK	HW xxv/4	Acts 1, 2 inc.; ?1st perf. Eszterháza, 16, 18 Sept 1770; ?1st movt of ov., cf J *106*	30, 31, 92, 99
11	XXVIII:5	L'infedeltà delusa (Liebe macht erfinderisch; Untreue lohnt sich nicht; Deceit outwitted) (burletta per musica, 2, M. Coltellini)	2 S, 2 T, B, 2 ob, 2 bn, 2 hn, timp, str, bc	[1773]	A, EK	HW xxv/5	perf. Eszterháza, 26 July 1773; ov., concert version, cf K *8*	36, 37, 92

12	XXIXa:1, 1a; XXIXb:2	Philemon und Baucis oder Jupiters Reise auf die Erde (Singspiel/marionette opera, 1, G. K. Pfeffel); Vorspiel: Der Götterrat (1, ? P. G. Bader)	2 S, 2 T, 4vv, ?2 fl, 2 ob, ?bn, 2 hn, ? 2 tpt, timp, str	[1773]	EK, signed lib. HL. A (frag., u)	HW xxiv/1	supposed ov. (cf J 50) and frag. of prelude extant; drama extant in rev. version; perf. Eszterháza, 2 Sept 1773; ov. to drama, Hfa:8; cf appx G.1, 1	37, 40
13	XXIXa:2	Hexenschabbas (marionette opera)	?	?1773	—	—	lost	40
14	XXVIII:6	L'incontro improvviso (Die unverhoffte Zusammenkunft; Unverhofftes Begegnen) (dramma giocoso, 3, K. Friebert, after Dancourt: La rencontre imprévue)	3 S, 2 T, 2 B, 2 ob/eng hn, 2 bn, 2 hn, 2 tpt, timp, perc, str, bc	[1775]	A, EK	HW xxv/6 (I, II)	perf. Eszterháza, 29 Aug 1775; ov., K 5	37, 92, 99
15	XXIXa:3	Dido (Singspiel/marionette opera, 3, Bader)	?	-1778 [?1776]	HL	—	music lost; perf. Eszterháza, ? March 1776, also aut. 1778; ?aria extant (G 13)	40
16a	XXIXa:4	Opéra comique vom abgebrannten Haus	?	?c1773-9	EK	?	lost or = no.16b	40
16b	XXIXb:A	Die Feuerbrunst (Singspiel/marionette opera, 2)	S, ?5 T, B, 4vv, 2 fl, 2 ob, 2 cl, 2 bn, 2 hn, 2 tpt, timp, str	?1775-8	?	(London, 1963) (vocal score)	? = no.16a; authenticity uncertain; dialogues lost; 1st, 2nd, ?3rd movts of ov. by I. Pleyel; cf K 8	
17	XXVIII:7	Il mondo della luna (Die Welt auf dem Monde) (dramma giocoso, 3, Goldoni)	2/3 S, 1/2 A, 2 T, B, 2 fl, 2 ob, 2 bn, 2 hn, 2 tpt, timp, str, bc	[1777]	A, EK, Sk	HW xxv/7 (I, II, III)	perf. Eszterháza, 3 Aug 1777; cf A 8, J 63, K 7, appx K 8, S 8, 9, 10, 12, 13	39, 99, 104
18	XXIXb:3	Die bestrafte Rachbegierde (Singspiel/marionette opera, 3, Bader)	?	?1779	lib	—	music lost; perf. Eszterháza, 1779	
19	XXVIII:8	La vera costanza (dramma giocoso, 3, F. Puttini)	?	-1779 [?April-Nov, 1778]	EK; Sk	—	music lost where not incl. in 2nd version; sketches, HW xxv/8, 356; perf. Eszterháza, 25 April 1779; ov., concert version, K 7	42, 45, 95
		2nd version (Der flatterhafte Liebhaber; Der Sieg der Beständigkeit; Die wahre Beständigkeit; List und Liebe; Laurette (P. U. Dubuisson) (HXXVIII: 8a))	3 S, 3 T, B, 1/2 fl, 2 ob, 2 bn, 2 hn, timp, str, bc	1785	A (partly in copyists' hands)	HW xxv/8	Count Errico's Act 2 scene = that in Anfossi's setting (1775)	

No.	H	Title, librettist	Forces	Date	Authentication	Edition	Remarks	
20	XXVIII:9	L'isola disabitata (Die wüste Insel) (azione teatrale, 2, Metastasio)	2 S, T, B, 2 ob, bn, 2 hn, timp, str, bc	1779	A (frags.), EK	(Vienna and Leipzig, 1909) (vocal score)	perf. Eszterháza, 6 Dec 1779, finale rev. 1802; ov., K 4, autograph fragment in PL-Kj	45, 99
21	XXVIII:10	La fedeltà premiata (Die belohnte Treue) (dramma pastorale giocoso, 3, after G. Lorenzi: L'infedeltà fedele)	4 S, 2 T, 2 B, fl, 2 ob, bn, 2 hn/tpt, timp, str, bc	1780	A, RC	HW xxv/10 (I, II)	perf. Eszterháza, 25 Feb 1781; cf J 73	45, 53, 99
22	XXVIII:11	Orlando paladino (Der Ritter Roland) (dramma eroicomico, 3, C. F. Badini, N. Porta)	3 S, 4 T, 2 B, fl, 2 ob, 2 bn, 2 hn/tpt, timp, str, bc	1782	A	HW xxv/11 (I, II)	perf. Eszterháza, 6 Dec 1782; ov., H1a:16; cf D 7; duetto H 16 arr. with text Quel cor umano e tenero (Da Ponte) (London, 1794-5)	45, 100
23	XXVIII:12	Armida (dramma eroico, 3)	2 S, 3 T, B, fl, 2 ob, 2 cl, 2 bn, 2 hn/tpt, timp, str, bc	1783	A	HW xxv/12	perf. Eszterháza, 26 Feb 1784; ov., H1a:14	45, 49, 98, 100, 111, 118
24	XXVIII:13	L'anima del filosofo ossia Orfeo ed Euridice (dramma per musica, 4/5, Badini)	2 S, T, B, 4vv, 2fl, 2 ob, 2 cl, 2 eng hn, 2 bn, 2 hn, 2 tpt, 2 trbn, timp, harp, str, bc	1791	A	HW xxv/13	ov., H1a:3, cf K 13	64, 107, 110
25	XXX:5	Alfred, König der Angelsachsen, oder Der patriotische König (J. W. Cowmeadow, after A. Bicknell):		1796	A		incidental music; perf. as Haldane, König der Dänen. Eisenstadt, 9 Sept 1796	
a		Triumph dir, Haldane (chorus)	3vv, 2 ob, 2 bn, 2 tpt, timp, str			(Leipzig, 1814) (vocal score)		
b		Ausgesandt vom Strahlenthrone (aria with spoken interjections)	S, 2 cl, 2 bn, 2 hn			(Salzburg, 1961)		
c		Der Morgen graut (duet)	2 T, (?harp), vn solo, str			—		
26	XXX:4	Fatal amour (aria with spoken interjections), F, G, E♭	S, fl, 2 ob, 2 bn, 2 hn, str	?c1796	A (u)	—	music from unknown comedy; quotes Aria alla polacca by J. Schuster	

Appendix E: Selected doubtful and spurious works

No.	H	Title, librettist	Edition	Remarks
1	XXIXa:5	Genovefens vierter Theil (Singspiel/marionette opera, 3, J. K. von Pauersbach)	—	music lost; by different composers according to HL, by Haydn according to HV; perf. Eszterháza, sum. 1777
2	XXIXb:F Add.	Die reisende Ceres (Singspiel, P.·M. Lindemayer)	—	music inc.
3	XXXII:2	Der Freibrief (Singspiel, 1, ? G. E. Lüderwald)	—	several versions; music lost; perf. Meiningen, 1789, with Haydn's music, ? arr. F. von Weber
4	XXXII:3	Alessandro il grande (opera seria, 3)	—	pasticcio arr. J. Schellinger from works by Haydn and others
5	XXXII:4	Der Äpfeldieb (Singspiel, 1, C. F. Bretzner)	—	music lost; by (?M.) Jast (Jost), other version by Kaffka; perf. Hamburg, 1791, with inserted music by Haydn
6	i, 577	Die [Das] Ochsenmenuett (Singspiel, 1, G. E. von Hofmann)	(Mainz, 1927)	pasticcio arr. von Seyfried from Haydn's works; perf. Vienna, 1823; see appx X.3, 8
7	—	Das Teebrett (comedy, E. Fischer), vv, kbd	(Berlin, 1914)	music from L'incontro improvviso (E 14), L'infedeltà delusa (E 11), Orlando paladino (E 22)
8	—	(Finale: ... sey voll edlen Stolzes)	—	2 coloraturas, S, orch; without author's name; MS (D-LEm) not a Haydn autograph

F: SECULAR VOCAL WITH ORCHESTRA

No.	H	Title	Forces	Date	Authentication	Edition	Remarks
1	XXIVb:A1	Aure dolci ch'io respiro, aria	?S/T, 2 fl, 2 ob, str	-?1762	F	—	vocal part lost
2	XXIVb:2	D'una sposa meschinella	S, 2 ob, 2 hn, str	?sum. 1777	A	(Salzburg, 1961)	aria for Paisiello: La Frascatana; ?by unknown composer, ?rev. Haydn; ? orig. = HXXIVb:2bis
3	XXIVb:8	Dica pure chi vuol dire	?S, 2 ob, bn, 2 hn, str	?1778/85	—	(Vienna, 1787) (vocal score)	aria for Anfossi: Il geloso in cimento: newly scored P. A. Pisk (Vienna, 1931)

No.	H	Title	Forces	Date	Authentication	Edition	Remarks
4	XXIVb:3	Quando la rosa . . . Finché l'agnello *	S, fl, bn, 2 hn, str	?July 1779	A (u)	(Salzburg, 1961) (1st stanza only)	aria for Anfossi: La Metilde ritrovata (L'incognita perseguitata); recit is by Anfossi
5	XXIVb:5	Dice benissimo	B, 2 hn, str	–?27 July 1780	A (frags, u)	(Salzburg, 1964)	aria for Salieri: La scuola de' gelosi; also with texts Männer ich sag es euch and Ja in dem Himmel
6	XXIVb:7	Signor voi sapete	S, 2 fl, 2 ob, 2 bn, 2 hn, str	–?3 July 1785	Sk, HE	(Salzburg, 1961)	aria for Anfossi: Il matrimonio per inganno; sketch in PL–Kj
7	XXIVa:7	Miseri noi . . . Funesto orror	S, 2 fl, 2 ob, 2 bn, 2 hn, str	–1786	SC	D 17 (1960)	cantata recit and aria
8	XXIVb:9	Sono Alcina	S, fl, 2 ob, 2 bn, 2 hn, str	[–18 June] 1786	A	(Salzburg, 1961)	cavatina for G. Gazzaniga: L'isola di Alcina; cf T 3
9	XXIVb:10	Ah tu non senti . . . Qual destra omicida	T, fl, 2 ob, 2 bn, 2 hn, str	[–4 July] 1786	A, Sk	(Salzburg, 1964)	recit and aria for Traetta: Ifigenia in Tauride
10	XXIVb:11	Un cor si tenero	B, 2 ob, 2 hn, str	[–April] 1787	A	(Salzburg, 1964)	aria for F. Bianchi: Il disertore
11	XXIVb:12	Vada adagio, signorina	S, 2 ob, 2 bn, 2 hn, str	–?3 June 1787	A (u pt.), C	(Salzburg, 1961)	aria for P. Guglielmi: La quacquera spiritosa: cf appx F.2, 3
12	XXIVb:13	Chi vive amante	S, fl, 2 ob, 2 bn, 2 hn, str	[–25/26 July] 1787	A	(Salzburg, 1961)	aria for F. Bianchi: Alessandro nell'Indie
13	XXIVb:14	Se tu mi sprezzi	T, 2 ob, 2 bn, 2 hn, str	[–9 March] 1788	A	(Salzburg, 1964)	aria for G. Sarti: I finti eredi
14	XXIVb:15	Infelice sventurata	S, 2 ob, 2 bn, 2 hn, str	[–Feb] 1789	A	(Salzburg, 1961)	aria for Cimarosa: I due supposti conti
15	XXXII:1	for Circe ossia L'isola incantata:		[–July] 1789			pasticcio by Naumann, Haydn and unknown composer; cf appx F.2, 19
a		Son due ore che giro, recit	T, fl, 2 ob, 2 bn, str, bc		A	(Budapest, 1960) (see Bartha–Somfai)	
b		Son pietosa, son bonina, aria	S, fl, 2 ob, 2 bn, 2 hn, str		C	D 19 (1959)	
c		Lavatevi presto, terzetto	2 T, B, fl, 2 ob, 2 bn, 2 hn, str		C	—	cf appx X.3, 2

16	XXIVb:16	Da che penso a maritarmi	T, fl, 2 ob, 2 bn, 2 hn, str	[-14 March] 1790	A	(Salzburg, 1964)	aria for Gassmann: L'amore artigiano, which incl. 2 other arias by Haydn: ?no.17, ?appx F.1, 5
17	XXIVb:19	La mia pace, oh Dio, perdei	S, fl, 2 ob, 2 bn, 2 hn, str	1790	A	—	see no.16
18	XXIVb:17	Il meglio mio carattere	S, fl, 2 ob, 2 bn, 2 hn, str	-?6 June 1790	C	(Salzburg, 1961)	aria for Cimarosa: L'impresario in angustie
19	XXIVb:18	La moglie quando è buona	S, fl, 2 ob, 2 bn, 2 hn, str	-?Aug/Sept 1790	HE, C	(Salzburg, 1961)	aria for Cimarosa: Giannina e Bernardone; cf appx H 13
20	XXIVb:22*	Tornate pur mia bella, aria	T, fl, 2 ob, 2 bn, 2 hn, str	-13 Aug 1790 [?1787]	—	—	with text Consola pur mia bella inserted in Guglielmi: La quacquera spiritosa, Vienna, 1790
21	XXIVb:23*	Via siate bonino, aria	S, fl, 2 ob, 2 bn, 2 hn, str	?c1785-95	—	—	
22	XXIVb:24	Cara deh torna, aria for (Giacomo) Davide	T, ob, bn (and ?)	-?16 May 1791	Gr, Dies	—	music lost
23	Add. —	Aria for Miss Poole	?S, ?	1791-5	Gr, Dies	—	lost/unidentified; ?sketch extant
24	—	Aria with full orch	?	1791-5	Gr, Dies		lost/unidentified
25	XXIVa:10	Berenice, che fai, cantata	S, fl, 2 ob, 2 cl, 2 bn, 2 hn, str	[-4 May] 1795	A	D 129 (1965)	scena from Antigono (Metastasio); composed in London for Brigida Giorgi Banti
26	XXIVb:20	Solo e pensoso, aria	S, 2 cl, 2 bn, 2 hn, str	1798	A	(Salzburg, 1961)	sonetto from Petrarch's Canzoniere (no.xxv)

Note: Ah come il core (HXXIVA, Anh. 4), see E 21 (HW xxv/10, 380); Quel cor umano e tenero (HXXVa, Anhang) = Quel tuo visetto amabile, see E 22 (HW xxv/11, 237); Sono le donne capricciose = Dice benissimo (no.5)

Frag., E(Eb), *MGG*, v, 1893, line 4 = Dice benissimo (no.5)

Unpubd secco recits, rev./composed Haydn, in A. Felici (?Sacchini): L'amore soldato, perf. Eszterháza, 1779, and Cimarosa: L'impresario in angustie, perf. Eszterháza, 1790

Recit and aria sung by Calcagni, London, 1792, and Cantata a voce sola con violino composed for the Duke of Bedford, unidentified or lost; see Landon, iii (1976)

Appendix F.1: Selected works attributed to Haydn

No.	H	Title	Forces	Date	Edition	Remarks
1	XXVb:5*	Pietà di me, benigni Dei, terzetto	2 S, T, eng hn solo, bn solo, hn solo, 2 hn, str	?	—	Haydn's name on MS copies added later; ? composed for Elisabeth Billington; considered as probably authentic by Landon, ii, iii (1978, 1976) and by Larsen (1941, rev. 1979)
2	XXIVb:6	Mora l'infido . . . Mi sento nel seno, recit and aria	S, orch	[1781]	—	extant are vocal part of recit, 2 vn (partly in Haydn's hand) and b of recit and aria; without author's name; incl. in Righini: Il convitato di pietra
3	XXVIb:1	Er ist nicht mehr! (Deutschlands Klage auf den Tod des grossen Friedrichs, Borussens König), cantata	?S, baryton (and ?)	1786–8	—	perf. Leipzig and Nuremberg, 1788, by Carl Franz; vocal part with bc extant; considered authentic by Landon, ii (1978)
4	XXIVb:21*	?(aria, ? of Giannina)	?S, 2 fl, 2 ob, 2 bn, 2 hn, str	~1788	—	vocal part lost; without author's name; incl. in G. Sarti: I finti eredi; cf appxs X.1, 7, Y.4. /
5	XXIVb:16bis	?Occhietti cari del mio tesoro, aria	?T, 2 ob, bn, 2 hn, str	~1790	—	vocal part lost; without author's name; incl. in Gassmann: L'amore artigiano
6	XXIVa:F1	Pianger vidi appresso un fonte, cantata	A, 2 ob, 2 hn, str	?	(Munich, 1942)	probably not authentic
7	XXIIId:B2	Veni tandem expectatus, aria	S, str	?	—	not sacred; without author's name; not a Haydn autograph

Note: several anon. arias from Viennese Singspiels of 1750s tentatively attrib. Haydn: 22 more arias from Esterházy archives listed in Bartha-Somfai (ii/1–22) as probably by Haydn, though no source with his name is known; more anonymous arias from same archives mentioned in Landon, ii (1978) as possibly by Haydn

Appendix F.2: Revisions (mostly in Haydn's hand) of operatic works by other composers

No.	H	Title	Forces	Date	Edition	Remarks
1	XXXIc:3	Vi miro fiso	?S, 2 ob, 2 hn, str	[aut. 1777]	—	aria from Dittersdorf: Arcifanfano re de' matti; altered and wind pts. added

2	—	Non per parlar d'amore	?S, orch	[July 1778]	—	aria by Salieri from pasticcio L'astratto; altered and 8 bars rewritten, Bartha–Somfai, iii/2
3	XXXIc:4	?Se provasse un pocolino	?S, ? 2 fl, 2 ob, 2 hn, str	[Feb 1780]	—	aria from Anfossi: La forza delle donne, inc.; wind pts. added and 2 vn rewritten; melody similar to F 11
4	XXXIc:5	Ah crudel, poiché lo brami	S, 2 fl, 2 hn, str	[April 1780]	(Salzburg, 1961)	aria from G. Gazzaniga: La vendemmia; 2nd half composed by Haydn
5	XXIVb:4	?(aria, ? of Carlotta)	S, 2 ob, 2 hn, str	[July] 1780	—	incl. in Salieri: La scuola de' gelosi; text lost; without author's name; score mostly rewritten and perhaps composed by Haydn
6	XXXIc:6	Gelosia d'amore è figlia (2 versions)	S, 2 ob, 2 hn, str	[July 1780]	—	aria from Salieri, ibid; altered, wind pts. added, 34 bars of score added or rewritten
7	XXXIc:7	Si promette facilmente	S, 2 ob, 2 hn, str	[Oct 1780]	—	aria from Anfossi, La finta giardiniera; completely rewritten
8	XXXIc:8	Vorrei punirti indegno	S, 2 ob, 2 hn, str	[Oct 1780]	—	aria from Anfossi, ibid; altered and wind pts. added
9	XXXIc:9	Non ama la vita	?S, orch	[April 1781]	—	aria from Anfossi: Isabella e Rodrigo ossia La costanza in amore; 2 bn and 6 bars added
10	XXXIc:10	Che tortora	S, 2 ob, 2 hn, str	[Aug 1781]	—	aria from N. Piccinni: Gli stravaganti ossia La schiava riconosciuta; 70 bars rewritten
11	XXXIc:11	Una semplice agnelletta	S, orch	[Aug 1781]	—	aria from Piccinni, ibid; altered, 14 bars added
12	—	Siam di cuor tenero	S, str (and ?)	[Aug 1781]	—	aria from Piccinni, ibid; 8 (?7 + 3) bars rewritten; see Bartha–Somfai, iii/14
13	—	Misera che farò	S, orch	[March 1782]	—	recit from Traetta: Il cavaliere errante; only 2 vn extant; not autograph; authenticity uncertain; see Bartha–Somfai, iii/23*
14	XXXIc:12	Deh frenate i mesti accenti	?S, 2 ob, 2 hn, str	[Sept 1782]	—	aria from Anfossi: Il curioso indiscreto; extensively rev., wind pts. added, 2 fl, bn omitted
15	—	Dove mai s'è ritrovato	S, orch	[March 1784]	—	aria from Anfossi: I viaggiatori felici; 6 bars rewritten; see Bartha–Somfai, iii/16
16	—	Ah mi palesa almeno	S, T, orch	[July 1786]	—	duet from Traetta: Ifigenia in Tauride; vocal parts and 2 bars of score rewritten; see Bartha–Somfai, iii/17
17	XXXIc:15	Se palpitar degg'io	S, ob, str (and ?)	[Aug 1788]	—	aria from Prati: La vendetta di Nino (Semiramide); 27 bars added

No.	H	Title	Forces	Date	Edition	Remarks
18	XXXIc:13	Se voi foste un cavaliere	S, str	[Feb 1789]	—	aria from Cimarosa: I due supposti conti; completely rewritten
19	—	Quasi in tutte le ragazze	S, orch	[July 1789]	—	anon. aria in pasticcio Circe (F 15); 12 bars rewritten; see Bartha–Somfai, iii/20
20	XXXIc:14	Silenzio, miei signori	T/B, orch	[June 1790]	—	from quintet in Cimarosa: L'impresario in angustie; 25 bars added

Note: hXXXIc:2 shows only minor alterations as do many other arias described in Bartha–Somfai; for added or altered parts not written by Haydn and the revision therefore of doubtful authorship see Bartha–Somfai, iii/8*, 10*, 11*, 18*

G: SOLO SONGS WITH KEYBOARD

No.	hXXVIa	Title, poet, key	Date	Authentication	Edition	Remarks
1–36	1–12	XII Lieder für das Clavier, ii:	–27 May 1781	OE, ?EK, HC	HW xxix/1, 2–16	103

1 Das strickende Mädchen (Sir Charles Sedley, trans. J. G. Herder), B♭; 2 Cupido (G. Leon), E; 3 Der erste Kuss (J. G. Jacobi), E♭; 4 Eine sehr gewöhnliche Geschichte (C. F. Weisse), G; 5 Die Verlassene, g; 6 Der Gleichsinn (G. Wither, trans. J. J. Eschenburg), A; 7 An Iris (J. A. Weppen), B♭; 8 An Thyrsis (1st stanza: C. M. Ziegler, rest anon.), D; 9 Trost unglücklicher Liebe, f; 10 Die Landlust (Stahl), C; 11 Liebeslied (Leon), D; 12 Die zu späte Ankunft der Mutter (Weisse), E♭

13–24		XII Lieder für das Clavier, ii:	1781 [?1780] –[?3 March] 1784	OE, EK (nos. 17, 24), A (no.18, u), Sk (no.19)	HW xxix/1, 17–31	103

13 Jeder meint, der Gegenstand (? P. G. Bader), F (? from Dido (E 15), cf appx Y.3, l); 14 Lachet nicht, Mädchen, B♭; 15 O liebes Mädchen, höre mich, G; 16 Gegenliebe (G. A. Bürger), G (cf J 73); 17 Geistliches Lied, g; 18 Auch die sprödeste der Schönen (F. W. Gotter), F; 19 O fliess, ja wallend fliess, E; 20 Zufriedenheit (J. W. L. Gleim), C; 21 Das Leben ist ein Traum (Gleim), E♭; 22 Lob der Faulheit (G. E. Lessing), a; 23 Minna (J. J. Engel), A; 24 Auf meines Vaters Grab, E

		Title	Date	Sources	HW	Notes	
25-30		VI Original Canzonettas (A. Hunter), i:	−3 June 1794	OE, Sk (nos. 29, 30)	HW xxix/1, 34-51		
		25 The Mermaid's Song, C; 26 Recollection, F; 27 Pastoral Song, A; 28 Despair, E; 29 Pleasing Pain, G (cf B 22); 30 Fidelity, f					
31-6		VI Original Canzonettas, ii:	−14 Oct 1795	RC (no.31), Sk (no.32), HE (nos.33-4), EK	HW xxix/1, 52-69		
		31 Sailor's Song, A; 32 The Wanderer (Hunter), g; 33 Sympathy (Metastasio, trans. from It.), E; 34 She never told her love (Shakespeare), Ab; 35 Piercing Eyes, G; 36 Transport of Pleasure [Content], A					
36b	36bis	Der verdienstvolle Sylvius (Ich bin der Verliebteste) (J. N. Götz), Ab	−1 Feb 1795	Sk, HE, Gr	HW xxix/1, 70	orig. version of HXXVIa:36	
37-47	37	Beim Schmerz, der dieses Herz durchwühlet, E	?c1765-75	A (u), HC, HV	HW xxix/1, 74	? part of dramatic work	
	38	Der schlau(e) und dienstfertige Pudel (v. T....), Bb	c1780-87	A (u), Gr, Dies	HW xxix/1, 76		
	39	Trachten will ich nicht auf Erden, E	−14 Dec 1790	A	HW xxix/1, 78	date on autograph is that of dedication	
	40	Der Feldzug	?	HC	HW xxix/1, —	lost or unidentified	
	41	The Spirit's Song (Hunter), f	−9 Sept 1800 [?c1795]	E, HV	HW xxix/1, 81		111
	42	O Tuneful Voice (Hunter), Eb	?c1795	Gr	HW xxix/1, 84		111
	43	Gott, erhalte [Franz] den Kaiser! (L. L. Haschka), G	Oct 1796–Jan 1797	A, Sk	HW xxix/1, 89	facs. often pubd; used as Austrian, German and W. German national anthem; cf D 11, O 62	71, 116
	44	Als einst mit Weibes Schönheit, A	?c1796-1800	A (u)	HW xxix/1, 90		
	45	Ein kleines Haus, E	−30 Aug 1800	A	HW xxix/1, 92	autograph signed later, 20 July 1807 (?1801); facs. see Sandberger (1942)	
	46	Antwort auf die Frage eines Mädchens, G	−June 1803	SC	HW xxix/1, 95	signed MS in PL-Kj; title Vergiß mein nicht not authentic	
	47	Bald wehen uns des Frühlings Lüfte, G	?	E (without author's name)	HW xxix/1, 98	2nd stanza lost	

No.	HXXVIa	Title, poet, key	Date	Authentication	Edition	Remarks
48–51	48a–d	Four German Songs: 48 Ich liebe, du liebest, E♭; 49 Dürre, Staub, B♭; 50 Sag'n allweil, C; 51 Kein besseres Leben, G	?	A (incipits only, u)	HW xxix/1, 99 (incipits)	lost; ? popular tunes arr. Haydn
52	XXXIc:17	The Lady's Looking-glass, D	c1791–5	A (u)	HW xxix/1, 97	composed/arr./copied by Haydn; followed by short kbd piece, D (X 7); ? part of larger work; cf S 15

Note: further songs, mentioned by Griesinger and Dies as composed in England, may be identical with some of those listed above; 7 songs mentioned by Rosenbaum as perf. 16 Oct 1799 ? = some of H 6–18

Appendix G.1: Arrangement

No.	H	Title, poet, key	Date	Authenti-cation	Edition	Remarks
1	ii, 443	Canzonetta: Ein Tag, der allen Freude bringt (G. K. Pfeffel), A	?1773	A (u)	HW xxiv/1, 98	arr. from aria in E 12

Appendix G.2: Selected spurious works

No.	HXXVIa	Title, poet, key	Edition	Remarks
1	F1	Abschiedslied, F	HW xxix/1, 79	by Gyrowetz
2	D4	Hymne an die Freundschaft, G	M 20/I, 111	arr. Küttner, based on II of J 75
3	D1	Liebes Mädchen, hör mir zu, D	M 20/I, 110	also known as Ständchen, 3vv (XXVb:G1), also attrib. Mozart
4	C1	Die Teilung der Erde (Schiller), C	M 20/I, 112	by F. Roser von Reiter
5	G1	A Prey to Tender Anguish (Ich habe viel gelitten), G	(London, 1797)	
6	Es4	Heiss mich nicht reden (Goethe), E♭	(Vienna, 1925)	by Zumsteeg

H: MISCELLANEOUS VOCAL WORKS WITH KEYBOARD

No.	H	Title, poet, key	Forces	Date	Authentication	Edition	Remarks	
1	XXVIb:2	Arianna a Naxos (Teseo mio ben), cantata	S, hpd/pf	–9 Feb 1790	A (lost), OE	(Salzburg, 1965)		68, 76
2a	—	Maccone (Gesänge) for Gallini	?	1791–5	Gr, Dies	—	lost	
2b	—	Italian catch	??vv, (?bc)	–2 June 1791	see Landon (1976)	—	lost. ? partly = no.2a	
3	XXVIb:3	Dr. Harington's Compliment (What art expresses; Der Tausenden), A	S, 4vv, pf	?2–6 Aug 1794	Gr	(Leipzig, 1806)	variations on song by Dr H. Harington	
4–5		2 Duetti of Nisa and Tirsi (C. F. Badini)	S, T, hpd	1796		D 35 (1960)		
	XXVa:2	Saper vorrei, G			RC			
	XXVa:1	Guarda/Senti qui, F			A			
6–18		Aus des Ramlers Lyrischer Blumenlese (13 partsongs):	3–4vv, bc (nos. 1–9)/hpd obbl (nos.10–13)	1796 (–?1799)	A	HW xxx	mentioned in letter to E. L. Gerber, 23 Sept 1799; Haydn used 1st bars of no.5 for his visiting-card; pf obbl for nos.1–9 added ? A. E. Müller	73
	XXVc:1	1 Der Augenblick (J. N. Götz), A	S, A, T, B, bc					
	XXVc:2	2 Die Harmonie in der Ehe (Götz), Bb	S, A, T, B, bc					
	XXVc:3	3 Alles hat seine Zeit (Athenaeus, trans. J. A. Ebert), F	S, A, T, B, bc					
	XXVc:4	4 Die Beredsamkeit (G. E. Lessing), Bb	S, A, T, B, bc					
	XXVc:5	5 Der Greis (F. W. L. Gleim), A	S, A, T, B, bc					
	XXVb:1	6 An den Vetter (C. F. Weisse), G	S, A, T, bc					
	XXVb:2	7 Daphnens einziger Fehler (Götz), C	T, T, B, bc					
	XXVc:6	8 Die Warnung (Athenaeus, trans. Ebert), Bb	S, A, T, B, bc					
	XXVb:3	9 Betrachtung des Todes (C. F. Gellert), a	S, T, B, bc					
	XXVc:7	10 Wider den Übermut (Gellert), A	S, A, T, B, hpd					

No.	H	Title, poet, key	Forces	Date	Authentication	Edition	Remarks
	XXVb:4	11 An die Frauen (Anakreon, trans. G. A. Bürger), F	T, T, B, hpd				
	XXVc:8	12 Danklied zu Gott (Gellert), E♭	S, A, T. B. hpd				
	XXVc:9	13 Abendlied zu Gott (Gellert), E	S, A, T, B, hpd				
19	XXVIb:4	The Battle of the Nile (Ausania trembling ... Blest leader; Pindarick Ode) (E. C. Knight), cantata	1v, hpd/pf	?6-9 Sept 1800	RC (part A)	(Berlin, 1931)	10 of 17 stanzas set
20-25	ii, 533	6 airs with variations (6 Admired Scotch Airs): 1 The blue bell(s) of Scotland (?Mrs Grant), D: 2 My love she's but a lassie yet (?H. Macneill), C: 3 Bannocks o' barley meal (? A. Boswell), G: 4 Saw ye my father? (? R. Burns), D: 5 Maggy Lauder. A: 6 Killicrankie (?Mrs Grant; ?Burns), C	1v, vn, vc, pf	1801/2-3	E (nos. 2-6, without text, orig. without author's name); no.1: A (without text; vn, vc missing) and E (vn, vc only)	(London, 1805), arr. vn, pf (?ff)	each with 3 variations: themes (? and texts) = or nearly = Z 37, 242, 15, 296, 208, 175; date on autograph, 6 Feb 1805, is that of dedication

Note: Cantata, 1v, vn (and ?), composed for Duke of Bedford, mentioned in Landon (1976), lost or unidentified

Appendix H: Arrangements

No.	H	Title, key	Forces	Date	Authentication	Edition	Remarks
1-12	XXXIc:16	12 Sentimental Catches and Glees: 1 I Know then this truth, A: 2 O say what is. G: 3 Hail to the myrtle shade, A: 4 Love free as air. D: 5 Ah no lasciarmi, C: 6 O ever beauteous, A: 7 Where shall a hapless, G; 8 Ye little loves, E♭; 9 Some kind angel, A; 10 I fruitless mourn, a; 11 Farewell my flocks, A; 12 The envious snow. C	3vv, harp/pf	1795	?Gr, ?Dies	(London, 1795)	melodies by Earl of Abingdon, acc. (? and 3vv settings) by Haydn; nos.3, 7, 8 glees, rest catches
13	ii, 217	La moglie quando è buona, aria, E♭	S, hpd	?c1790-98	C	—	arr. of F 19

116

I. CANONS

HXXVII	Title, poet, key, forces	Date	Authentication	Edition	
a: 1–10	**Die Heiligen Zehn Gebote als Canons (The Ten Commandments):** 1 Canon cancrizans: Du sollst an einen Gott glauben, C, 3/4vv; 2 Du sollst den Namen Gottes nicht eitel nennen, G, 4vv; 3 Du sollst Sonn- und Feiertag heiligen, B♭, 4vv; 4 Du sollst Vater und Mutter verehren, E♭, 4vv; 5, 5b Du sollst nicht töten, g, 4vv (2 versions, 5b in unsigned autograph and sketch); 6 Du sollst nicht Unkeuschheit treiben, C, 5vv; 7 Du sollst nicht stehlen, a, 5vv; 8 Du sollst kein falsch Zeugnis geben, E, 4vv; 9 Du sollst nicht begehren deines Nächsten Weib, C, 4vv; 10 Du sollst nicht begehren deines Nächsten Gut, f, 4vv	c1791–5	A. Sk (nos.1, 5b, ?)	HW xxxi, 3–18; cf critical commentary, 8ff; 5b missing, see *Haydn-Studien*, iv (1976), 53	75
b: 1–47	40 (recte: 46/47) **Sinngedichte als Canons bearbeitet:**	c1791–9	except nos.45–6: A (u)/HV/HC, SC/Sk (? some versions) for inc.	HW xxxi, 21–65; critical commentary, 16 (no.47) and *passim* (sketches)	73

1 Hilar an Narziss (F. von Hagedorn), G, 3vv; 2 Auf einen adeligen Dummkopf (G. E. Lessing), E♭, 3vv; 3 Der Schuster bleib bei seinem Leist (Das Sprichwort; Canone in carricatura) (K. von Eckartshausen), F, 8vv; 4 Herr von Gänsewitz zu seinem Kammerdiener (G. A. Bürger), c, 4vv; 5 An den Marull (Lessing), F, 5vv; 6 Die Mutter an ihr Kind in der Wiege, E♭, 3vv (4th v added M. Haydn, cf HW, critical commentary, 23); 7 Der Menschenfreund (Gellert), E♭, 4vv; 8 Gottes Macht und Vorsehung (Gellert), G, 3vv; 9 An Dorilis (K. F. Kretschmann), F, 4vv; 10 Vixi (Horace), B♭, 3vv; 11 Der Kobold (M. G. Lichtwer), E♭, 4vv; 12 Der Fuchs und der Marder (Lichtwer), a, 4vv; 13 Abschied, B♭, 5vv; 14 Die Hofstellungen (F. von Logau), b, 3vv; 15 Aus Nichts wird Nichts (Nichts gewonnen, nichts verloren) (A. Blumauer, after M. Richey), C, 5vv

16 Cacatum non est pictum (Bürger), A, 4vv; 17 Tre cose (G. A. Federico), E♭, 3vv; 18 Vergebliches Glück (trans. from Arabic A. Tscherning), A, 2vv; 19 Grabschrift (P. W. Hensler), g, 4vv (?originally planned as partsong); 20 Das Reitpferd (Lichtwer), E♭, 3vv; 21 Tod und Schlaf (Logau), f, 4vv; 22 An einen Geizigen (Lessing), D, 3vv; 23, 23b Das böse Weib (Lessing), G, 3vv, ?C, 2vv (2 versions); 24 Der Verlust (Lessing), E, 3vv; 25 Der Freigeist, G, 3vv; 26 Die Liebe der Feinde (Gellert), A, 2vv; 27 Der Furchtsame (Lessing), c, 3vv; 28 Die Gewissheit (Lessing), E♭, 4vv; 29 Phöbus und sein Sohn (Lichtwer), G, 4vv

30 Die Tulipane (Lichtwer), ?C, 2vv; 31 Das grösste Gut, ?C, 2/3vv; 32 Der Hirsch (Lichtwer), d, 5vv; 33 Überschrift eines Weinhauses (trans. from Lat. M. Opitz), E, 4vv; 34 Der Esel und die Dohle (Lichtwer), C, 8vv; 35 Schalksnarren (Logau), B♭, 6vv; 36 Zweierlei Feinde (trans. from Arabic A. Tscherning), F/G, 3vv; 37 Der Bäcker und die Maus (Lichtwer), d, 5vv; 38 Die Flinte und der Hase (Lichtwer), G, 4vv; 39 Der Nachbar (Lichtwer), g, 4vv; 40 Liebe zur Kunst (Logau), G, 4vv; 41 Frag und Antwort zweier Fuhrleute (Die Welt), g, 5vv; 42 Der Fuchs und der Adler (Lichtwer), ?C, 3vv; 43 Wunsch (Hagedorn), g, 4vv; 44 Gott im Herzen, F (cancelled, incl. in Missa Sancti Bernardi, A 9), 3vv; 45 Turk was a faithful dog (V. Rauzzini), B♭, 4vv; 46 Thy voice o harmony, C, 3/4vv (arr. of no.a:1); 47 Canon without text, G, ?vv

116

Note: canon Der Spiess, listed in Landon, v (1977), 317, misquoted; *recte* Der Hirsch, no.32

2: INSTRUMENTAL

(I, II, III, IV = no. of movt)

J: SYMPHONIES

Hl	Key	Forces	Date	Authentication	Edition	Remarks	
1	D	2 ob, 2 hn, str	-25 Nov 1759	HV, Gr	P i, 37	MS copy, *A-ST*, with spurious Minuet	15, 89
2	C	2 ob, 2 hn, str	-1764 [-?1761]	EK	P i, 51		90
3	G	2 ob, 2 hn, str	-1762	EK	P i, 71		89
4	D	2 ob, 2 hn, str	-1762 [-?1760]	EK	P i, 89		90
5	A	2 ob, 2 hn, str	-1762 [-?1760]	HV, F	P i, 107	ed. M i/l with order of I and II reversed	
6	D	fl, 2 ob, bn, 2 hn, str	?1761	HV	P i, 125	'Le matin': title probably authentic	89
7	C	fl, 2 fl/ob, bn, 2 hn, str	1761	A	P i, 157	'Le midi': title authentic; facs. edn. (Budapest, 1972)	89
8	G	fl, 2 ob, bn, 2 hn, str	?1761	HV	P i, 197	'Le soir': title probably authentic; IV: 'La tempesta'	89
9	C	2 fl/ob, bn, 2 hn, str	?1762	A (lost), EK	P i, 231	?orig. ov. to unidentified vocal work	
10	D	2 ob, 2 hn, str	-1766 [-?1761]	HV, F	P i, 243		89
11	E♭	2 ob, 2 hn, str	-1769 [-?1760]	HV, F (?= RC)	P i, 259		90
12	E	2 ob, 2 hn, str	1763	A	P i, 279		90
13	D	fl, 2 ob, 4 hn, (timp), str	1763	A	P ii, 3		89
14	A	2 ob, 2 hn, str	-1764	HV, JE	P ii, 29	II also used in N *14*	90
15	D	2 ob, 2 hn, str	-1764 [-?1761]	EK	P ii, 43		
16	B♭	2 ob, 2 hn, str	-1766	HV	P ii, 65		
17	F	2 ob, 2 hn, str	-1765	EK	P ii, 79	date on MS in *CS-N*	
18	G	2 ob, 2 hn, str	-1766	EK	P ii, 97	ed. M i/2 with order of I and II reversed	
19	D	2 ob, 2 hn, str	-1766	EK	P ii, 113		89
20	C	2 ob, 2 hn, 2 tpt, timp, str	-1766	EK	P ii, 127		
21	A	2 ob, 2 hn, str	1764	A	HW i/4, 1; P ii, 155		90
22	E♭	2 eng hn, 2 hn, str	1764	A	HW i/4, 15; P ii, 173	'The Philosopher'; another version, 3 movts, incl. doubtful Andante grazioso (P ii, 189)	90
23	G	2 ob, 2 hn, str	1764	A	HW i/4, 31; P ii, 197		90
24	D	fl/2 ob, 2 hn, str	1764	A	HW i/4, 48; P ii, 217		89
25	C	2 ob, 2 hn, str	-1766 [-?1760]	F	P ii, 237	authentic MS in *D-RUl*	
26	d	2 ob, 2 hn, str	-1770	EK	P ii, 253	'Lamentatione': title ?authentic; title Weihnachtssymphonie (M i/2) of no apparent relevance	31, 93

No.	Key	Instrumentation	Date	Source	References	Remarks	Pages
27	G	2 ob, 2 hn, str	–1766 [–?1761]	EK	P ii, 271		89
28	A	2 ob, 2 hn, str	1765	A	HW i/4, 65; P iii, 3	cf R 20	90
29	E	2 ob, 2 hn, str	1765	A	HW i/4, 80; P iii, 21		89
30	C	fl, 2 ob, 2 hn, str	[–?13 Sept] 1765	A	HW i/4, 96; P iii, 41	'Alleluja'; Gregorian Easter Alleluia quoted in I; cf Q 64	89
31	D	fl, 2 ob, 4 hn, str	[–?13 Sept] 1765	A	HW i/4, 109; P iii, 57	'Hornsignal'; title 'Auf dem Anstand' (M i/3) of no apparent relevance	89
32	C	2 ob, 2 hn, 2 tpt, timp, str	–1766 [–?1760]	EK	P iii, 95		89
33	C	2 ob, 2 hn, 2 tpt, timp, str	–1767 [–?1760]	EK	P iii, 117		
34	d/D	2 ob, 2 hn, str	–1767	EK (with incipit of II)	P iii, 143	MS copy, CS-Bm, with doubtful Andante	90
35	Bb	2 ob, 2 hn, str	1 Dec 1767	A	HW i/6, 1; P iii, 165		31
36	Eb	2 ob, 2 hn, str	–1769 [?c1761–5]	EK	P iii, 187		89
37	C	2 ob, 2 hn (/2 tpt, timp), str	–?1758	EK	P iii, 211		89
38	C	2 ob, 2 hn, (2 tpt, timp), str	–1769	EK	P iii, 227		31
39	g	2 ob, 4 hn, str	–1770 [?1765]	EK	P iii, 253		31, 93
40	F	2 ob, 2 hn, str	1763	A	P iii, 277		90
41	C	fl, 2 ob, 2 hn, (2 tpt, timp), str	–1770	EK	P iv, 3	date on MS in D-Tsch	31
42	D	2 ob, 2 bon, 2 hn, str	1771	A	HW i/6, 43; P iv, 41		31
43	Eb	2 ob, 2 hn, str	–1772	EK	P iv, 73	'Mercury'	31, 93, 94
44	e	2 ob, 2 hn, str	–1772	EK	P iv, 107	'Trauersinfonie'	31, 93
45	f♯	2 ob, bn, 2 hn, str	1772	A	HW i/6, 69; P iv, 139	'Farewell'; facs. edn. (Budapest, 1959)	31, 35, 93
46	B	2 ob, 2 hn, str	1772	A	HW i/6, 104; P iv, 175		
47	G	2 ob, bn, 2 hn, str	1772	A	HW i/6, 125; P iv, 199	cf W 24	93
48	C	2 ob, 2 hn (/2 tpt, timp), str	–?1769	EK	P iv, 233	'Maria Theresia'	94
49	f	2 ob, 2 hn, str	1768	A	HW i/6, 24; P iv, 271	'La passione': 'Il quakuo di bel' humore'	31, 93
50	C	2 ob, 2 hn, 2 tpt, timp, str	1773	A	HW i/7, 1; P v, 3	I and II supposedly composed as ov. to Vorspiel: Der Götterrat (E 12); autograph in PL-Kj	
51	Bb	2 ob, 2 hn, str	–1774	EK	P v, 31	1st of the 2 trios missing in some sources	
52	c	2 ob, (bn), 2 hn, str	–1774	EK	P v, 57		31, 93

H1	Key	Forces	Date	Authentication	Edition	Remarks	
53	D 3 versions:	fl, 2 ob, bn, 2 hn, (timp), str	?1778/9	EK (slow introduction)	P v, 97	'Imperial', 'Festino', 3rd finale (P v, 150; cf H: C', C''), spurious; other combinations dubious (H: D, E', E'')	
B''	(i)	finale: 2 ob, 2 bn, 2 hn, str		HV	finale: P v, 135	no slow introduction; finale uses concert version of ov., cf K 3; cf no.62	
B'	(ii)	finale: as (i)			finale: as (i)	as (i), with introduction	
A	(iii)	finale: as other movts		JE	finale: P v, 124	as (ii), with new finale	
54	G	2 fl, 2 ob, 2 bn, 2 hn, 2 tpt, timp, str	1774	A	HW i/7, 28; P v, 163	slow introduction apparently an afterthought; fl, tpt, timp pts. added later	94, 95
55	Eb	2 ob, bn, 2 hn, str	1774	A	HW i/7, 63; P v, 201	'The Schoolmaster'	
56	C	2 ob, bn, 2 hn, 2 tpt, timp, str	1774	A	HW i/7, 86; P v, 229		
57	D	2 ob, 2 hn, str	1774	A	HW i/7, 126; P v, 271		
58	F	2 ob, 2 hn, str	-1775 [-?1767/8]	EK	P vi, 3	see Q 52	
59	A	2 ob, 2 hn, str	-1769	EK	P vi, 21	'Fire'; cf appx K 1	31
60	C	2 ob, 2 hn, (2 tpt), timp, str	-1774	EK	P vi, 43	'Il distratto'; title authentic; cf K 2	39
61	D	fl, 2 ob, 2 bn, 2 hn, timp, str	1776	A	HW i/8, 175; P vi, 75		101
62	D	fl, 2 ob, (2) bn, 2 hn, str	-1781 [?1780]	EK	P vi, 127	I is rev. version of Finale B from no.53	
63	C	fl, 2 ob, bn, 2 hn, str	-1781 [?1779]	EK	P vi, 198	'La Roxelane', 'Roxolana': title authentic, refers to II; I is altered version of ov. to Il mondo della luna (E 17); earlier version uses finale of frag. K 1; for 'Versione prima', see appx K 4	
64	A	2 ob, 2 hn, str	-1778 [-?c1773]	EK	P vi, 235	'Tempora mutantur': title probably authentic	
65	A	2 ob, 2 hn, str	-1778 [?c1769-72]	EK	P vi, 259		47
66	Bb	2 ob, 2 bn, 2 hn, str	-1779 [?c1775/6]	EK	HW i/8, 135; P vii, 3		47
67	F	2 ob, 2 bn, 2 hn, str	-1779 [?c1774/5]	EK	HW i/8, 47; P vii, 55		47
68	Bb	2 ob, 2 bn, 2 hn, str	-1779 [?c1775/5]	EK	HW i/8, 1; P vii, 109	order of II and III sometimes reversed as in H; abridged version (HW i/8, 228), doubtful	
69	C	2 ob, 2 bn, 2 hn, 2 tpt, timp, str	-1779 [?c1775/6]	EK	HW i/8, 93; P vii, 163	'Laudon', 'Loudon': title approved by Haydn	

No.	Key	Scoring	Date	Sources	Edition	Remarks	Ref
70	D	fl, 2 ob, bn, 2 hn, 2 tpt, timp, str	–18 Dec 1779 [?1778/9]	EK, A (timp pt, u)	P vii, 217	timp (? and tpts) added later by Haydn	101
71	B♭	fl, 2 ob, bn, 2 hn, str	–1780 [?1778/9]	EK	P vii, 249		89
72	D	fl, 2 ob, bn, 4 hn, (timp), str	–1781 [?c1763–5]	EK	P vii, 305		
73	D	fl, 2 ob, 2 bn, 2 hn, (2 tpt, timp), str	–1782 [?1781]	EK. A (u frag.)	P vii, 331	'La chasse': title authentic, refers to IV, orig. composed as ov. to La fedeltà premiata (E 21); II uses song, Gegenliebe (G 16); autograph fragment in PL-Kj	103
74	E♭	fl, 2 ob, bn, 2 hn, str	–22 Aug 1781 [?1780]	EK	P viii, 3		
75	D	fl, 2 ob, bn, 2 hn, (2 tpt, timp), str	–1781 [?1779]	EK	P viii, 53		101
76	E♭	fl, 2 ob, 2 bn, 2 hn, str	?1782	EK	P viii, 101	nos.76–8 apparently for Haydn's planned visit to England, 1783; see Haydn's letter, 15 July 1783	47, 101

nos.82–7: Paris syms.

No.	Key	Scoring	Date	Sources	Edition	Remarks	Ref
77	B♭	fl, 2 ob, 2 bn, 2 hn, str	?1782	EK	P viii, 153		47
78	c	fl, 2 ob, 2 bn, 2 hn, str	?1782	EK	P viii, 207		47
79	F	fl, 2 ob, 2 bn, 2 hn, str	–?20 Nov 1784	HV, RC	P viii, 255		47
80	d	fl, 2 ob, 2 bn, 2 hn, str	–8 Nov 1784	HV, SC	P viii, 311		47
81	G	fl, 2 ob, 2 bn, 2 hn, str	–8 Nov 1784	EK	P viii, 363		47
82	C	fl, 2 ob, 2 bn, 2 hn/tpt, timp, str	1786	A, A (u frag.)	P ix, 3	'L'ours', 'The Bear'; orig. version of Trio, L i/9, 308	49, 50, 106 / 105
83	g	fl, 2 ob, 2 bn, 2 hn, str	1785	A	HW i/12, 91; P ix, 61	'La poule', 'The Hen'	105
84	E♭	fl, 2 ob, 2 bn, 2 hn, str	1786	A, Sk	HW i/12, 107	'La poule', 'The Hen'	105
85	B♭	fl, 2 ob, 2 bn, 2 hn, str	?1785	A (u frag.), HV, SC	HW i/12, 49; P ix, 161	'La reine', 'The Queen [of France]'	105
86	D	fl, 2 ob, 2 bn, 2 hn, 2 tpt, timp, str	1786	A, Sk	P ix, 207	sketch for Minuet and Trio, L i/9, 336	105
87	A	fl, 2 ob, 2 bn, 2 hn, str	1785	A	HW i/12, 1; P ix, 261		105

nos.88–9 composed for J. Tost.

No.	Key	Scoring	Date	Sources	Edition	Remarks	Ref
88	G	fl, 2 ob, 2 bn, 2 hn, 2 tpt, timp, str	?1787	EK	P x, 3		52, 105

nos.90–92 composed for Comte d'Ogny and Prince Oettingen-Wallerstein

No.	Key	Scoring	Date	Sources	Edition	Remarks	Ref
89	F	fl, 2 ob, 2 bn, 2 hn, str	1787	A	P x, 59	II and IV use lira conc., T 4	52 / 105
90	C	fl, 2 ob, 2 hn, (2 tpt, timp), str	1788	A	P x, 109		
91	E♭	fl, 2 ob, 2 bn, 2 hn, str	1788	A	P x, 167		

H	Key	Forces	Date	Authentication	Edition	Remarks	
92	G	fl, 2 ob, 2 bn, 2 hn, (2 tpt, timp), str	1789	A	P x, 223	'Oxford'; unpubd version of II and IV for fl, 2 ob, 2 hn, str in later MS authorized copy	49, 59, 61, 108
		nos.93–104: London syms.					
93	D	2 fl, 2 ob, 2 bn, 2 hn, 2 tpt, timp, str	1791	A (lost), EK	P xi, 3	perf. London, 17 Feb 1792	108
94	G	2 fl, 2 ob, 2 bn, 2 hn, 2 tpt, timp, str	1791	A	P xi, 49	'The Surprise'; perf. London, 23 March 1792; 1st version of II without 'surprise', P xi, 116; cf C 6	108
95	c	fl, 2 ob, 2 bn, 2 hn, 2 tpt, timp, str	1791	A	P xi, 121	perf. London, 1791	
96	D	2 fl, 2 ob, 2 bn, 2 hn, 2 tpt, timp, str	1791	A (incl. Sk)	P xi, 171	'The Miracle'; perf. London, 1791; sketch for II, P xi, 219	65
97	C	2 fl, 2 ob, 2 bn, 2 hn, 2 tpt, timp, str	1792	A	P xi, 223	perf. London, 3/4 May 1792	
98	B♭	fl, 2 ob, 2 bn, 2 hn, 2 tpt, timp, hpd obbl, str	1792	A	P xi, 301	perf. London, 2 March 1792; autograph in PL-Kj	
99	E♭	2 fl, 2 ob, 2 cl, 2 bn, 2 hn, 2 tpt, timp, str	1793	A, Sk	HW i/17, 1; P xii, 3	perf. London, 10 Feb 1794; autograph in PL-Kj; sketches for Finale, critical commentary to HW i/17, 49a, P xii, 402; cf appx Y.1, 5	66, 67
100	G	(2) fl, 2 ob, 2 cl, 2 bn, 2 hn, 2 tpt, timp, perc, str	1793/4	A	HW i/17, 145; P xii, 59	'Military'; perf. London, 31 March 1794; II uses Romance of lira conc., T 5; cf K 12	67, 108
101	D	2 fl, 2 ob, 2 cl, 2 bn, 2 hn, 2 tpt, timp, str	1793/4	A, Sk	HW i/17, 59; P xii, 139	'The Clock'; perf. London, 3 March 1794; autograph in PL-Kj; sketches for Minuet and Trio, critical commentary to HW i/17, 57a, P xii, 406; cf appx Y.1, 3	67, 108
102	B♭	2 fl, 2 ob, 2 bn, 2 hn, 2 tpt, timp, str	1794	A	HW i/18, 1; P xii, 205	perf. London, 2 Feb 1795; II= Adagio of pf trio, V 24	68
103	E♭	2 fl, 2 ob, 2 cl, 2 bn, 2 hn, 2 tpt, timp, str	1795	A	HW i/18, 59; P xii, 265	'Drumroll'; perf. London, 2 March 1795; 1st version of closing section, HW i/18, 224, P xii, 326	68, 108
104	D	2 fl, 2 ob, 2 cl, 2 bn, 2 hn, 2 tpt, timp, str	1795	A, Sk	HW i/18, 129; P xii, 333	'London', 'Salomon'; perf. London, 4 May 1795	68, 108

105	Concertante, B♭	soli: vn, vc, ob, bn; fl, ob, bn, 2 hn, 2 tpt, timp, str	1792	A (incl. Sk)		HW ii; P x, 287	perf. London, 9 March 1792; sketch for I, P x, 371	61
106	D	2 ob, 2 hn, str	?1769	EK		HW xxv/4, 289	only I extant, as III of K 5; supposedly composed as ov. to Le pescatrici (E 10); cf K 5 sym. 'A'; cf appx Q.3, I; also attrib. Wagenseil sym 'B'
107	B♭	2 ob, 2 hn, str	-1762 [-?1761]	F		P i, 3	
108	B♭	2 ob, bn, 2 hn, str	-1765	HV		P i, 19	

Note: single movts, see K 1, 10; c150 spurious syms. listed in H

K: MISCELLANEOUS ORCHESTRAL

No.	H	Title, key	Forces	Date	Authentication	Edition	Remarks
1	i, 87	Menuet, Trio, Finale, C	2 ob, 2 hn, 2 tpt, timp, str	-?1773	A (u frag.)	P vi, 184	finale used for earlier version of sym. J 63; cf no.8
2	XXX:3	Incidental music: Der Zerstreute (comedy, 5, ? J. B. Bergopzoomer, after J. F. Regnard: Le distrait)	see J 60	-30 June 1774	Pressburger Zeitung, 23 Nov 1774	see J 60	ov., entr'actes and final music = sym. J 60
3	Ia:7	Sinfonia, D	2 ob, 2 hn, str	1777	A, A (frag.)	P v, 135	1 movt only; ov. to unidentified work; used as Finale B of sym. J 53; cf appx K 5
4-9		6 sinfonie [overtures]:					
4	Ia:13	g	fl, 2 ob, bn, 2 hn, str	-29 Sept 1782	OE	(London, 1959)	ov. to L'isola disabitata (E 20)
5	Ia:6	D	2 ob, 2 hn, str			HW xxv/6, 1	ov. to L'incontro improviso (E 14); tpts, timp, perc omitted; ? earlier version uses I of J 106 for III
6	Ia:10	G	fl, 2 ob, 2 hn, str			HW xxv/3, 1	ov. to Lo speziale (E 9)
7	Ia:15	B♭	2 ob, bn, 2 hn, str			HW xxv/8, 1	ov. to La vera costanza (E 19); with added III compiled from Introduzione of same opera and balletto from Il mondo della luna (E 17)

No.	H	Title, key	Forces	Date	Authentication	Edition	Remarks
8	Ia:1	C	2 ob, 2 hn, timp, str		A (u frag.)	HW xxv/5, 1	ov. to L'infedeltà delusa (E 11); with altered II and added III almost identical with III of ov. to Die Feuerbrunst (E 16b); ?earlier version with altered II, uses no.1 as III and IV
9	Ia:2	c/C	2 ob, 2 bn, 2 hn, 2 tpt, timp, str			HW xxviii/1, 1	ov. to Il ritorno di Tobia (C 3); with altered final bars
10	Ia:4	Finale, D	fl, 2 ob, 2 bn, 2 hn, str	?1777–86 [?1782–4]	A, EK	D 51 (1959)	from unidentified work (?sym., J 73); sometimes connected with sym. J 53
11	XX/1 A	Musica instrumentale sopra le 7 ultime parole del nostro Redentore in croce ossiano 7 sonate con un'introduzione ed al fine un terremoto	2 fl, 2 ob, 2 bn, 4 hn, 2 tpt, timp, str	–11 Feb 1787 [?1786]	OE, Sk, RC	HW iv	composed for Cádiz; ?1st Viennese perf. 26 March 1787; some sketches in critical commentary to HW iv, 41; cf. C 4, appx O.1, 1
12	i, 206	Piece for military band, C	fl, 2 ob, 2 cl, 2 bn, 2 hn, tpt, serpent, perc	?1794/5	A (u)	HW i/17, 227	arr. of II of sym. J 100
13	–	Overtura Coventgarden	?	1791–5	Gr, Dies	—	lost or = Hla:3, ov. to Orfeo (E 24); ?perf. as ov. to J. P. Salomon's opera Windsor Castle; cf appx K 6
14	i, 590	?, E	?	?c1763–9	A (u)	—	b only of sequence of 9 pieces; see critical commentary to HW xiii, 12

Note: ovs. listed as Hla:3, 5, 8, 14, 16, 17 Add. are taken from Haydn's operas without alteration; Ia:11 is not a separate piece

Appendix K: Doubtful and spurious works or arrangements

No.	H	Title, librettist, key	Forces	Date	Edition	Remarks
1	XXX:2	Incidental music: Die Feuerbrunst (? G. F. W. Grossmann)	?	1774	—	not verified; not identical with E 16a/b; ? = sym. J 59

No.	H	Title, key	Forces	Date	Authentication	Edition	Remarks
2	XXX:B	Incidental music: Hamlet (Shakespeare)	?	?c1774-6	—		not verified
3	XXX:C	Incidental music: Götz von Berlichingen (Goethe)	?	-?1776	—		not verified; also attrib. M. Haydn
4	XXX:D	Incidental music: Soliman II, oder Die drei Sultaninnen (? F. X. Huber, after C. S. Favart)	?	?c1777	—		not verified; hypothetical reconstruction (P vi, 165: '1st version' of sym. J 63) combines altered ov. to Il mondo della luna (E 17), II of J 63 and frag. K 1
5	Ia:7bis	Overture, D	?	-1783	—		2nd version of K 3; extant in various arrs. only; inclusion in sym. J 53 doubtful
6	ii, 435	Overture to Salomon's opera Windsor Castle, D	?	1795	—		in MS (J-Tn) and in vocal score of opera (London, n.d.), as by Salomon; cf K 13
7	XXX:A; Ia:9	Incidental music: King Lear (Shakespeare)	2 fl, 2 ob, bn, 2 hn, 2 tpt, timp, str	-1806	—		ov. and entr'actes, without author's name; ov. attrib. W. G. Stegmann (? C. D. Stegmann); ? by J. von Blumenthal (i)
8	Ia:12	Overture, g	2 ob, bn, 2 hn, str	-1799	—		combination and arr. of pieces from Il mondo della luna (E 17)
		Fantaisie, d, see appx X.3, 16					

39

L: DANCES, MARCHES FOR ORCHESTRA/MILITARY BAND

No.	H	Title, key	Forces	Date	Authentication	Edition	Remarks
1	IX:1	[12] Minuetti (with 3 Trios)	2 ob, 2 hn, 2 vn, b	-?1760	A	—	'Seitenstetten' minuets
2	IX:3	[12] Menuetti (with 4 Trios)	(?2) fl, 2 ob, (?2) bn, 2 hn, 2 vn, b	-1767	—	—	lost; pf arr. extant, cf appx X.2, 1
3	—	4 [?cycles of] Menuetti	?	-?1765	EK	—	? partly = nos. 1 and 2: otherwise lost
4	iii, 315	Marche regimento de Marshall, G	2 ob, 2 hn, 2 bn	-1772	—	D 34, 2 (1960)	
5	IX:23	?24 Dances (?12 Minuets and 12 Trios)	2 fl, 2 ob, 2 vn, b and ?	-?c1773	A (frag.)	—	only nos.23-4 extant
6	IX:5	[6] Menuetti (with 2 Trios)	fl, 2 ob, bn, 2 hn, 2 vn, b	1776	A	—	? = 1st pt. of longer cycle; cf appx L 5

No.	H	Title, key	Forces	Date	Authentication	Edition	Remarks
7	IX:6a Add.	12 Menuets	?	-11 Feb [-?9 Jan] 1777	see Thomas: 'Haydns Tanzmusik' (1973)	—	lost or ? identical with no.6; for the Redoutensäle, Vienna
8	IX:6b Add.	18 Menuets	?	-8 Feb [-?9 Jan] 1780	see Thomas, op cit	—	lost or unidentified; for the Redoutensäle, Vienna
9	IX:7	Raccolta de' [14] menuetti ballabili (with 6 Trios)	fl, 2 ob, 2 bn, 2 hn, timp, 2 vn, b	-31 Jan 1784	—	D 301 (1970)	
10	IX:8	XII Menuets (with 5 Trios)	?	-9 April 1785	—	—	lost; pf arr. extant, cf appx X.2, 3
11	IX:9	6 Allemandes (6 deutsche Tänze)	fl, 2 ob, bn, 2 hn, 2 tpt, timp, 2 vn, b	-15 Nov 1786	—	D 52 (1960)	
12	IX:9d, e Add.	Unos 24 minués y otras tantas [= 24] contradanzas	?	-22 April 1789	see Solar-Quintes	—	sent to Duchess of Osuna (Madrid); lost or unidentified
13	IX:9c	12 ganz neue Tanz Menuetts mit 12 Trios begleitet	?	-11 Jan 1790	Haydn's letters	—	promised to Prince Oettingen-Wallerstein, 21 Oct 1789; lost or unidentified
14	IX:16	24 Menuetti (with 24 Trios)	fl pic, 2 fl, 2 ob, 2 cl, 2 bn, 2 hn, 2 tpt, timp, perc, 2 vn, b	?c1790–1800	—	D 299 (1974)	
15	VIII:6	Marcia, E♭	2 cl, 2 hn, 2 bn	-1793 [?c1780–90]	A (u)	HW xxv/12, 316; D 34, 4 (1960)	
16	VIII:7	March, E♭	2 cl, 2 bn, 2 hn, tpt, serpent	?c1792	A (u frag.)	D 34, 5 (1960)	only 1st 8 bars extant
17a	VIII:3	March, E♭	2 cl, 2 bn, 2 hn, tpt, serpent	1792	A (as pt. of no.17b); Sk	D 34, 6 (1960)	? = March for the Prince of Wales mentioned by Gr and Dies
17b	VIII:3bis	March, E♭	2 fl, 2 cl, 2 bn, 2 hn, 2 tpt, str	1792	A	D 98 (1961)	2nd version of no.17a; for Royal Society of Musicians
18	IX:11	[12] Menuetti di ballo (Redout Menuetti; Katharinentänze) (with 11 Trios)	fl pic, 2 fl, 2 ob, 2 cl, 2 bn, 2 hn, 2 tpt, timp, 2 vn, b	-25 Nov 1792	A (u pt.); Sk	(Lippstadt, 1959)	for Pensionsgesellschaft bildender Künstler; for pf arr., see appx X.2, 4
19	IX:12	12 deutsche Tänze (Tedeschi di ballo) (with Trio and Coda)	2 fl, 2 ob, 2 cl, 2 bn, 2 hn, 2 tpt, timp, 2 vn, b	-25 Nov 1792	Sk	(Lippstadt, n.d.)	for Redoute as above; for pf arr., see appx X.2, 5

20	—	24 Minuets and German Dances	?	1791–5	Gr, Dies	—	lost or ? = nos.*18* and *19*
21	iii, 323	4 and 2 Countrydances	?	1791–5	Gr, Dies	—	lost; for ? pf arr. of one or two, see X 7, appx X.3, *6*
22	VIII:1–2	2 [Derbyshire] Marches, E♭, C	2 cl, 2 bn, 2 hn, tpt, serpent, perc	1795	A, A (u)	D 34, 8–9 (1960)	for pf arr. of March in C see appx X.2, 7
23	VIII:4	Hungarischer National Marsch, E♭	2 ob, 2 cl, 2 bn, 2 hn, tpt	[–27 Nov] 1802	A	D 34, 10 (1960)	
24	i, 541	March, E♭	str	after 1791	?A	—	lost
25	i, 541	March, E♭	2 cl, 2 hn, 2 bn	?	?A	—	lost or ? = no.*15*

Note: sketches to unknown minuets in H i, 561–3, ?remnants of lost dances; 3 unidentified minuets (with 3 trios) composed for Haydn by J. Eybler in 1789

Appendix L: Selected doubtful and spurious works or arrangements

No.	H	Title	Forces	Date	Edition	Remarks
1	i, 547	VI Menuets (with 6 Trios) and VI Allemandes	(fl, ob), 2 hn, 2 vn, b	–1787	(Berlin and Amsterdam, 1787)	by Haydn and Vanhal; minuets by Vanhal; allemandes identical with L *11*
2	i, 547	12 Contratänze	fl, 2 ob, 2 bn, 2 hn, 2 vn, b	–1799	—	lost; ?arr. from various works by Haydn; see Thomas: 'Haydns Tanzmusik' (1973)
3	IX:2	VI Menuetti	2 hn, 2 vn, b	–?1766	—	lost
4	IX:4	[12] Minuetti da ballo (with 12 Trios)	2 fl, 2 hn, 2 vn, b	–1766	(Amsterdam, 1766)	
5	IX: 6, nos.1–8	XII Menuetti (with 4 Trios)	fl, 2 ob, 2 bn, 2 hn/tpt, timp, 2 vn, b	?	—	HIX:6, nos.9–12 = HIX:5, nos.1–4; see L *6*
6	IX:9b	12 Deutsche (dell'opera L'arbore di Diana)	fl, 2 ob, cl, bn, 2 hn, 2 vn, b	1787–99	—	lost; pf arr. ? extant as appx X.3, *4*
7	IX:14	13 Menuetti (with 4 Trios)	fl pic, 2 fl, 2 ob, 2 bn, 2 hn, 2 vn, b	?	—	
8	IX:15	[6] Menuetti (with 6 Trios)	2 fl, 2 ob, 2 cl, 2 bn, 2 hn, 2 tpt, timp, 2 vn, b	?	—	
9	IX:17	[17] Deutsche Tänze	fl pic, fl, 2 ob, 2 bn, 2 hn, 2 vn, b	?	—	lost
10	IX:18	IX Menuette (with Trios) fürs Orchester	?	?	—	1st incipit = L *10*, no.7, rest unknown

No.	H	Title	Forces	Date	Edition	Remarks
11	IX:19	[13] Menuetti (with 4 Trios)	2 vn, b	–?1777	—	theme of no.1 similar to III of S 3; no.11 uses III of S 6
12	IX:24	Menuetto and Trio	2 vn, b	?	—	unsigned draft MS not Haydn's autograph; for pf arr. see appx X.3, 13; for orch arr. see no.14
13	IX:25	?Minuet	str	?	—	?movt of spurious sym. or str qt
14	i, 580	10 Menuette	orch	?	(Kassel, 1950)	orch arr. of no.12 and minuets arr. from syms. and str qts
15	i, 580	12 deutsche Tänze, 2 versions	i orch, ii 2 vn, vc	?	i (Kassel, 1950); ii HM, xli (1967)	minuets arr. from syms. and str qts
16	—	12 Menuette	2 vn, vc	?	(Wolfenbüttel, 1938)	from str trios, baryton trios and Scherzandi
17	iii, 323	XII [recte XIV] Menuette (with 5 Trios)	2 fl pic/fl/ob, 2 hn, 2 vn, b	?	—	see Landon: "Survey of the Haydn Sources' (1961), 70
18	IX:22a Add.	[12] Menuetti (with 1 Trio)	2 ob, 2 hn, 2 vn, b	?	—	see Thomas: 'Haydns Tanzmusik' (1973), 23

Note: for doubtful works extant only in pf arrs., see appx X.3

M: CONCERTOS FOR STRING OR WIND INSTRUMENTS

No.	H	Title, key	Forces of orchestral accompaniment	Date	Authentication	Edition	Remarks
1–4	VIIa	[4] Concerti per il violino:					
1	1	C	str	–1769 [?c1761–5]	EK	HW iii/1,1	for Luigi [Tomasini]
2	2	D	(2 ob, 2 hn), str	?c1761–5	EK	—	lost; incipit in HW iii/1, VI
3	3	A (Melker Konzert)	str	–1771	EK	HW iii/1, 32	title not authentic
4	4*	G	str	[?c1765–70] –1769	—	HW iii/1, 71	
5–7	VIIb	[2/3] Concerti per il violoncello:					
5	1	C	2 ob, 2 hn, str	?c1761–5	EK	HW iii/2, 1	erroneously attrib. A. Kraft; 47, 48, 101, 118
6	2	D	2 ob, 2 hn, str	1783	A	HW iii/2, 57	rev. version by F. A. Gevaert
7	3	C	?	?c1761–5	EK	—	lost or = no.5

No.	H	Title, key	Forces of orchestral accompaniment	Date	Edition		Remarks
8	VIIc:1	Concerto per il violone (contraviolone)		?1763	EK	—	lost
9–10	XIII	[2] Concerti per il pariton [baryton]:					
9	1	D	(? 2 vn, b)	?c1765–70	EK	—	lost
10	2	D	(? 2 vn, b)	?c1765–70	EK	—	lost
11	XIII:3	Concerto per 2 pariton, D	?	?c1765–70	EK	—	lost
12	VIIf:1	Concerto per il flauto, D	?	?c1761–5	EK	—	lost
13	i, facs, V	Concert für Fagott	?	?	see remark	—	lost; mentioned in Haydn's short work-list, c1803–4
14–15	VIId	[2] Concerti per il corno di caccia:					
14	1	D	?	?c1761–5	EK	—	lost
15	3*	D (no.1)	2 ob, str	1762	A	(London, 1959)	89
16	VIId:2	Concerto a 2 corni, Eb	?	?1784	HV	—	lost
17	VIIe:1	Concerto per il clarino, Eb	2 fl, 2 ob, 2 bn, 2 hn, 2 tpt, timp, str	1796	A	(London, 1951)	

Note: concs. for 2 lire organizzate, see group T; Concertante, see J 105; concs. for vn, org/hpd, see U 3; ? conc. for vn planned in 1799, see Landon, iii (1976)

Appendix M: Selected doubtful and spurious works

No.	H	Title, key	Forces of orchestral accompaniment	Date	Edition	Remarks
1	VIIa:D1	Violin concerto, D	2 ob, 2 hn, str	–c1777	(Paris, c1777), as by Stamitz	by C. Stamitz
2	VIIa:G1	Violin concerto, G	str	–1771	—	? by M. Haydn
3	VIIa:A1	Violin concerto, A	?	–c1777	(Paris, c1777), as by Giornovichi	by Giornovichi
4	VIIa:B1	Violin concerto, Bb	str	1760	D 3 (1960), as by M. Haydn	by M. Haydn
5	VIIa:B2	Violin concerto, Bb	str	–1767	(Leipzig, 1915)	by Christian Cannabich
6	VIIb:4*	Cello concerto, D	str	–1772	(Leipzig, 1894)	also attributed (?G.B.) Costanzi
7	VIIb:5*	Cello concerto, C	2 fl, 2 ob, 2 cl, 2 bn, 2 hn, str	?c1899	(Berlin, 1899)	'nach einer Skizze ausgeführt und herausgegeben von David Popper': sketch never found
8	VIIb:g1	Cello concerto, g	str	–1773	—	lost
9	VIIf:D1	Flute concerto, D	str	–1771	(Munich, 1955)	by L. Hofmann

No.	H	Title, key	Forces of orchestral accompaniment	Date	Edition	Remarks
10	VIIg:C1	Oboe concerto, C	2 ob, 2 hn, 2 tpt, timp, str	?c1800	(Wiesbaden, 1954)	
11	VIId:4*	Horn concerto (no.2), D	str	-1781	(London, 1954)	
12	—	Concerto for 2 horns, Eb	2 ob, 2 hn, str	?	(Amsterdam, 1966)	D-HR, orig. without author's name; 'par Michael Heiden added later

N: DIVERTIMENTOS ETC FOR 4+ STRING AND/OR WIND INSTRUMENTS
(str qts, works with baryton, lira organizzata excepted)

No.	HII	Title, key	Forces	Date	Authentication	Edition	Remarks
1-4		[4] Divertimentos (Cassations) a 9:					
1	9	G	2 ob, 2 hn, 2 vn, 2 va, b	-1764	EK	—	also erroneously attrib. M. Haydn
2	20	F	+ (bn)	-1763 [-?1757]	EK	D 56 (1962)	
3	17	C	? 2 cl instead of 2 ob	-c1765	EK	D 23 (1960), ed. H. Steppan	
4	G1	G		-1768 [?c1760]	—	D 47 (1959)	sometimes attrib. M. Haydn; version a 5 without IV (Copenhagen, 1953)
5-10		[6] miscellaneous works:					
5	24*	[V] Variations on a minuet, Eb	fl, 2 eng hn, bn, 2 hn, vn solo, 2 hn, vc, vle,	?1761-2	A (u)	—	? movt of larger work
6	2	Divertimento (Cassation) a 5, G	2 vn, 2 va, b	-1763 [?1753/4]	EK	(Wolfenbüttel, 1958)	
7	10	Divertimento a 6 (Der [verliebte] Schulmeister), D	?	-c1765	EK	—	lost
8	13	Divertimento (? a 6), D	?	-c1765	EK	(Leipzig and Berlin, 1953)	
9	8	Divertimento (Cassation) [a 7]	2 fl, 2 hn, 2 vn, b	-1767	EK		lost
10	D22 Add.	Cassation, D	4 hn, vn, va, b	?c1763	—	D 66 (1960)	

159

		Title	Scoring	Date		Publication	Notes
11–12		[2] Divertimentos (Cassations) a 6	2 hn, 2 vn, va, b				for spurious arrs. as str qts, see appx O.3, 2–3 title in Berlin edn.; some sources incl. added variations of 2nd trio
11	21*	Eb (Eine Abendmusik)		–1763 [–?1761]	EK	(Berlin, 1936)	
12	22*	D		–1764 [–?1760]	EK	(Frankfurt, 1962)	
13–14		[2] Divertimentos (Cassations) [a 6]:	fl, ob, 2 vn, vc, db				
13	1	G		–1768	EK	NM 129 (1937)	pubd as qt for fl, vn, va, b/gui; orig. version unpubd
14	11	C (Der Geburtstag)		–1765	EK	D 57 (1961)	II: 'Mann und Weib'; cf also J 14; spurious version for fl, vn, va, b (Amsterdam, 1768) other versions probably spurious
15–20		6 Scherzandos (Sinfonias, Divertimentos):	fl/2 ob, 2 hn, 2 vn, b	–1765		D 71–6 (1961)	
15	33*	F					
16	34*	C			−		
17	35*	D			−		
18	36*	G			−		
19	37*	E			−		
20	38*	A			EK		
21–6		[6] Divertimentos [a 6]:					
21	15	F (Parthia)	2 ob, 2 hn, 2 bn	1760	A	D 29 (1959)	facs. of autograph in Haydn Yearbook, i, 257
22	23*	F (Parthia)		–1765 [?1760]	A (u frag.)	D 30 (1959); (London, 1959), in F/G	added movt of doubtful authenticity, D 30, 8 and London edn., p.8
23	7	C (Feld-Parthie)		–1765	EK	D 31 (1959)	
24	3	G (Parthie)		–1766	EK	D 84 (1960)	
25	D18	D (Cassation)		–1765 [?c1760]	−	D 33 (1959)	added (?spurious) movt, D 33, 8
26	G9/C12 Add.	G/C (Parthia)		–1766 [?c1760]	−	D 85 (1960)	
27–32		[6] Divertimentos [a 4–8]:					
27	16	F (Feld-Parthie)	2 eng hn, 2 hn, 2 vn, 2 bn	1760	A	(Leipzig, 1954)	
28	12	Eb (Feld-Parthie) (? a 6)	(?2) eng hn, and ?	–c1765	EK	—	
29	20bis	A (Feld-Parthie)	?	–?c1765	EK	—	lost; probably not in Bb as in H
30	14	C	2 cl, 2 hn	1761	A	—	lost
31	4	F (?D), a 5	2 cl, 2 hn, bn	–?c1765	EK	D 32 (1959) —	lost

No.	HII	Title, key	Forces	Date	Authentication	Edition	Remarks
32	5	F (?D), a 5 (? a 4)	2 cl, 2 hn, (?bn)	–?c1765	EK	—	lost; version for 2 hn, baryton, va, b extant; cf R 26

Note: for arrs. of works composed for baryton or lira organizzata, see groups R and T; 2 Divertimenti a più voci (Gr, Dies) probably = London versions of T 8 and T 13

Appendix N: Selected doubtful and spurious works

No.	HII	Title, key	Forces	Date	Edition	Remarks
1	18	Divertimento (Notturno), D	fl, 2 hn, vn, va, b	?	—	probably by Vanhal, though incipit in HV
2	19	Divertimento (Notturno), G	fl, (2 hn), vn, va, b	?	—	probably by Vanhal, though incipit in HV
3	24* a	Minuet with variations, D	2 fl, 2 ob, (bn), 2 hn, 2 vn, va, b	?	—	lost; minuet from P 15
4	24* b	Minuet with variations, A	2 fl, 2 ob, 2 hn, 2 vn, va, b	?	—	lost; minuet from P 7
5	39*	Divertimento (Echo, Sextett), Eb	4 vn, 2 b	–1766/7	(Wilhelmshaven, 1957)	
6	40*	Sextetto, Eb	ob, bn, hn, vn, va, b	–1781	(London, 1957)	
7–12	46*	6 Divertimentos (Feldparthien), Bb	2 ob, 2 hn, 3 bn, serpent	–1784	(New York, 1960)	II: St Antony chorale, basis for Brahms's Haydn variations, op.56; arr. for 5 wind insts (London, 1942)
8	42*	Bb	2 ob, 2 cl, 2 hn, 2 bn		—	
9	41*	Eb	2 ob, 2 cl, 2 hn, 2 bn		(Vienna, 1931)	
10	45*	F	2 ob, 2 hn, 3 bn, serpent		—	
11	43*	Bb	2 ob, 2 cl, 2 hn, 2 bn		(Mainz, 1970)	
12	44*	F	2 ob, 2 hn, 3 bn, serpent		—	
13	47*	Toy Symphony (Kindersinfonie; Berchtolsgadener Sinfonie; Symphonie burlesque), C/G	(2 hn), 2 vn (or vn, va), b, children's insts	–1786	(Mainz, 1952); D 300 (1974), as by L. Mozart	various versions extant; sometimes without author's name, sometimes with names of M. Haydn, L. Mozart, or Angerer; version by L. Mozart with added movts

No.	Cat.	Title, key	Instrumentation	Date	Edition	Remarks
14	D5	[12] Notturni (Quartetto), D	2 fl, 2 hn	?	(Leipzig and Berlin, 1952)	
15	D6	Divertimento, D	fl, vn, va, b	–1767	(Frankfurt, 1971)	probably by L. Hofmann
16	D8	Divertimento, D	fl, 2 vn, va, b	?	(Zurich, 1940)	
17	D9	Quatuor, D	fl, vn, va, b	–1768	(London, 1960)	
18	F2	Cassation, F	ob, bn, 2 hn, vn, va, b	?	(Leipzig, 1970)	
19	F7	Parthia (Harmonie; Octett), F	2 ob, 2 cl, 2 hn, 2 bn	–1802	(Leipzig, 1902)	probably by Wranitzky
20	F10	Quartetto, F	3 vn, vc	–1799	(Augsburg, c1799), as by Ferandini	probably by Ferandini; see Marrocco (1972)
21	F12	Parthia, F	2 ob, 2 hn, bn	?	(London, 1961)	
22	G4	Quatuor, G	fl, vn, va, b	–1768	(London, 1960)	
23	A1	Divertimento, A	2 vn, 2 va, b	–1762	—	considered authentic by Landon, i(1980) supposed autograph not authentic; also attrib. C. F. Abel and J. C. Bach
24	B4	Divertissement, Bb	ob, vn, va da gamba, b	?		
25	—	Quatro, C	fl, vn, va, vc	?	(Zurich, 1969)	
26	D23 Add.	Divertimento, D	2 ob, 2 hn, 2 bn	?	D 86 (1960)	?authentic

Note: more doubtful and spurious works listed in hII; for arrs. for lute/gui, vn, va, vc, see O 8

O: STRING QUARTETS

No.	hIII	Op.	Title, key	Date (pubd)	Authentication	Edition	Remarks	
1–10			[10] Divertimentos (Cassations, Notturnos):	(1764–6)				17, 32
1	1	1/1	Bb	–1762 [?c1757–9]	EK	HW xii/1,1		
2	2	1/2	Eb	–1762 [?c1757–9]	EK	HW xii/1, 9	'La chasse'	87, 88
3	3	1/3	D	–1762 [?c1757–9]	EK	HW xii/1, 18		
4	4	1/4	G	–1764 [?c1757–9]	EK	HW xii/1, 27		
5	II:6	1/0	Eb	–1764 [?c1757–9]	EK	HW xii/1, 39		
6	6	1/6	C	–1762 [?c1757–9]	HV, F	HW xii/1, 50	arrs. for lute/gui, vn, vc, not authentic	
7	7	2/1	A	–1763 [?c1760–62]	EK	HW xii/1, 59		
8	8	2/2	E	–1765 [?c1760–62]	EK	HW xii/1, 69	arrs. (in D) for lute/gui, vn, va, vc, not authentic	
9	10	2/4	F	–1762 [?c1760–62]	EK	HW xii/1, 80		
10	12	2/6	Bb	–1762 [?c1760–62]	EK	HW xii/1, 91		

No.	hIII	Op.	Title, key	Date (pubd)	Authentication	Edition	Remarks
11–16			6 Divertimentos:	−1771 [?1769/70]	EK		32, 95
11	22	9/4	d			HW xii/2,3	
12	19	9/1	C			HW xii/2, 13	
13	21	9/3	G			HW xii/2, 24	
14	20	9/2	Eb			HW xii/2, 35	cf X 3
15	23	9/5	Bb			HW xii/2, 45	
16	24	9/6	A			HW xii/2, 57	
17–22			6 Divertimentos:	1771 (1772)	A		32, 95
17	26	17/2	F			HW xii/2, 69	
18	25	17/1	E			HW xii/2, 84	
19	28	17/4	c			HW xii/2, 99	
20	30	17/6	D			HW xii/2, 115	
21	27	17/3	Eb			HW xii/2, 129	'Recitative'
22	29	17/5	G			HW xii/2, 140	'Sun' Quartets
23–8			6 Divertimentos:	1772 (1774)	A		32, 95
23	35	20/5	f			HW xii/3, 3	
24	36	20/6	A			HW xii/3, 21	
25	32	20/2	C			HW xii/3, 36	
26	33	20/3	g		Sk	HW xii/3, 54, 191 (incl. sketch for III)	96
27	34	20/4	D			HW xii/3, 70	
28	31	20/1	Eb			HW xii/3, 89	
29–34			6 Quatuors (Quartetti):	1781 (1782)	HV, OE, SC (title, frag. of no.29)		'Russian' Quartets, 'Jungfernquartette'; date 1778–81 is incorrect 46, 53, 102, 106
29	41	33/5	G		C	HW xii/3, 105	'How do you do?'; for pf arr. of IV, see appx X.2, 2
30	38	33/2	Eb		C	HW xii/3, 120	'The Joke'
31	37	33/1	b		C	HW xii/3, 133	
32	39	33/3	C			HW xii/3, 147	'The Bird'
33	42	33/6	D		C	HW xii/3, 163	
34	40	33/4	Bb			HW xii/3, 175	
35	43	42	Quartetto, d	1785 (1786)	A	HW, xii/4	51

	No.	Hob.	Key	Type	Date	HV, OE, SC	HW, xii/4	Nickname / cross-ref	pp.
36–41				6 Quartetti:	1787 [−16 Sept] (1787)			'Prussian' Quartets	51, 106
36	44	50/1	B♭						
37	45	50/2	C						
38	46	50/3	E♭						
39	47	50/4	♯						
40	48	50/5	F					II: 'Ein Traum'	
41	49	50/6	D					'The Frog'	
42–7				6 Quatuors:	−?22 Sept 1788 (1789, 1790)	HV, ?Haydn's letters	HW, xii/4	'Tost' Quartets, i–ii	51, 52, 106
42	57	54/2	C					cf appx Y.1, 1	
43	58	54/1	G						
44	59	54/3	E						
45	60	55/1	A						
46	61	55/2	f			A (u frag.)		'The Razor'	
47	62	55/3	B♭			A (u frag.)			
48–53				6 Quartetti:	1790 (1791)			'Tost' Quartets, iii	51, 52, 106, 108
48	65	64/1	C			A	HW xii/5, 3		
49	68	64/2	b			A	HW xii/5, 18		
50	67	64/3	B♭			A	HW xii/5, 33		
51	66	64/4	G			HV	HW xii/5, 53		
52	64	64/6	E♭			A	HW xii/5, 68		
53	63	64/5	D			A, Sk	HW xii/5, 83, 218 (incl. sketch for I)	'The Lark'; cf appx Y.1, 4	
54–9				6 Quartetti:	1793 (1795, 1796)			'Apponyi' Quartets	66, 68, 108
54	69	71/1	B♭			A	HW xii/5, 101		
55	70	71/2	D			Sk	HW xii/5, 119, 222 (incl. sketch for III)		
56	71	71/3	E♭				HW xii/5.135		
57	72	74/1	C				HW xii/5, 155		
58	73	74/2	F			Sk	HW xii/5, 177, 220 (incl. sketch for IV)	cf appx Y.1, 2	
59	74	74/3	g				HW xii/5, 198	'The Rider'; for kbd arr. of II, see appx X.2, 6	109

No.	hIII	Op.	Title, key	Date (pubd)	Authentication	Edition	Remarks
60–65			6 Quartetti:	?14 June 1797 (1799)	HV, OE	HW, xii/6	'Erdödy' Quartets
60	75	76/1	G				75, 108, 111, 112
61	76	76/2	d				
62	77	76/3	C	–28 Sept 1797	HE (= E) Sk		'Fifths'; 'Emperor'; II uses Gott erhalte Franz den Kaiser, D 11; cf appx X,2, 8; date 1796 incorrect
63	78	76/4	Bb		HE (= E)		'Sunrise'
64	79	76/5	D				
65	80	76/6	Eb		HE (= E)		
66–7			2 Quartetti:	1799 (1802)	A	HW, xii/6	'Lobkowitz' Quartets, facs. edn. (Budapest, 1972, 2/1980): arr. A. E. Müller for fl/vn, pf (Leipzig, 1803)
66	81	77/1	G				75, 111, 112
67	82	77/2	F				112
68	83	103	Unfinished Quartet, d (not Bb)	–1803 (1806)	A, Sk	HW, xii/6	movts II and III only; 75, 112

Note: Haydn apparently wrote ?2 small str qts for Spain in 1784, now lost, not identical with hIII:B4, G5, C8, F2, D2 or g 1, which are by Gallus-Mederitsch; unpubd sketch, d, c1795, not identified

Appendix O.1: Arrangements for string quartet

No.	H	Title, key	Date	Authentication	Edition	Remarks
1	III:50–56	Musica instrumentale sopra le 7 ultime parole del nostro Redentore in croce ... ridotte in quartetti, op.51	–14 Feb 1787	OE	(London, 1956)	arr. of orch version (K 11)
2	—	Quartetti: La vera costanza	–1799 [?c1790]	E	—	16 pieces arr. from opera (E 19) ? by Haydn or with his approval
3	—	Quartetti: Armida	–1799 [?c1790]	E	—	18 pieces arr. from opera (E 23) ? by Haydn or with his approval

Note: arrs. of other Haydn operas and oratorios for str qt or qnt, not authenticated; VI Fugen ... von G. J. Werner ... herausgegeben von ... J. Haydn (Vienna, 1804) not arr. but only issued by Haydn

Appendix O.2: Selected spurious works

No.	hIII	Op.	Title, key	Date	Edition	Remarks
1-6			6 Quatuors:	-1777	(London, n.d.)	? by R. Hoffstetter, though in HV
1	13	3/1	E			
2	14	3/2	C			
3	15	3/3	G			
4	16	3/4	Bb			
5	17	3/5	F			
6	18	3/6	A			II: 'Serenade'
7	D 3	—	Divertimento, D	-1763	(Mainz, 1955)	by Albrechtsberger
8	E 2	—	E	-1768	HM, xcviii (1936)	

Note: further spurious qts listed in hIII, and Feder (1974)

32

Appendix O.3: Spurious arrangements

No.	H	Op.	Key	Date	Edition	Remarks
1	III:5	1/5	Bb	-1770/71	(London, n.d.)	arr. of sym. J *107;* spurious though in HV
2	III:9	2/3	Eb	-1766	(London, n.d.)	arr. of N *11;* spurious though in HV
3	III:11	2/5	D	-1766	(London, n.d.)	arr. of N *12;* spurious though in HV

87

P: STRING TRIOS (DIVERTIMENTOS)
(baryton trios excepted; for 2 vn, vc (b), unless otherwise stated)

HV	Key	Forces	Date	Authentication	Edition	Remarks
1	E		-1767	EK	(Paris, c1768)	
2	F		-1767	EK	(Vienna, 1803)	
3	b		-1767	EK	(Leipzig, 1932) (2 vn, pf, vc ad lib)	
4	Eb	?	-1767	EK	D 904 (1981)	
5	B		-?1765	EK	—	lost
6	Eb		-?1764	EK	—	other versions: III, I, II, or I, II without III; see H iii, 308, 309
7	A		[-?1761] -?1765	EK	(Mainz, 1955)	incl. variations on Ich liebe, du liebest (G *48*); cf appx N *4*

165

hV	Key	Forces	Date	Authentication	Edition	Remarks
8	B♭	vn, va, b	–1765	EK	(München-Gräfelfing, 1971)	
9	E♭	?	–?1765	EK		lost
10	F		–1767	EK	(Paris, c1768)	wrongly attrib. M. Haydn in catalogue Rayhrad, 1771
11	E♭		–1765	EK	D 923 (1981)	
12	E		–1767	EK	D 911 (1981)	
13	B♭		–?1765	EK	—	
14	b	?	–?1765	EK	—	lost
15	D		–1762	EK	D 914 (1981)	cf appx N 3
16	C		–1766	EK	D 915 (1981)	see remark for no.11
17	E♭		–1766	EK	(Leipzig, 1932) (arr. as no.3)	see remark for no.11
18	B♭		–1765	EK	(Paris, c1765; Amsterdam, 1767)	
19	E		–1765	EK	as no.18	sometimes wrongly attrib. M. Haydn
20	G		–1766	EK	(Leipzig, 1932) (arr. as no.3)	
21	D		?c1765	EK	(Vienna, 1803)	

Appendix P: Selected works for 2 violins, bass, attributed to Haydn (early works if authentic)

No.	hV	Key	Edition	Remarks
1	D3	D	D 920 (1981)	probably authentic
2	F1	F	D 928 (1981)	probably authentic
3	G1	G	D 921 (1981)	probably authentic; attrib. M. Haydn in catalogue Rayhrad, 1771
4	A2	A	—	probably authentic; see previous remark
5	A3	A		?authentic
6	D1	D	D 924 (1981)	?authentic
7	B1	B♭	D 927 (1981)	?authentic
8	G3	G	(Mainz, 1955)	I and II ?authentic; III and IV (from one MS copy) doubtful
9	G4	D	—	?authentic though also attrib. C. d'Ordonez; see A. P. Brown, *AcM*, xlvi (1974), 225

No.	Code	Key	Publication	Remarks
10	C3	C	—	doubtful; nos.*10–14* considered authentic by Landon, i (1980), nos.*10*. *12–14* as possibly authentic by Larsen (1941, rev. 1979)
11	C2	C	—	doubtful; see previous remark
12	C1	C	—	doubtful; see remark for no.*10*
13	C4	C	6 Weinzierler Trios (Wolfenbüttel, 1938), no.1	doubtful; see remark for no.*10*
14	C5	C	—	doubtful; see remark for no.*10*
15	Es4	E♭	—	doubtful
16	C6	C	—	probably not authentic
17	C7	C	5 Eisenstädter Trios (Wiesbaden, 1954), no.3	probably not authentic
18	C8	C	—	probably not authentic
19	D4	D	6 Weinzierler Trios (Wolfenbüttel, 1938), no.5	probably not authentic
20	—	d	—	*A-Wst*; probably not authentic
21	Es2	E♭	—	probably not authentic
22	Es3	E♭	—	probably not authentic
23	Es5	E♭	12 Menuette (Wolfenbüttel, 1938), nos.9, 12	probably not authentic; 5 movts; only 2 minuets pubd
24	Es11	E♭	(?Paris, n.d.)	probably not authentic
25	E2	E	—	probably not authentic
26	F7	F	as no.*24*	probably not authentic
27	—	F	—	*CS-Bm* (2 vn, vle); probably not authentic
28	G5	G	as no.*24*	probably not authentic
29	—	A	—	*Pnm*; probably not authentic
30	B3	B♭	—	probably not authentic
31	B4	B♭	—	probably not authentic
32	Es1	E♭	(München-Gräfelfing, 1969)	by M. Haydn; for vn, va, vc
33	G2	G	(Leipzig, 1932)	by M. Haydn; edn. as no.*3*
34	A1	A	(Leipzig, 1932)	by M. Haydn; edn. as no.*3*
35	Es9	E♭	6 Weinzierler Trios (Wolfenbüttel, 1938), no.6	probably by L. Hofmann

Note: other works in HV, probably by other composers, incl. D2, E1, B2: ? by M. Haydn: C9 (lost), D5, Es8, F5 (lost, ?3str qt), G6, A7: ? by L. Hofmann; Es12, F2, F6: ? by Kammel; Es10: ? Asplmayr; F3: ? by Asplmayr/Ivanschiz; Es7: ? by P. Gasparini; Es13 (lost): ? by Auffmann; F4: ? by J. C. Bach (qt); A5: ? by Enderle; A6: ? by Filtz; B5: ? by Chiesa; incipits of 7 lost and doubtful works: HV: D6, Es6, E3, F8, G7, A4, B6; see also pf sonatas, W *40–42*

Q: BARYTON TRIOS (DIVERTIMENTOS)

(for baryton, va, b; WT = 6 leichte Wiener Trios, Wolfenbüttel, 1939)

No. HXI		Key	Date	Authentication	Edition	Remarks
1-24: Book i						
1		A	-14 Jan 1767 [c1765/6]	EK	HW xiv/1, 1	bound by that date; preserved singly edn. with II and III reversed and added Presto as IV
2a	—	?1st version, A		I: EK	HW xiv/1, 6	3 movts
2b	2	2nd version, A		I: EK; III, IV: A (u)	HW xiv/1, 6	4 movts; facs. of autograph frag. in Unverricht (1969)
2c	2bis	spurious version, G		—	WT, no.4	3 movts as 2a but in order II, III, I; for vc, va, b, and other arrs.; cf appx X.3, 9a–c
	3	A	-1770		HW xiv/1, 16	
	4	A		I: EK	HW xiv/1, 21	
5a	—	?1st version, A		I: EK	HW xiv/1, 24	3 movts as 5c; I quotes Gluck: Che farò senza Euridice
5b	—	?2nd version, A		I: EK; III: A (u)	HW xiv/1, 24	like 5d but in 3 movts; Adagio from 5c, in D, as II; facs. of autograph frag. in Unverricht (1969)
5c	i, 596	spurious version, G		—	WT, no.2	for 2 vn, b; also in D, arr. fl, vn, b
5d	(below)	inc. reconstruction, A		I: EK; II: A (u)	HW xiv/1, 24	2 movts
	6	A	-1769		HW xiv/1, 28	spurious version omits II and incl. III from 5b
	7	A	-1769		HW xiv/1, 34	
	8	A			HW xiv/1, 40	
	9	A	-1770		HW xiv/1, 46	
	10	A	-1772	A (frag., u)	HW xiv/1, 51	not for 2 barytons, b, as stated in H
	11	D	-1772		HW xiv/1, 56	
	12	A			HW xiv/1, 61	
	13	A			HW xiv/1, 70	only I extant or identified; edn. in B♭, for 2 vn, vc
	14	D			HW xiv/1, 72	
	15	A			HW xiv/1, 78	
	16	A	-1772		HW xiv/1, 84	lost or unidentified
	17	D	-1772		HW xiv/1, 88	
	18	A	-1772		—	
	19	A			HW xiv/1, 96	
	20	D	-1771		HW xiv/1, 102	
	21	A			HW xiv/1, 108	only I extant or identified; edn for 2 vn, vc
	22	A			HW xiv/1, 113	lost or unidentified; cf appx Q 2
	23	D			—	
	24	D	1766	A (inc.)	HW xiv/1, 115	edn with Trio of Minuet and III, both missing in H

169

No.	Key	Date	EK	HW	Notes
25–48: Book ii		–11 Oct 1767 [c1766/7]	EK		bound by that date
25	A	–1772		HW xiv/2, 1	
26	G			HW xiv/2, 6	uses minuet of appx X.1, 2; II and III reversed in H
27	D			HW xiv/2, 13	
28	D			HW xiv/2, 19	I uses theme from La canterina (E 8)
29	A			HW xiv/2, 25	another version (?not authentic) has 4 movts, incl. Adagio from no.5
30	G			HW xiv/2, 32	
31	D			HW xiv/2, 37	
32	G			HW xiv/2, 43	
33	A			HW xiv/2, 49	
34	D	–1776 [–?1775]		HW xiv/2, 56	
35	A	–1771		HW xiv/2, 61	I uses W 3
36	D	–1776		HW xiv/2, 65	
37	D	–1776		HW xiv/2, 70	
38	G	–1776		HW xiv/2, 77	
39	A	–1776		HW xiv/2, 83	
40	D		A (frag.)	HW xiv/2, 88	
41	D		A	HW xiv/2, 93	
42	D	1767	A (frag.)	HW xiv/2, 98	
43	D			HW xiv/2, 104	
44	D			HW xiv/2, 109	
45	D			HW xiv/2, 114	
46	A			HW xiv/2, 120	
47	G			HW xiv/2, 125	
48	D			HW xiv/2, 131	
49 72: Book iii		–7 July 1768 [c1767/8]	EK		bound by that date
49	G			HW xiv/3, 1	
50	D			HW xiv/3, 7	
51	A			HW xiv/3, 14	
52	d/D			HW xiv/3, 18	minuet and trio based on movt in sym. J 58
53	G	1767	A	HW xiv/3, 24	
54	D			HW xiv/3, 29	
55	G			HW xiv/3, 33	
56	D	1768		HW xiv/3, 38	
57	A		A	HW xiv/3, 44	
58	D			HW xiv/3, 48	
59	G		Sk	HW xiv/3, 53	
60	A		Sk	HW xiv/3, 59	for sketch, see critical commentary to HW xiv/3, 32

No.	HXI	Key	Date	Authentication	Edition	Remarks
	61	D		Sk	HW xiv/3, 65	for sketch, see critical commentary to HW xiv/3, 35
	62	G			HW xiv/3, 72	
	63	D			HW xiv/3, 77	
	64	D			HW xiv/3, 83	I uses Alleluia theme of sym. J 30
	65	G			HW xiv/3, 88	
	66	A			HW xiv/3, 93	
	67	G			HW xiv/3, 100	
	68	A		A	HW xiv/3, 106	
	69	D		A	HW xiv/3, 111	
	70	G			HW xiv/3, 116	
	71	A			HW xiv/3, 122	
	72	D			HW xiv/3, 128	
73–96: Book iv						
	73	G	–22 Dec 1771	EK, SC	HW xiv/4, 1	paper for copying ordered by that date; bound by 3 Feb 1772
	74	D	[c1768–71]		HW xiv/4, 5	
	75	A	–1772		HW xiv/4, 11	
	76	C			HW xiv/4, 16	
	77	G			HW xiv/4, 21	
	78	D			HW xiv/4, 26	
	79	D	1769	A	HW xiv/4, 30	
	80	G		A (frag.)	HW xiv/4, 35	
	81	D			HW xiv/4, 41	
	82	C			HW xiv/4, 46	
	83	F			HW xiv/4, 52	
	84	G			HW xiv/4, 58	
	85	D			HW xiv/4, 64	
	86	A			HW xiv/4, 70	
	87	a			HW xiv/4, 76	
	88	A			HW xiv/4, 82	
	89	G			HW xiv/4, 87	vn instead of va
	90	C			HW xiv/4, 93	vn instead of va
	91	D			HW xiv/4, 100	vn instead of va
	92	G			HW xiv/4, 106	
	93	C	–1774		HW xiv/4, 111	
	94	A			HW xiv/4, 116	
	95	D			HW xiv/4, 123	
	96	b			HW xiv/4, 130	

97–126*: Book v

No.		Date	Copyist	HW ref	Notes
97	D	−8 Nov 1778 [c1771–8] [?1766]	EK	HW xiv/5, 1	paper for copying ordered by that date; preserved singly; 'per la felicissima nascita di S.Al.S. Prencipe Estorhazi'; cf S 11
98	D		EK	HW xiv/5, 15	
99	G		EK	—	
100	F		EK	HW xiv/5, 22	lost
101	C		EK	HW xiv/5, 30	
102	G		EK	HW xiv/5, 37	
103	A		EK	HW xiv/5, 44	based on U 15; see also R 6, V 6
104	D		EK	HW xiv/1, 126	MS discovered 1976, see Fisher (1978)
105	G	1772	A	HW xiv/5, 50; xiv/1, 132	III discovered 1976, see Fisher (1978)
106	D		EK	HW xiv/5, 55	autograph erroneously mentioned in H is that of no.105
107	D		EK	HW xiv/5, 61	
108	A		EK	HW xiv/5, 68	
109	C		A, EK	HW xiv/5, 74	
110	C		EK	HW xiv/5, 80	I and II based on U 13
111	G		EK	HW xiv/5, 87	in HV 'a cinque'
112	D		EK	HW xiv/5, 92	
113	D		HV, JE	HW xiv/5, 99	
114	D		EK	HW xiv/5, 106	
115	D		EK	HW xiv/5, 113	
116	G		EK	HW xiv/5, 119	
117	F		EK	HW xiv/5, 125	
118	D		EK	HW xiv/5, 132	
119	G		EK	HW xiv/5, 139	
120	D		EK	HW xiv/5, 141	only baryton pt. extant
121	A		HV, C	HW xiv/5, 146	
122	A		EK	HW xiv/5, 153	
123	G		EK	HW xiv/5, 159	
124	G		EK	HW xiv/5, 166	
125	C		EK	HW xiv/5, 174	
126*			EK	HW xiv/5, 180	

Appendix Q: String (probably baryton) trios attributed to Haydn

No.	hXI	Title, key	Forces	Edition	Remarks
1	D1	Adagio cantabile, D; Menuetto (with Trio), A/a (I, II)	2 vn, vc	HW xiv/1, 120, 122	probably authentic; ? II, III of Q 13
2	iii, 327	Finale (Presto assai), D	2 vn, vc	HW xiv/1, 124	probably authentic; ? III of Q 23
3	iii, 327	Menuetto (with Trio), E♭	2 vn, vc	HW xiv/1, 123	probably authentic, but transposed; ? II of Q 23
4	D2	Divertimento, D	baryton, va, vc	—	doubtful
5	A1	Terzetto (a tre), A	baryton, va, b	—	doubtful
6	C3	Trio, C	vc, va, b	DTÖ, cxxiv (1972), 71, as by Tomasini	baryton trio by Luigi Tomasini

Note: for hXI:C1–2, see appx S 27, 26; see also appx S 1

R: WORKS FOR 1–2 BARYTONS

No.	H	Title, key	Forces	Date	Authentication	Edition	Remarks
1–5		[5] Divertimenti per il pariton solo:					
1	XII:20	G	?with vc	c1765/6	EK	—	lost
2	XII:21	D	?with vc	c1765/6	EK	—	lost
3	XII:22	A	?with vc	c1765/6	EK	—	lost
4	XII:23	G	?with vc	c1766–9	EK	—	lost
5	XII:18	A	with vc		EK	—	lost
6–7		[2] Soli per il pariton:					
6	XII:13	D	with vc	?1770–75	EK	—	lost; probably based on U 15; theme identical with III of V 6
7	XII:14	D	baryton, vc	?1770–75 ?c1775	EK	—	lost
8–13		6 Sonate:					
8	XII:7	D			EK	—	lost
9	XII:8	C			EK	—	lost
10	XII:9	G			EK	—	lost
11	XII:10	A			EK	—	lost
12	XII:11	D			EK	—	lost
13	XII:12	G			HV	—	lost

14–16			?	HV		
		[3] Sonate: baryton, vc			—	lost; for authenticity see critical commentary to HW xiii, 11; ?incl. in '16 Duetten für den Bariton' in Haydn's short work-list, c1803/4 (H i, facs., p.V)
14	XII:15	F				
15	XII:16	D				
16	XII:17	D				
17–22		**[6] Duetti:** 2 barytons				
17	X:11	D	c1764–9	EK	HW xiii, 2	only extant in unauthentic arr. for fl, vn, b
18	XII:4	G		EK, JE	HW xiii, 6	
19	XII:1	A		EK	HW xiii, 10	as no.*17*
20	XII:5 + 3	D		EK	HW xiii, 16	as no.*17*; finale uses Trio from sym. J 28
21	XII:6	G		EK	—	lost
22	XII:2	G		HV	—	lost
23	XII:19	12 Cassations-Stücke (Divertimento), 2 barytons, b	c1765/6	EK, A (small frag, u); JE	HW xiii, 20	
24	X:9	Divertimento, D, 2 hn, baryton, va, b	?1765–70	EK	—	lost
25–6		**[2] Divertimentos (Quintetti):**				'3 Quintetten' according to Haydn's short work-list, c1803/4 (H i, facs., p.V)
25	X:7	D	c1767/8	EK	—	lost
26	X:10	D	c1767/8 [?c1771]	EK	HW xiii, 29	uses theme of N 32
27–33		**[7] Divertimentos a 8:** 2 hn, 2 vn, baryton, va, vc, vle				
27	X:2	D	?1775	EK	HW xiii, 38	1st edn. with fl instead of baryton; only extant in arrs. without baryton
28	X:5	G	1775	EK, A	HW xiii, 62	
29	X:3	a/A	1775	EK, A	HW xiii, 87	
30	X:4	G	?1775	EK	HW xiii, 109	as for no.*27*
31	X:1	D	1775	EK, A	HW xiii, 131	autograph in *PL-Kj*
32	X:6	A	?1775	EK	HW xiii, 157	as for no.*27*
33	X:12*	G	?1775	—	HW xiii, 177	as for no.*27*

Note: ᵃX:8 probably = XI:111 (*Q 111*); XII:24 probably = XI:114 (*Q 114*); XII:25* has not been verified

S: MISCELLANEOUS CHAMBER MUSIC FOR 2–3 STRING AND/OR WIND INSTRUMENTS

No.	H	Title, key	Forces	Date	Authentication	Edition	Remarks
1–6		6 Violin Solo mit Begleitung einer Viola (Sonatas; Duos):	vn, va	–1777 [–?1769]	EK	(Mainz, 1970)	versions for 2 vn and vn, vc, doubtful
1	VI:1	F					
2	VI:2	A					
3	VI:3	Bb			A (u vn)		cf. appx L 11
4	VI:4	D			A (u vn)		
5	VI:5	Eb					
6	VI:6	C					cf. appx L 11
7	IV:5*	Divertimento a 3 per il corno di caccia, Eb	hn, vn, vc	1767	A	D 1 (1957)	
8–13		6 Divertimentos a 3 (Divertissements):	vn/fl, vn, vc	1784	SC	(Leipzig, 1926), as op.100	
8	IV:6*	D					I arr. from Il mondo della luna, no.12 (E 17); II uses no.15
9	IV:7*	G					I uses no.24 of E 17
10	IV:8*	C					II uses no.25 of E 17
11	IV:9*	G					arr. of 3 movts from Q 97
12	IV:10*	A					III arr. from no.23 of E 17
13	IV:11*	D					III uses no.14 of E 17
14–17		[?4] Trios:	2 fl, vc	1794/5			orig. versions of nos.15–17 uncertain
14	IV:1	C		1794	A	(Leipzig, 1959), ed. K. H. Köhler	2, not 3 versions of II, both in edn., but 2nd version spoiled; wrong description in Landon, iii (1976), 406
15	IV:2	G			A (u)	as no.14	1 movt only; II only final variation of I; in autograph without title or 'Fine' remark; contrary statement in H wrong; uses song The Lady's Looking-glass (G 52); 1st pubd with added III from no.16 (London, 1799)
16	IV:3	G (no.2)			A (u)	as no.14	autograph in PL-Kj
17	IV:4*	G (no.3)			E	NM 71 (1954)	1 movt only; MS title in Haydn's hand, not signed by him, no author's name; also with no.15 added as II

Appendix S: Works attributed to Haydn

No.	H	Title, key	Forces	Date	Edition	Remarks
1	IV:G2	Divertimento a 3, G	fl, vn, vc	?1762	—	?authentic; 1 movt only; ?arr. of otherwise lost baryton composition; date on MS copy
2	VI:C4	Violino solo (Arioso + 7/8 variations), C	vn, b	–1768	—	doubtful
3–5	VI, Anhang	3 movts (each 2nd trio of Minuet): i F; ii Bb; iii c	2 vn	i –1800 ii–iii –1802	i (Paris, 1800); ii–iii (Leipzig, 1917)	doubtful; ?arr. from unknown works
6	VI:G2	Solo con basso, G	vn, b	?	—	doubtful
7	VI:Es2 Add.	23 variations, Eb	vn, b	?	—	doubtful; MS copy, *A-SEI*
8	IV:D2	Cassation, D	fl, vn, b	?	(Frankfurt, 1973) (with added hpd)	doubtful; arr. for fl, vn, str, hpd (Frankfurt, 1973)
9	IV:D1	Trio, D	fl, vn, b	–1768	—	doubtful
10–12	—	3 Terzetti:	fl/vn, vn, va, vc/bn	?	—	probably not authentic; MS copy, *HE*
10	—	C				
11	—	F				
12	—	Bb				
13	IV:F1	Divertimento (Trio), F	3 fl	?	—	probably not authentic
14	IV:F2	Sonata a 3, F	lute, vn, b	?	(Antwerp, 1973)	probably not authentic
15–17		3 Trios	clarinetto d'amour, vn, b	–1781	(Leipzig, 1977)	probably not authentic
15	IV:Es1	Eb				
16	IV:Es2	Eb				
17	IV:B1	Bb				
18	VI:G4	Ein musikalischer Scherz, G	2 vn	?	(Offenbach, 1896)	probably not authentic
19	IV:D3	Divertimento, D	hn, va, vle	?	ed. W. Rainer, D 274 (1969), as by M. Haydn	? by M. Haydn
20–23		4 Duos:	vn, va	1783	(Leipzig, 1911), as by M. Haydn	by M. Haydn
20	VI:C1	C				
21	VI:E1	E				
22	VI:F2	F				
23	VI:D3	D				

No.	H	Title, key	Forces	Date	Edition	Remarks
24–5		[2] Divertimenti da camera:				
24	IV:G1	G	vn/fl, vn, b	?	(Wolfenbüttel, 1972)	probably by Haver (?Gregor Hauer)
25	IV:A1	A	fl, vn, b			
26	XI:C2	Divertimento, C	fl, vn, b	?	(London, 1851)	probably by Haver
27	XI:C1	Divertissement, C	vn/fl, vn, b	–1771	(London, 1936) (for vn, pf)	probably by Dittersdorf (2 vn, b)
28	VI:D1	Duett, D	vn, vc	?	(Leipzig, 1902)	probably by L. Hofmann
29–34		6 Sonatas:	2 vn	–1770	(Mainz, 1953)	also attrib. Campioni; probably by Kammel
29	VI:G1	G				
30	VI:A1	A				
31	VI:B1	B♭				
32	VI:D2	D				
33	VI:Es1	E♭				
34	VI:F1	F				
35	IV, Anhang	Gioco filarmonico, D	2 vn/fl, b	–1781	(Naples, –1790)	by M. Stadler; also pubd for pf
36	i, 509	Divertimento, E♭	vn, va d'amore, vc	?	NM 52 (1930)	spurious arr. of Q 56, I: 34, II (trio of minuet by Gassmann); 78, III

Note: 6 vn duettos mentioned by A. Fuchs, doubtful and lost (hVI:G3, D4, A2, C2, F3, C3); arr. for lute/gui, vn, vc, see O 6; 3 ob duettos, no.1 on Teldec 6.42416 AW, doubtful

T: WORKS FOR 2 LIRE ORGANIZZATE

107

No.	H	Title, key	Forces	Date	Authentication	Edition	Remarks
1–5		[?5] Concerti per la lira organizzata:	2 lire, 2 hn, 2 vn, 2 va, vc				1 conc., ?in C, possibly lost
1	VIIh:1*	C		?1786–7	HE (= C)	HW vi, 1	
2	VIIh:4*	F		[1786]	HE	HW vi, 35	only extant MS copy without author's name but rev. Haydn; II uses cavatina Sono Alcina (F 8)
3	VIIh:2*	G		?1786–7	HC	HW vi, 75	

107

4	VIIh:5*	F			?1786-7	HC	HW vi, 113	only extant MS copy without author's name but rev. Haydn; cf J 89
5	VIIh:3*	G			?1786-7	A (u. frag.); HC	HW vi, 141	only extant MS without author's name but partly written by Haydn; cf J 100
[?8] Notturni:								
6-13 6	II:25*	C	C	2 lire, 2 cl, 2 hn, 2 va, b	c1788-90	HE (= C)	HW vii, 1	?1 notturno missing
7	II:26*	F	F	2 lire, 2 cl, 2 hn, 2 va, b	c1788-90	HC	HW vii, 25	only extant MS copy without author's name but from Haydn's collection
8	II:32*	C, i orig. version	2 lire, 2 cl, 2 hn, 2 va, b	?1790	RC	HW vii, 48 (based on both versions)	MS copy without author's name but rev. Haydn
		ii London version	2 fl, 2 vn, 2 hn, 2 va, vc, db	?1792	RC		MS copy without Haydn's name but rev. Haydn
9	II:31*	(Divertimento), C i orig. version	2 lire, 2 cl, 2 hn, 2 va, vc	1790	A, Sk	HW vii, 78	sketch for I, HW vii, 188
		ii 1st London version	fl, ob, 2 cl/vn, 2 hn, 2 va, vc	?1792	SC, RC	HW vii, 78	
		iii 2nd London version	fl, ob, 2 vn, 2 hn, 2 va, vc	?1794	corrections in A	HW vii, 78	
10	II:29*	C, i ?orig. version	?2 lire, ?2 cl, ?2hn, ?2 va, ? vc	?1790	—	[HW vii, 98]	
		ii extant version	fl, ob, 2 hn, 2 va, vc/b	?1791	HE	[HW vii, 98]	
11	II:30*	G	2 lire, 2 cl, 2 hn, 2 va, vc	?1790	HC, C	HW vii, 116	finale lost; only extant MS copy without author's name
12	II:28*	F, i ?orig. version	?2 lire, ?2 hn, ?2 vn, ?2 va, ? vc	?1790	Sk	[HW vii, 130]	sketch for I, HW vii, 196
		ii London version	fl, ob, 2 hn, 2 vn, 2 va, vc, db	?1792	SC	HW vii, 130	
13	II:27*	(Divertimento), G i orig. version	2 lire, 2 hn, 2 vn, 2 va, vc	?1790	A	HW vii, 158 (based on both versions)	
		ii London version	fl, ob, 2 hn, 2 vn, 2 va, vc, db	?1792	corrections in A, SC		

U: KEYBOARD CONCERTOS/CONCERTINOS/DIVERTIMENTOS

No.	H	Title, key	Forces	Date	Authentication	Edition	Remarks
1-2		[2] Concerti per il clavicembalo:					
1	XVIII:1	(Concerto per l'organo, no.1), C	org/hpd, 2 ob, (2 tpt/?hn, ? timp), str	?1756	A, EK	(Wiesbaden, 1953)	17, 87
2	XVIII:2	D	org/hpd (2 ob, 2 tpt, timp), str	-1767	EK	—	wrongly attrib. Galuppi in MS copy, D-B
3	XVIII:6*	Concerto per violino e cembalo, F	org/hpd, vn solo, str	-1766	EK	(Kassel, 1959)	
4-6		[3] Concerti per il clavicembalo:					
4	XVIII:3	F	hpd, (?2 hn), str	-1771	EK	(Mainz, 1958)	
5	XVIII:4	G	hpd/pf, (?2 ob, ?2 hn), str	-1781	EK	(Leipzig, 1958)	
6	XVIII:11*	D	hpd/pf, 2 ob, 2 hn, str	[?c1770] -1784	—	(Leipzig, 1931)	47, 48, 101
7-13		[7] Concertinos/Divertimentos:					
7	XIV:11*	Concertino, C	hpd, 2 vn, b	1760	A (lost)	(Munich, 1969); D 21 (1959)	
8	XIV:10*	Divertimento no.1 con violini	hpd, (2) vn, (b)	?c1764-7	JE	—	hpd only extant; finale uses that of kbd sonata, appx W.1, 11; facs. in Landon, i (1980), 546
9	XIV:4	Divertimento (Concerto), C	hpd, 2 vn, b	1764	A	(Frankfurt, 1972)	
10	XIV:3	Divertimento (Concertino, Sonate), C	hpd, 2 vn, b	-1771 [-c1767]	EK	(Leipzig, 1952)	wrongly attrib. L. Hofmann; not identical with conc. by Hofmann in H i, 672
11	XIV:7*	Divertimento, C	hpd, 2 vn, vc	-c1767	HE	(Frankfurt, 1972)	str pts. ?not authentic, see Brown (1972)
12	XIV:9*	Divertimento, F	hpd, 2 vn, vc	-c1767	HE	(Frankfurt, 1972)	
13	XIV:8*	Divertimento, C	hpd, 2 vn, vc	c1768-72	HE	(Frankfurt, 1973)	cf Q 110
14	XIV:1	Divertimento, Eb	hpd, 2 hn, vn, b	-1766	EK	HW xvii/1, 157	
15	XIV:2	Divertimento, F	hpd, 2 vn, baryton	?c1767-71	EK	—	lost; versions as pf trio (V 6) and baryton trio (Q 103) extant; cf R 6

Appendix U: Works attributed to Haydn

No.	H	Title, key	Forces	Date	Edition	Remarks
1	XVIII:5*	Concerto, C	org/hpd (?2 ob, ?2 tpt/hn), 2 vn, b	-1763	NM 200 (1959)	probably authentic; ?EK; also attrib. Wagenseil in MS copy, Burgenländisches Landesmuseum, Eisenstadt
2	XVIII:8*	Concerto (no.2), C	org/hpd, (2 hn/tpt, timp), 2 vn, b	-1766	D 80 (1962)	probably authentic; ?EK; originally attrib. (L.) Hofmann in MS copy, D-B
3	XVIII:10*	Concertino (Concerto), C	org/hpd, 2 vn, b	-1771	(Munich, 1969)	probably authentic; ?EK; only extant MS copy, A-Wgm, as by 'Heyden'
4	XIV:12*	Concerto (Partita, Concertino), C	hpd, 2 vn, b	-1772 [-c1767]	(Munich, 1969); D 323 (1969)	probably authentic
5	XIV:13*	Concerto (Concertino), G	hpd, 2 vn, b	-c1767	(Munich, 1969; Mainz, 1956)	probably authentic, date 1765 not in Göttweig catalogue, contrary to preface in Mainz edn.
6	XVIII:F2	Concerto (Concertino), F	hpd, 2 vn, b	-c1767	(Munich, 1969); D 324 (1969)	probably authentic
7	XIV:C2	Divertimento, C	hpd, 2 vn, b	-c1767	D 325 (1969)	probably authentic; edn. without III, preserved in CS-KRa (MS A-4792)
8	XIV:C1	Divertimento, C	hpd, (?2) vn, b	-1772 [-c1767]	D 534 (1976)	?authentic; allegedly not approved by Haydn in 1803; ?vn 1 lost; in edn. as pf trio
9	XVIII:G2	Concerto duetto, G	2 hpd/pf, 2 hn, 2 vn, b	-1782	(London, 1782)	by J. A. Šteffan (Šetková no.135)
10	XVIII:7*	Concerto, F	org/hpd, 2 vn, b	-1766	(Amsterdam, 1962)	doubtful; considered probably authentic by Larsen (1941, rev. 1979); I and III later versions of pf trio, appx V.1, 8; orig. attrib. Wagenseil in MS copy, CS-KRa
11	XIV:G1	Partita (Divertimento), G	hpd, 2 vn, b	-1774	—	lost, doubtful; allegedly not approved by Haydn in 1803; not with 2 bn as in H
12	XVIII:9*	Concerto, G	hpd, 2 vn, b	-1767	(Mainz, 1967)	doubtful; considered probably authentic by Larsen (1941, rev. 1979)
13	XVIII:Es1	Concerto, E♭	hpd, str	?	—	probably not authentic; orig. without author's name in only extant MS copy, D-B
14	XVIII:G1	Concerto, G	hpd, 2 fl/ob, 2 hn, 2 vn, b	?	—	probably not authentic
15	—	Concertino, D	hpd, 2 vn, vc	?	—	probably not authentic; MS copy, CS-KRa

No.	H	Title, key	Forces	Date	Edition	Remarks
16	XVIII:F1	Concerto, F	hpd, 2 fl, str	c1779/80	(Berlin, 1927)	by G. J. Vogler (6 leichte Clavierconcerte, no.6)
17	XVIII:F3	Concerto, F	hpd, str	1766	—	probably by (J. G.) Lang
18	—	Concerto (Kleines Konzert), F	hpd, (2 hn), str	1775	(Heidelberg, 1962)	by L. Hofmann; see Mf, xvii (1964), 461
19	XIV:C3	Concerto (Quattro), C	hpd, 2 vn, b	1766	(Paris, c1776), as by Wagenseil	by Wagenseil
20	XIV:Es1	Divertimento, Eb	hpd, 2 vn, b	?	—	by J. A. Steffan (orig. for hpd solo)
21	XIV:F1	Quartetto concertant, F	hpd/harp, fl, vn/va, vc	1774	(Paris, 1777)	by J. Schmittbauer; orig. for hpd/pf, fl, vn, vc
22	XIV:F2	Concertante, F	pf, ob, vn, va, vc	1782	(London, ?c1785), as by J. C. Bach	not a Haydn autograph; by J. C. Bach

V: KEYBOARD TRIOS

No.	HXV	Title, key	Forces	Date	Authentication	Edition	Remarks	
1	5	Sonata, G	hpd, vn, b	-25 Oct 1784	A (frag.), SC	HW xvii/2, 1	no.3 of 3 Sonatas, nos.1 and 2 spurious; see appx V.2, 1-2	104
2-4		3 Sonatas:	hpd, vn, vc					104
2	6	F		1784	A (lost frag.), OE	HW xvii/2, 22		
3	7	D		1785	A (incl. Sk)	HW xvii/2, 39	sketch of III, HW xvii/2, 260	
4	8	Bb		-26 Nov 1785	OE	HW xvii/2, 55		
5-7		3 Sonatas:	hpd, vn, vc					104
5	9	A		1785	A, EK, SC	HW xvii/2, 73		
6	2	(Divertimento), F	(hpd, vn, b)	?c1767-71	SC	HW xvii/1, 141	uses lost divertimento U 15; cf R 6	
7	10	Eb		-28 Oct 1785	SC	HW xvii/2, 88		104
8-10		3 Sonatas:	hpd/pf, vn, vc					104
8	11	Eb		-8 March 1789 [-?16 Nov 1788]	OE	HW xvii/2, 106		104
9	12	e		-8 March 1789 [1788/9]		HW xvii/2, 124		
10	13	c	hpd/pf, vn, vc	[-29 March] 1789		HW xvii/2, 148		104
11	14	Sonata, Ab	hpd/pf, fl, vc	-[?11 Jan] 1790	OE	HW xvii/2, 169		104
12	16	Trio, D		-[28 June] 1790	OE	HW xvii/2, 195		104

13	15	Trio, G	hpd/pf, fl, vc	[–28 June] 1790	OE	HW xvii/2, 220	sketch for I in *Belb 1973–7*	104
14	17	Trio, F	hpd/pf, fl/vn, vc	–?20 June 1790	Sk, ?OE	HW xvii/2, 245	?originally for pf, vn	104
15	32	Sonata, G	pf, vn, vc	–14 June 1794	HV, ?Gr, Dies	D 481 (1970)		
16–18		3 Sonatas:	pf, vn, vc	–15 Nov 1794	HV, ?Gr, Dies	D 482–4 (1970)		
16	18	A						
17	19	g						
18	20	B♭						
19–21		3 Sonatas:	pf, vn, vc	–23 May 1795	HV, Gr, Dies	D 485–7 (1970)		
19	21	C						
20	22	E♭			SC of II (pf only)		SC shows slightly different earlier version ?1794/5, ?for pf solo and printed thus in D 486, p.36	
21	23	d						
22–4		3 Sonatas:	pf, vn, vc	–9 Oct 1795	HV, ?Dies	D 488–90 (1970)		
22	24	D						
23	25	G			Sk		III: Gypsy rondo (all' ongarese) see sym. J 102	
24	26	f♯		[?1794]				
25–7		3 Sonatas:	pf, vn, vc	–20 April 1797 [–?Aug 1795]	HV	D 493–5 (1970)		109, *110*
25	27	C						
26	28	E						
27	29	E♭						
28	31	Sonata, e♭	pf, vn, vc	1795	A	D 491 (1970)	II called 'Jacob's Dream' in autograph, ?orig. a separate work, see H i, 727; whole sonata formerly thought to be for pf, vn	
29	30	Sonata, E♭	hpd/pf, vn, vc	–7 Oct 1797 [?16 April– 9 Nov 1796]	A (u frag.); E; OE	D 492 (1970)		

Note: Haydn apparently composed no sonatas for pf, vn, except perhaps no.*15*; extant edns. are arrs, see especially O *66–7*, V *15, 28*, W *22–4, 37*

Appendix V.1: Early works for harpsichord, violin and bass attributed to Haydn

No.	H	Title, key	Date	Authentication	Edition	Remarks
1	XV:36*	Partita (Concerto), E♭	-1774 [-?1760]	H 1803	HW xvii/1, 1	not verified by Haydn in 1803; attrib. Wagenseil in one MS copy (see Scholz-Michelitsch, no.449); early edn. with spurious minuet and trio
2	XV:C1	Divertimento, C	-1766 [-?1760]	—	HW xvii/1, 13	
3	XV:37*	Divertimento (Trio, Concerto), F	-1766 [-?1760]	H 1803	HW xvii/1, 31	
4	XV:38*	Divertimento, B♭	-1769 [-?1760]	H 1803	HW xvii/1, 45	
5	XV:34*	Partita (Divertimento), E	-1771 [-?1760]	H 1803, F	HW xvii/1, 57	
6	XV:f1	Partita, f	-?1760	F	HW xvii/1, 67	
7	XV:41*	Divertimento, G	-1767 [-?1760]	H 1803	HW xvii/1, 81	
8	XV:40*	Divertimento (Partita), F	[?c1760]	—	HW xvii/1, 97	one MS copy with spurious Adagio (see D 4, p.8) instead of minuet; see appx U 10
9	XV:1	Partita (Divertimento), g	-1766 [?c1760-62]	H 1803	HW xvii/1, 109	
10	XV:35*	Divertimento (Capriccio), A	-1771 [?c1764/5]	HE, H 1803	HW xvii/1, 123	
11	XV:33*	Divertimento, D	-1771 [-?1760]	H 1803	HW xvii/1, 175 (incipits)	lost
12	XV:D1	Divertimento, D	-1771	—	HW xvii/1, 175 (incipits)	lost; doubtful, not verified by Haydn in 1803; according to Pohl, for hpd, 2 vn, vc

Appendix V.2: Doubtful and spurious works and arrangements

No.	H	Title, key	Forces	Date	Edition	Remarks	
1	XV:3	Sonata, C	hpd/pf, vn, vc	-1784	HW xvii/2, appx, 261	probably by Pleyel, though one MS copy signed by Haydn; orig. without vc; see critical commentary, HW xvii/2, and V 1	104
2	XV:4	Sonata, F	hpd/pf, vn, vc	-1784	HW xvii/2, appx, 280	probably by Pleyel; see above remarks	104
3	XV:C2	Grand bataille, C	pf, vn, vc	c1800	(Paris, c1804-14)	arr. from syms. J 48, I, J 76, III, J 81, III, with spurious movts added	

4	XIV:6	Sonata, G	hpd, vn, vc	−1767	D 523 (1977)	arr. from sonata W 1
5	XV:39*	Sonata, F	hpd, vn, vc	−1767	D 524 (1977)	arr. from sonatas appx W.1, 11, 10, 2, with spurious Andante
6	XV:D42* Add.	Variazioni, D	hpd, vn, b	?	D 533 (1976)	apparently arr. from otherwise unknown movt (see appx X.1, 3) and from appx X.1, 4; see Landon's piano trio list, no.15

Note: see also appx U 8

W: KEYBOARD SONATAS

Editions: *J. Haydn: Sämtliche Klaviersonaten*, i–iii, ed. C. Landon (Vienna, 1964–6) [WU]
J. Haydn: Sämtliche Klaviersonaten, i–iii, ed. G. Feder (Munich, 1972) [HU], mostly identical with HW xviii/1–3

No.	H	Title, key	Instrument	Date	Authentication	Edition	Remarks
1	XVI:6	Partita (Divertimento), G	hpd	−1766 [−?1760]	A (no IV)	HU i, 34; WU 13	
2	XVI:14	Parthia (Divertimento), D	hpd	−1767 [−?1760]	EK	HU i, 26; WU 16	
3	XVI:3	Divertimento, C	hpd	[?c1765]	EK	HU i, 98; WU 14	see baryton trio Q 37
4	XVI:4	Divertimento, D	hpd	[?c1765]	EK	HU i, 104; WU 9	III and IV in H not part of this work; orig. III apparently lost
5	XVI:2a	Divertimento, d	hpd	[?c1765–70]	EK	—	lost; WU 21
6	XVI:2b	Divertimento, A	hpd	[?c1765–70]	EK	—	lost, WU 22
7	XVI:2c	Divertimento, B	hpd	[?c1765–70]	EK	—	lost; WU 23
8	XVI:2d	Divertimento, Bb	hpd	[?c1765–70]	EK	—	lost; WU 24
9	XVI:2e	Divertimento, e	hpd	[?c1765–70]	EK	—	lost; WU 25
10	XVI:2g	Divertimento, C	hpd	[?c1765–70]	EK	—	lost; WU 26
11	XVI:2h	Divertimento, A	hpd	[?c1765–70]	EK	—	lost; WU 27
12a	XVI:47 bis Add.	Divertimento, e	hpd	[?c1765]	EK	HU i, 108; WU 19	earlier and probably orig. version of no.*12b*
12b	XVI:47	Sonata, F	hpd/pf	−1788	HV	WU 57	doubtful, though apparently authorized version of no.*12a*; Moderato added as I, Minuet omitted

14

No.	H	Title, key	Instrument	Date	Authentication	Edition	Remarks	
13	XVI:45	Divertimento, Eb	hpd	1766	A	HU i, 116; WU 29		33, 97, 98
14	XVI:19	Divertimento, D	hpd	1767	A	HU i, 130; WU 30		33, 97, 98
15	XIV:5 = XVI:5a Add.	Divertimento, D	hpd	[c1767–70]	EK, A (u frag.)	HU i, 143; WU 28	frag.; only I (inc.) and II extant	
16	XVI:46	Divertimento, Ab	hpd	–1788 [c1767–70]	EK	HU i; 147; WU 31		33, 97, 98
17	XVI:18	Sonata, Bb	hpd	–1788 [c1771–3]	A (u frag.), HV	HU i, 162; WU 20	rev. Haydn for Breitkopf edn. (1799)	
18	XVI:44	Sonata, g	hpd	–1788 [c1771–3]	HV	HU i, 171; WU 32		
19–24		6 Sonatas:	hpd	–Feb 1774	OE, EK	(Vienna, 1774)	op.13: ?1st orig. pubn authorized by Haydn	34, 43, 98
19	XVI:21	C		1773	A	HU ii, 1; WU 36		
20	XVI:22	E		1773	A	HU ii, 12; WU 37		
21	XVI:23	F		1773	A (frag.)	HU ii, 22; WU 38		
22	XVI:24	D		?1773		HU ii, 34; WU 39	formerly better kpown with added vn pt. by Burney	
23	XVI:25	Eb		?1773		HU ii, 44; WU 40	as above	
24	XVI:26	A		1773	A (frag.)	HU ii, 52; WU 41	as above; minuet and trio arr. from sym. J 47	
25–30		6 Sonatas (Divertimentos):	hpd	–1776	EK, H 1799–1803		op.14	34, 43, 98
25	XVI:27	G				HU ii, 60; WU 42		
26	XVI:28	Eb				HU ii, 70; WU 43		
27	XVI:29	F		1774	A (frag.)	HU ii, 82; WU 44		
28	XVI:30	A				HU ii, 96; WU 45		
29	XVI:31	E				HU ii, 106; WU 46		
30	XVI:32	b				HU ii, 116; WU 47		
31–6		6 Sonatas:	hpd/pf		OE, HV		op.30	102
31	XVI:35	C		–31 Jan 1780		HU ii, 126; WU 48		
32	XVI:36	c#		–31 Jan 1780 [?c1770–75]		HU ii, 138; WU 49		
33	XVI:37	D		–31 Jan 1780		HU ii, 146; WU 50		
34	XVI:38	Eb		–31 Jan 1780 [?c1770–75]		HU ii, 154; WU 51		
35	XVI:39	G		–8 Feb 1780		HU ii, 162; WU 52		
36	XVI:20	c		1771	A (frag., incl. Sk)	HU ii, 174; WU 33		98
37–9		[3] Sonatas:	hpd (/pf)					
37	XVI:43	Ab		–26 July 1783	—	HU iii, 1; WU 35	formerly better known in spurious arr. for pf, vn, G (hXVI:43bis)	

No.	H	Title, key		Date	Authentication	Edition	Remarks	
38	XVI:33	D		-17 Jan 1778	—	HU iii, 12; WU 34	date on MS in A-Wn rev. Haydn for Breitkopf edn. (1799)	102
39	XVI:34	e		-15 Jan 1784	HV	HU iii, 22; WU 53	also known in doubtful arr. for str trio	
40-42		3 Sonatas:	pf	-1784	HV			
40	XVI:40	G				HU iii, 33; WU 54		
41	XVI:41	Bb				HU iii, 40; WU 55		
42	XVI:42	D				HU iii, 48; WU 56		
43	XVI:48	Sonata, C	hpd (/pf)	-5 April [-?10 March] 1789	OE; HV	HU iii, 56; WU 58		105
44	XVI:49	Sonata, Eb	pf	1789-[1 June] 1789	A	HU iii, 68; WU 59		105
45	XVI:52	Sonata, Eb	pf	1794	A	HU iii, 84; WU 62		110
46	XVI:50	Sonata, C	pf	[c1794/5]	H 1799-1803 (II only)	HU iii, 100; WU 60	earlier version of II appeared 1794 (WU iii, 121)	110
47	XVI:51	Sonata, D	pf	[?c1794/5]	?OE	HU iii, 114; WU 61		110

Note: sketch for inc. sonata, HU iii, 122; 'Sonata Pianoforte für den Nelson', mentioned in Eissler, *Haydn's vollendete Compositionen*, A-Sm, not verified, ? = H 19

Appendix W.1: Early harpsichord sonatas attributed to Haydn

No.	H	Title, key	Date	Authentication	Edition	Remarks
1	XVI:16	Divertimento, Eb	[?c1750-55]	—	HU i, 1	doubtful
2	XVI:5	Divertimento, A	-1763 [?c1750-55]	H 1803	HU i, 6; WU 8	doubtful; 1st pubd with added vn pt. and erroneously attrib. Pleyel
3	XVI:12	Divertimento, A	-1767 [?c1750-55]	H 1803	HU i, 14; WU 12	? I doubtful; see above remark
4	XVI:13	Parthia (Divertimento), E	-1767 [-?1760]	? H 1803	HU i, 19; WU 15	Haydn's statements in 1803 concerning his authorship were contradictory; for 1st pubn see remark for no.2
5	XVI:2	Partita (Parthia), Bb	[-?1760]		HU i, 44; WU 11	
6	XVI:Es2 Add.	Parthia, Eb	[?c1755]		HU i, 53; WU 17	doubtful
7	XVI:Es3 Add.	Parthia, Eb	[?c1764]		HU i, 60, 187; WU 18	doubtful; also attrib. otherwise unknown Mariano Romano Kayser
8	XVI:1	Partita (Divertimento), C	[?c1750-55]		HU i, 68; WU 10	
9	XVI:7	Partita (Parthia, Divertimento), C	-1766 [-?1760]	H 1803	HU i, 74; WU 2	
10	XVI:8	Parthia (Divertimento), G	-1766 [-?1760]	H 1803	HU i, 77; WU 1	

No.	H	Title, key	Date	Authentication	Edition	Remarks
11	XVI:9	Divertimento, F	−1766 [−?1760]	H 1803	HU i, 80; WU 3	see Divertimento U 8
12	XVI:10	Divertimento, C	−1767 [−?1760]	H 1803	HU i, 84; WU 6	for 1st pubn see remark for no.2
13a	XVI:G1	Divertimento, G	[−?1760]	—	HU i, 90; WU 4	
13b	XVI:11	Divertimento, G	?	H 1803	WU 5	?later combination of III of no.13a and 2 other movts; see appx X.1, 1–2
14	XVII: D1	Variazione, D	?	—	HU i, 94; WU 7	3 movts: variations, minuet, finale

Appendix W.2: Selected spurious works

No.	H	Title, key	Date	Edition	Remarks
1	XVI:15	Sonata, C	−1785	M xiv/1, 80	arr. of Divertimento N 14; spurious though in Breitkopf & Härtel's Oeuvres de Haydn; also with added vn pt.
2	XVI:17	Sonata, Bb	−1768	M xiv/1, 91	probably by J. G. Schwanenberger though authenticated by Haydn c1799–1803 according to Pohl
3	XVI:C1	Sonata, C	?	—	4 apparently heterogeneous movts
4	XVI:C2 Add.	Sonata, C	?	—	1 movt only
5	XVI:D1	Sonata militare (The conquest of Oczakow), D	17 Dec 1788– 11 April 1789	Mw, xxxvi (1970), 53	by Kauer
6	i, 731	Sonata, Eb	−1789	(London, 1789)	with vn ad lib
7	XVI:BI	Sonata, Bb	?	(Paris, before 1800)	
8	XVII:G2	Caprices (Fantasie et variations), G	?	(Wolfenbüttel, 1934)	by Hoffmeister
9–11	i, 733	[3] Göttweiger Sonaten, C, A, D	?	(London, 1964)	?19th-century forgery
12	—	Children's Concerto (Concerto de bébé), C	−?1876		

X: MISCELLANEOUS KEYBOARD WORKS

Editions: J. Haydn: Klavierstücke, ed. S. Gerlach (Munich, 1969) [HU]
J. Haydn: Klavierstücke, ed. F. Eibner and G. Jarecki (Vienna, 1975) [WU]

No.	H	Title, key	Instrument	Date	Authentication	Edition	Remarks
1	XVII:1	Capriccio: Acht Sauschneider müssen sein, G	hpd	1765	A	HU, 5; WU, 1	
2	XVII:2	20 Variazioni, A	hpd	-1771 [?c1765]	EK	HU, 16; WU, 22 (in G)	first pubd 1788/9 as Arietta con 12 variazioni (WU, 41)
3	XVII:3	12 Variations, E♭	hpd	-1774 [c1770–74]	HV	HU, 28; WU, 33	theme arr. from minuet of str qt O 14; first pubd 1788/9 as Arietta con 12 variazioni
4	XVII:4	Fantasia (Capriccio), C	pf	[-?29 March] 1789	OE, HV	HU, 37; WU, 12	
5	XVII:5	6 Variations, C	pf	-9 Feb 1791 (?Nov 1790)	OE, HV	HU, 48; WU, 48	
6	XVII:6	Sonata (Un piccolo divertimento; Variations), f	pf	1793	A	HU, 54; WU, 53	
7	XXXIc:17b	(Untitled piece), D	(pf)	[?1791–5]	A (u)	HW xxix/1, 97	written with song G 52; ? country dance
8	XVIIa:1	Divertimento (Il maestro e lo scolare), F	hpd (4 hands)	-1778 [?c1768–70]	EK	WU, 78	

Note: for further works see pf trio V 20 (WU, 70) and pf sonata W 46

Appendix X.1: Selected works attributed to Haydn

No.	H	Title, key	Instrument	Date	Authentication	Edition	Remarks
1	XVI:11 "	Andante, g	hpd	[?c1755]	—	HW xviii/1, 181	extant as II of sonata appx W.1, 13b
2	XVI:11 "'	Minuet, G, Trio, c	hpd	[?c1755]	—	HW xviii/1, 182	extant as III of appx W.1, 13b; ?trio doubtful; cf Q 26
3	XVII:D2 Add.	Allegro molto, D	hpd	[-?1765]	—	HW xviii/1, 184	frag.;?finale of sonata; extant in one MS copy only as introduction to no.4, acc. vn. b; see appx V. 2, 6
4	XVII:7*	5 Variations, D	hpd	-1766 [?c1750–55]	H 1803	HU, 65	
5	IX:26	Minuetto, F♯	pf	-1785	—	HW xviii/1, 186	?movt of pf sonata

No.	H	Title, key	Date	Authentication	Edition	Remarks
6	XVII:9*	Adagio, F	hpd/pf	–1786	Sk	HU, 68; WU, 69	authentic; sketch in PL–Kj
7	—	Variationes, C	hpd/pf	?	—	—	variations on theme of aria, appx F.1, 4; orig. without author's name; see Schmid (1970); cf also appx Y.4, 1; probably spurious
8	XVII:11*	Andante, C	hpd	–1807	—	(?Vienna, 1807)	not verified
9	XVII:12*	Andante con variazioni, B♭	pf	–1807	—	(Bryn Mawr, 1974)	probably spurious
10	XVIIa:2	Partita, F	hpd (4 hands)	[?c1768–70]	—	(Bryn Mawr, 1956)	
11–13	XVII:C2	3 Praeambula, C, C, G	org	?	—	(Hilversum, 1979)	doubtful
14	XVII:F2	Andante, F	org	?	—	(Hilversum, 1979)	Probably spurious

Note: more works, probably spurious, listed in hXVII as C1 etc

Appendix X.2: Arrangements

No.	H	Title, key	Date	Authentication	Edition	Remarks
1	IX:3	[12] Menuetti (with 4 Trios)	[c1763–7]	A (u)	(Vienna, 1935) (nos.5, 8, 7 only)	see L 2; cf appx X. 3, 10
2	i, 799	Allegretto, G	1781–6	A (u)	HW xii/3, 189; WU, 76	arr. of finale of O 29
3	IX:8	XII Menuets (with 5 Trios)	–9 April 1785	—	(Wilhelmshaven, n.d.)	trio of minuet no.11 doubtful; cf L 10
4	IX:11	[12] Menuetti di ballo (12 neue Redout Menuette) (with 11 Trios)	–22 Dec 1792	E	(Zurich, 1941)	arr. on request of the empress; cf L 18
5	IX:12	XII neue deutsche Tänze (with Trio and Coda)	–22 Dec 1792	A (u)	(Mainz, 1937)	see L 19 and previous remark
6	—	(Largo assai), E	c1793	A (u frag.)	HW, xii/5, 223	arr. of II of O 59; only frags. extant
7	VIII:2	March, C	c1795	A (u)	—	see L 22, March in C; edn. in Landon: Haydn (1972), 81, not Haydn's arr.
8	i, 430	Variations sur le thème Gott erhalte den Kaiser, G	1797–9	A (u)	WU, 64	arr. of II of O 62; later erroneously attrib. J. Gelinek

Note: arrs. of Loudon sym. (J 69) and the Seven last Words (K 11) not made but rev. Haydn; MS arr. of sym. J 96 described in IMSCR, vii Cologne 1958, 197, not autograph; authenticity of many printed arrs. not verified

Appendix X.3: Selected doubtful and spurious arrangements

No.	H	Title, key	Date	Edition	Remarks
1	IX:9a	6 Minuetti	–Aug 1787	—	lost or unidentified: ? = L 11
2	XVI:Es1	Sonata (Terzetto; Die Belagerung Belgrads), Eb	c1789–93	—	arr. (?by P. Polzelli) of terzetto F 15c
3	IX:13	12 deutsche Tänze (with 5 Trios, Coda) aus dem k.k. Redouten Saale	1792 or later	—	first 2 pages of MS copy by J. Schellinger
4	IX:10	XII deutsche Tänze	–1793	(Mainz, 1937)	arrs. of melodies from opera L'arbore di Diana by Martin y Soler; probably = appx L 6
5	XVII:10*	Allegretto, G	–1794	WU, 74	
6	IX:31 Add.	The Princess of Wales's Favorite Dance (Country Dance)	?1795	MT, cii (1961), 693	arr. of piece for flute-clock (Y 11)
7	IX:28	[8] Zingarese	–1799	Strache xxvi (Vienna, 1930), 9	
8	IX:27	Ochsenmenuett (Menuet du boeuf)	c1805	(Mainz, n.d.)	taken from or gave rise to the following stage works: (?lost) vaudeville Le menuet du boeuf, ou Une leçon d'Haydn, 1805, by J. B. Constantin; (?lost) vaudeville Haydn, ou Le menuet de boeuf, 1812, by J. J. Gabriel and A. J. M. Wafflard; pasticcio Die Ochsenmenuett, 1823, see appx E 6
9a	i, 794	Variations, A	?	—	one of 3 different arrs. of variations in Q 2c
9b	XVII:8*	Variations, D	?	—	see remark for no.9a
9c	i, 794	Variations, C	?	—	see remark for no.9a; differs widely from orig.
10	IX:20; XVII:F1	[18] Menuetti (with 7 Trios, Aria)	?	Strache xxvii (Vienna, 1930), 10; H XVII:F1 in HW xviii/1, 186	no.2 from appx X.2, 1, no.10; no.18 from sonata W 2; aria ? from lost early sonata
11	IX:21	[12] Menuets (with 5 Trios) de la redoute	?	—	
12	IX:22	Ballo tedescho (10 deutsche Tänze)	?	(Zurich, n.d.)	listed in H as minuets
13	IX:29; IX:24	[5] Contredanze (Contredanse) (with Quadrille, Minuet)	?	Strache xxvi (Vienna, 1930), 5	
14	IX:30	Englischer Tanz	?	—	
15	i, 580	[3] Minuetti	?	Strache xxvii (Vienna, 1930), 5	from pf trios: appx V.1, 4, 8, 3
16	—	Fantaisie pour l'orchestre, d	?	(Paris, 1855)	arr. pf, 4 hands, by E. T. Eckhardt; see Mies (1962)

No.	H	Title, key	Date	Edition	Remarks
17	IX:4a Add.	6 Minuetti (with 6 Trios)	–?1770	—	arr. of Mozart K 61f

Y: WORKS FOR FLUTE-CLOCK

Edition: *J. Haydn. Werke für das Laufwerk (Flötenuhr)*, ed. E. F. Schmid (Kassel, 1954) [S]

(dates based on research by S. Gerlach)

No.	HXIX	Title, key	Date	Authentication	No.: year of clock	Edition	Remarks
1	17	C	–1792 [?c1789]	A (u)	I: 1792	S 1	
2	10	Andante, C	–1792 [?c1789]	A (u)	I: 1792	S 2	
3	18	Presto, C	–1792 [?c1789]	A (u)	I: 1792	S 3	
4	16	Fuga, C	1789	A	III: ?1796 (not 1772)	S 24	
		rev. version	?1793	—	II: 1793	—	
5	11	C	–1793 [?1789]	A	III: ?1796 (not 1772)	S 19	
		rev. version	?1793	E (without author's name)	II: 1793	—	
6	12	Andante, C	–1793 [?1789]	A	III: ?1796 (not 1772)	S 20	
		rev. version	?1793	E (without author's name)	II: 1793	—	
7	13	C (?orig. version)	?1789		III: ?1796 (not 1772)	—	
		?rev. version	?1789	E (without author's name)	II: 1793	S 21	
8	14	C (?orig. version)	?1789		III: ?1796 (not 1772)	—	
		?rev. version	?1793	E (without author's name)	II: 1793	S 22	
9	15	C (?orig. version)	?1789		III: ?1796 (not 1772)	—	
		?rev. version	?1793	E (without author's name)	II: 1793	S 23	
10	31	Presto, C	–?1794/5 [?1789]	A		S 31	
11	27	Allegretto, G	?1793	A (u)	II: 1793	S 27	cf appx X.3, 5

Appendix Y.1: Adaptations for flute-clock

No.	HXIX	Title, key	Date	Authenti-cation	No.: year of clock	Edition	Remarks
1	9	Menuet, C	1788–92 [?c1789]	A (u)	I: 1792	S 11	uses III of O 42
2	28	Allegro, C	[1793]	A (u)	II: 1793	S 28	adapted from IV of O 55

No.	HXIX	Title, key			No.: year of clock	Edition	Remarks
3	29	C	[1793]	A (u)	II: 1793	S 29	adapted from III of J 101
4	30	Presto, G	1790–93 [?1793]	A (u)	II: 1793	S 30	adapted from IV of O 53
5	32	Allegro, F	1793 or later	A (u)	—	S 32	adapted from IV of J 99; Haydn specially sketched the scale to be used, A-Wgm

Appendix Y.2: Doubtful works

No.	HXIX	Title, key	No.: year of clock	Edition	Remarks
1	24	Presto, C	I: 1792	S 12	MS copy without author's name
2	21	G	I: 1792	S 7	no written source known
3	7	C	I: 1792	S 8	no written source known
4	8	C	I: 1792	S 6	no written source known
5	2	F	III: ?1796 (not 1772)	S 14	no written source known

Appendix Y.3: Doubtful adaptations

No.	HXIX	Title, key	No.: year of clock	Edition	Remarks
1	19	C	I: 1792	S 4	adapted from G 13; no written source known
2	20	C	I: 1792	S 5	uses III of J 85; no written source known
3	25	Marche, D	II: 1793	S 25	adapted from L 15
4	1	F	III: ?1796 (not 1772)	S 13	uses aria no.4 in E 17; no written source known
5	3	F	III: ?1796 (not 1772)	S 15	uses II of J 53; no written source known
6	5	F	III: ?1796 (not 1772)	S 17	adapted from III of Q 82; no written source known
7	6	F	III: ?1796 (not 1772)	S 18	adapted from III of Q 76; no written source known

Appendix Y.4: Spurious arrangements

No.	HXIX	Title, key	No.: year of clock	Edition	Remarks
1	22	C	I: 1792	S 9	aria by unidentified author (see appx F.1, 4); no written source known
2	23	C	I: 1792	S 10	from IV of HI-C6, sym. by Dittersdorf; no written source known
3	26	Andante, Allegro, E	II: 1793	S 26	Allegro: Aria alla polacca by J. Schuster; see E 26
4	4	C	III: ?1796 (not 1772)	S 16	Air or Dance russe by Giornovichi in Das Waldmädchen, ballet by P. Wranitzky and J. Kinsky (1796); originally Russian folk-song 'Kamarinskaja', see Beethoven, WoO 71; no written source known

3. FOLKSONG ARRANGEMENTS

Z. ARRANGEMENTS OF BRITISH FOLKSONGS

Editions: *A Selection of Original Scots Songs*, compiled W. Napier, ii–iii (London, 1792–5) [N]
A Select Collection of Original Scottish Airs, compiled G. Thomson, i–iv (London and Edinburgh, 1802–5); v (London and Edinburgh, 1818); suppl. to v as *25 Additional Scottish Airs* (Edinburgh, 1826) [TT]
The Select Melodies of Scotland, compiled G. Thomson, i, ii, v (London and Edinburgh, 1822); vi as *Thomson's Collection ... united to the Select Melodies of Scotland ... Ireland and Wales* (London and Edinburgh, 1824); suppl. as *20 Scottish Melodies* (Edinburgh, 1839) [TS]
A Select Collection of Original Welsh Airs, compiled G. Thomson, i–iii (London and Edinburgh, 1809–17) [TW]
A Select Collection of Original Irish Airs, compiled G. Thomson (London and Edinburgh, 1814) [TI]
A Collection of Scottish Airs, compiled W. Whyte, i–ii (Edinburgh, 1804–7) [W]

(for 1v unless otherwise stated; HXXXIa = Scottish, b = Welsh; key sometimes uncertain; dates based on research by I. Becker-Glauch)

No.	HXXXI	Tune/Title, key	Accompaniment	Date	Authentication	Edition (no. = no. of piece except in HW)
		Adieu to Llangollen, see Happiness lost				
1	a:131	Ae fond kiss, e (?Celtic air)	vn, bc	1795	HV	N iii, 31
		Age & youth, see What can a young lassie do				
		Aileen a roon, see Robin Adair				
		Alas! Yat I came o'er the moor, see Last time I came o'er the muir				
2	b:48	Allurement of love, The, D	vn, vc, pf	1804	HV	—
		Anna, see Shepherds, I have lost by love				
		Answer, The, see My mither's ay glowran				
3	a:164	An thou wert mine ain thing, A	vn, vc, pf	1800	SC, HV	T iii, 20
4	a:164bis	An thou wert mine ain thing, A	vn, vc, pf	?1804	HV	W ii, 49
		An ye had been where I hae been, see Killicrankie				
		Argyll is my name, see Bannocks o' barley meal				
5	b:9	Ar hyd y nos, A (duet)	vn, vc, pf	1803	HV	TW i, 12
6	b:55	Aria di guerra e vittoria, D	vn, vc, pf	1804	HV	—
7	a:114	As I cam down by yon castle wa', e	vn, bc	1795	HV	N iii, 14
		As I came o'er the Cairney mount, see Old highland laddie				
		As Sylvia in a forest lay, see Maid's complaint				
8	a:184	Auld gudeman, The, Bb	vn, vc, pf (hpd)	1801	A (u), HV	T iii, 47
9	a:218	Auld lang syne, F	vn, vc, pf	1802/3	HV	W i, 24
10	a:168	Auld Robin Gray, D	vn, vc, hpd	1800	HV	T iii, 26
11	a:192	Auld Rob Morris, Eb (duet)	vn, vc, hpd	1801	A (2nd version of coda only, u), HV	T i, 17
12	a:195	Auld wife ayont the fire, The, Eb	vn, vc, pf	1801	A (u)	T i, 39

No.	hXXXI	Tune/Title, key	Accompaniment	Date	Authentication	Edition (no. = no. of piece except in HW)
47	a: 172	Bonny Jean, D	vn, vc, pf	1800	HV	T iii, 31
		Bonny Jean, see Willie was a wanton wag				
48	a:94	Bonny Kate of Edinburgh, G	vn, bc	~1792	HV	N ii, 94; HW xxxii/1, 98
		Bonny, roaring Willie, see Rattling roaring Willy				
		Bonny Scot-man, The, see Boatman				
49	a:200	Braes of Ballenden, The, G	vn, vc, pf	1801	HV	T ii, 84
50	a:200bis	Braes of Ballenden, The, G	vn, vc, pf	1802/3	A (u)	W i, 27
51	a:207	Braes of Yarrow, The, A	vn, vc, pf	1802/3	A (u)	W i, 5
		Braw lads of Galla water, see Galla water				
		Bridegroom greets when the sun gangs down, The, see Auld Robin Gray				
		Bride's song, The, see Blithsome bridal				
52	a:46	Brisk young lad, The, g	vn, bc	~1792	HV	N ii, 46; HW xxxii/1, 49
53	a:46bis	Brisk young lad, The, e	vn, vc, hpd	1801	HV	T iv, 191
54	b:51	Britons, The, c	vn, vc, pf	1804	HV	
55	a:170	Broom of Cowdenknows, The, Eb (with chorus 2vv)	vn, vc, hpd	1800	HV	T iii, 28
		Broom, the bonny broom, see Broom of Cowdenknows				
56	a:204	Bush aboon Traquair, The, Bb (duet)	vn, vc, pf	1802/3	—	W i, 2
		Busk ye, busk ye, see Braes of Yarrow				
		Butcher boy, The, see My Goddess woman				
		By the stream so cool and clear, see St Kilda song				
		Captain Cook's death, see Highland Mary				
57	a:224	Captain O'Kain, e (?Irish air)	vn, vc, pf	?1802/3	HV	W i, 37
		Captain's lady, The, see Mount your baggage				
		Carron side, see Frae the friends and land I love				
58	b:26	Castell Towyn, Eb	vn, vc, pf	1803	HV	TW ii, 38
		Cauld frosty morning, see Cold frosty morning				
59	a:55	Cauld kail in Aberdeen, D	vn, bc	~1792	HV	N ii, 55; HW xxxii/1, 58
60	a:55bis	Cauld kail in Aberdeen, D (duet)	vn, vc, pf	1801	A (u)	T i, 31
		Caun du delish, see Oran gaoil				
61	b:39	Cerdd yr hen-wr or coed, F (duet)	vn, vc, pf	1804	HV	TW iii, 67
		Charming highlandman, The, see Lewie Gordon				
62	b:12	Codiad yr haul, Bb (duet)	vn, vc, pf	1803	HV	TW i, 17
63	b:1	Codiad yr hedydd, Bb	vn, vc, pf	1803	HV	TW i, 1
64	a:107	Cold frosty morning, A, F	vn, bc	1795	HV	N iii, 7
		Collier's [bonnie] dochter, The, see Collier's bonny lassie				
65	a:213	Collier's bonny lassie, The, F	vn, vc, pf	?1802/3	HV	W i, 14
		Collier's lass, The, see Collier's bonny lassie				
66	a:97	Colonel Gardner, Bb	vn, bc	~1792	HV	N ii, 97; HW xxxii/1, 100

Come kiss wi' me, come clap wi' me, see Now westlin winds
Comin thro' the rye, see If a body meet a body
Comin thro' the rye, see Auld lang syne

67	b:21	Cornish may song, The, E♭	vn, vc, pf	1803	HV	TW ii, 31
68	a:216	Corn riggs, A (duet)	vn, vc, pf	1802/3	—	Wi, 20
69	a:144	Cornwallis's lament, see Sensibility				
69	a:144	Country lassie, A, D	vn, bc	1795	HV	N iii, 44
70	a:193	Cragieburn Wood, D	vn, vc, pf	1801	A (u)	T i, 32
		Crooked horn ewe, The, see Ewie wi' the crooked horn				
		Cuckoo, The [The cuckoo's nest], see I do confess thou art sae fair				
71	a:47	Cumbernauld House, E♭	vn, bc	–1792	HV	N ii, 47; HW xxxii/1, 50
72	b:4	Dafydd y Garreg-Wen, g	vn, vc, pf	1804	HV	TW i, 6
73	a:32	Dainty Davie, D	vn, bc	–1792	A (u, frag.); HV	N ii, 32; HW xxxii/1, 33
74	a:259	Day returns, The, E♭ (duet)	vn, vc, pf	?1804	HV	W ii, 47
75	a:136	Dear Silvia, E♭	vn, bc	1795	HV	N iii, 36
76	a:138	Death of the linnet, The, E♭	vn, bc	1795	HV	N iii, 38
77	a:138bis	Death of the linnet, The, D (duet)	vn, vc, hpd	1801	A (2nd version of coda only, u), HV	T iii, 39
		Deil's awa wi' the exciseman, The, see Looking glass				
78	a:229	Deil tak the wars, B♭	vn, vc, pf	1801	HV	T iv, 157
79	b:59	Departure of the king, The, e	vn, vc, pf	1804	HV	—
80	b:34	Digan y pibydd coch, c (2 versions)	vn, vc, pf	1803	HV	TW ii, 56
81	a:217	Donald, B♭ (?Irish air)	vn, vc, pf	?1802/3	HV	W i, 21
82	a:139	Donald and Flora, D	vn, bc	1795	HV	N iii, 39
83	a:139bis	Donald and Flora, E♭	vn, vc, pf	1802/3	—	W i, 15
		Donocht Head, see The minstrel				
84	b:50	Door clapper, The, G (duet)	vn, vc, pf	1804	HV	—
85	b:14	Dowch i'r frwydr, B♭ (duet)	vn, vc, pf	1803	HV	TW i, 19
86	a:152	Down the burn, Davie, F (duet)	vn, vc, hpd	1800	HV	T iii, 3
		Drunken wife o' Galloway, The, see Hooly and fairly				
87	a:26	Duncan Davison, C	vn, bc	–1792	HV	N ii, 26; HW xxxii/1, 27
88	a:34	Duncan Gray, G	vn, bc	–1792	HV	N ii, 34; HW xxxii/1, 35
		Dutchess of Buccleugh's reel, see The sutor's daughter				
		Earl Douglas's lament, see Lady Randolph's complaint				
89	a:234	East Neuk o' Fife, The, F	vn, vc, pf	1801	HV	T iv, 165
		Eire a ruin, see Robin Adair				
90	a:74	Eppie Adair, e	vn, bc	–1792	HV	N ii, 74; HW xxxii/1, 78
91	b:27	Erddigan caer y waun, G	vn, vc, pf	1803	HV	TW ii, 39
92	a:203bis	Erin-go-bragh, C	vn, vc, pf	?1802/3	HV	W i, 16
93	b:20	Eryri wen, b	vn, vc, pf	1804	HV	TW i, 28
		Ettrick banks, see On Ettrick banks				
94	a:188	Ewe-bughts, The, d	vn, vc, pf	1801	HV	T i, 8
95	a:116	Ewie wi' the crooked horn, The, F	vn, bc	1795	HV	N iii, 16

No.	HXXXI	Tune/Title, key	Accompaniment	Date	Authentication	Edition (no. = no. of piece except in HW')
96	a:116bis	Ewie wi' the crooked horn, The, G	vn, vc, hpd	1800	HV	T iii, 6
		Exile of Erin, The, see Erin-go-bragh				
		Failte na miosg, see My heart's in the highlands				
97	a:117	Fair Eliza, e (Gaelic air)	vn, bc	1795	HV	N iii, 17
98	a:236	Fair Helen of Kirkconnell, B♭	vn, vc, pf	1804	HV	T iv, 168
		Fairwell, thou fair day, see My lodging is on the cold ground				
99	a:156	Fee him, father, F	vn, vc, pf	1800	HV	T iii, 10
100	b:13	Ffarwel Ffranses, E♭	vn, vc, pf	1804	HV	TW i, 18
101	b:40	Ffarwel jeuengetid, E♭	vn, vc, pf	1804	HV	TW iii, 74
102	a:29	Fife and a' the lands about it, D	vn, bc	-1792	HV	N ii, 29; HW xxxii/1, 30
103	b:58	Flower of north Wales, The, C	vn, vc, pf	1804	HV	—
104	a:90	Flowers of Edinburgh, The, E♭	vn, bc	-1792	HV	N ii, 90; HW xxxii/1, 94
105	a:90bis	Flowers of Edinburgh, The, F	vn, vc, pf	1801	HV	—
106	a:212	Flowers of the forest, The, B♭	vn, vc, pf	?1802/3	HV	W i, 13
107	a:222	For the lack of gold, B♭	vn, vc, pf	?1802/3	HV	W i, 34
		14th of October, see Ye Gods!				
108	a:105	Frae the friends and land I love, E♭	vn, bc	1795	HV	N iii, 5
109	a:7	Fy! gar rub her o'er wi' strae, e	vn, bc	-1792	HV	N ii, 7; HW xxxii/1, 7
110	a:7bis	Fy! gar rub her o'er wi' strae, e (duet)	vn, vc, pf	1801	A (2nd version of introduction only, u), HV	T ii, 53
		Ey, let us a' to the bridal [wedding], see Blithsome bridal				
		Gaberlunzie (Gaberlunyie) man, The, see Brisk young lad				
111	a:179	Galashiels, E♭	vn, vc, hpd	1800	HV	T iii, 41
112	a:15	Galla water, D	vn, bc	-1792	HV	N ii, 15; HW xxxii/1, 15
113	a:15bis	Galla water, D	vn, vc, pf	?1802/3	HV	W i, 30
114	a:15ter	Galla water, D	vn, vc, pf	1803	HV	—
		Gardener's march, The, see Gard'ner wi' his paidle				
115	a:45	Gard'ner wi' his paidle, The, A	vn, bc	-1792	HV	N ii, 45; HW xxxii/1,48
		Gentle swain, The, see Johnny's gray breeks				
116	a:225	Gilderoy, g (duet)	vn, vc, pf	?1802/3	HV	W i, 39
117	a:196	Gil Morris [Morrice], E♭	vn, vc, hpd	1801	HV	T i, 45
		Gin you meet a bonny lassie, see Fy! gar rub her o'er wi' strae				
118	a:88	Glancing of her apron, The, D	vn, bc	-1792	HV	N ii, 88; HW xxxii/1, 92
		Gordons has [had] the guiding o't, The, see Strephon and Lydia				
119	b:2	Gorhoffedd gwyr Harlech, G	vn, vc, pf	1803	HV	TW i, 2
		Go to the ew-bughts, Marion, see Ewe-bughts				
120	a:13	Gramachree, E♭(Irish air)	vn, bc	-1792	HV	N ii, 13; HW xxxii/1, 13
121	a:13bis	Gramachree, D (Irish air)	vn, vc, pf	1801	HV	T i, 18

No.	hXXXI	Tune/Title, key	Accompaniment	Date	Authentication	Edition (no. = no. of piece except in HW)
149	a:80	If a body meet a body, G	vn, bc	–1792	HV	N ii, 80; HW xxxii/1, 84
150	a:80bis	If a body meet a body, G	vn, vc, pf	1801	HV	T iii, 23
151	a:95	If e'er ye do well it's a wonder, D	vn, bc	–1792	HV	N ii, 95; HW xxxii/1, 99
152	a:17	I had a horse, b	vn, bc	–1792	HV	N ii, 17; HW xxxii/1, 17
153	a:17bis	I had a horse, c	vn, vc, pf	?1804	HV	W ii, 50
154	a:205	I'll never leave thee, D	vn, vc, pf	1802/3	—	W i, 3
155	a:3	I love my love in secret, G	vn, bc	–1792	HV	N ii, 3; HW xxxii/1, 3
156	a:30	I'm o'er young to marry yet, B♭	vn, bc	–1792	HV	N ii, 30; HW xxxii/1, 31
157	a:177	I wish my love were in a myre, B♭	vn, vc, hpd	1800	HV	T iii, 37
158	a:231	Jacobite air, A, B♭ (duet)	vn, vc, pf	1801	HV	T iv, 160
159	a:79	Jamie, come try me, D	vn, bc	–1792	HV	N ii, 79; HW xxxii/1, 83
160	a:132	Jenny drinks nae water, B♭	vn, bc	1795	HV	N iii, 32
161	a:252	Jenny's bawbie, G	vn, vc, pf (hpd)	1801	A (u)	T iv, 197
		Jenny's lamentation, see Jockie and Sandy				
162	a:99	Jenny was fair, E♭	vn, bc	–1792	HV	N ii, 99; HW xxxii/1, 102
163	a:263	Jingling Jonnie, F	vn, vc, pf	1801	HV	T ii (1817), 79 (in E♭)
		Jockey was the blythest lad, see Young Jockey				
164	a:91	Jockie and Sandy, G	vn, bc	–1792	HV	N ii, 91; HW xxxii/1, 95
		Jock the laird's brither, see Auld Rob Morris				
165	a:2	John Anderson, my jo, g	vn, bc	–1792	HV	N ii, 2; HW xxxii/1, 2
166	a:2bis	John Anderson, my jo, g	vn, vc, pf	?1802/3	HV	W i, 26
167	a:41	John, come kiss me now. E♭	vn, bc	–1792	HV	N ii, 41; HW xxxii/1, 44
168	a:109	Johnie Armstrong, G	vn, bc	1795	HV	N iii, 9
169	a:154	Johnny's gray breeks, B♭/g	vn, vc, pf	1800	HV	T iii, 8
170	a:24	John of Badenyon, g	vn, bc	–1792	HV	N ii, 24; HW xxxii/1, 24
171	a:24bis	John of Badenyon, g	vn, vc, pf	1801	HV	T iv, 184
		Joyful widower, The, see Maggy Lauder				
172	a:220	Katherine Ogie, g	vn, vc, pf	1802/3	—	W i, 31
		Katy's answer, see My mither's ay glowran				
173	a:148	Kellyburn braes, E♭	vn, bc	1795	HV	N iii, 48
174	a:148bis	Kellyburn braes, D	vn, vc, hpd	1801	HV	T iv, 182
175	a:169	Killicrankie, C (cf H 25)	vn, vc, hpd	1801	HV	T iii, 27
		Kind Robin loves me, see Robin, quo' she				
		King James' march to Ireland, see Lochaber				
		Kirk wad let me be, The, see Blithsome bridal				
		Lads of Leith, The, see She's fair and fause				
		Lady Badinscoth's reel, see My love she's but a lassie yet				
176	b:45	Lady Owen's delight [favourite], F	vn, vc, pf	1803	HV	—
177	a:127	Lady Randolph's complaint, G	vn, bc	1795	HV	N iii, 27

		Title	Instr.	Date	HV	References
		Laird and Edinburgh Kate, The, see My mither's ay glowran				
178	b:43a	Lamentation of Britain, The, g (duet)	vn, vc, pf	1803	HV	—
179	b:43b	Lamentation of Cambria, The, g (duet)	vn, vc, pf	?1804	—	—
180	a:235	Langolee, G	vn, vc, pf	1801	HV	T iv, 167
181	b:57	La partenza dal paese e dalli amici, a	vn, vc, pf	1804	HV	—
		Lasses of the ferry, The, see Auld lang syne				
		Lass gin ye lo'e me, tell me now, see I canna come ilke day				
182	a:272	Lassie wi' the gowden hair, d	vn, vc, pf	1803	HV	N ii, 23; HW xxxii/1, 23
183	a:23	Lass of Livingston, The, c	vn, bc	-1792	HV	W i, 7
184	a:209	Lass of Lochroyan, The, a	vn, vc, pf	?1802/3	HV	T iii, 17
185	a:160	Lass of Patie's mill, The, C	vn, vc, pf	1800	HV	W ii, 43
186	a:160bis	Lass of Patie's mill, The, C (duet)	vn, vc, pf	?1804	HV	T ii, 80
187	a:199	Last time I came o'er the muir, The, D	vn, vc, pf	1801	A (u)	W i, 25
188	a:199bis	Last time I came o'er the muir, The, D	vn, vc, pf	1802/3	A (u)	N ii, 27; HW xxxii/1, 28
189	a:27	Leader haughs and yarrow, F	vn, bc	-1792	HV	N ii, 31; HW xxxii/1, 32
190	a:31	Lea-rig, The, F	vn, bc	-1792	HV	T iv, 195 (in G)
191	a:31bis	Lea-rig, The, F	vn, vc, hpd	1800	E (without author's name)	
192	a:31ter	Lea-rig, The, G	vn, vc, pf	?1802/3	HV	W i, 8
193	a:61	Let me in this ae night, d	vn, bc	-1792	HV	N ii, 61; HW xxxii/1, 64
194	a:61bis	Let me in this ae night, d	vn, vc, pf	1801	HV	T iv, 156
195	a:215	Lewie Gordon, G	vn, vc, pf	?1802/3	HV	W i, 19
196	a:83	Lizae Baillie, F	vn, bc	-1792	HV	N ii, 83; HW xxxii/1, 87
197	b:7	Llwyn Onn, G	vn, vc, pf	1803	HV	TW i, 10
198	a:190bis	Lochaber, F	vn, vc, pf	?1804	HV	W ii, 60
199	a:163	Logan water, g	vn, vc, pf	1800	HV	T iii, 16
200	a:73	Logie of Buchan, g/Bb	vn, bc	-1792	HV	N ii, 73; HW xxxii/1, 77
201	a:175	Lone vale, The, Bb (highland air)	vn, vc, hpd	1801	HV	T iii, 34
202	a:158	Looking glass, The, G	vn, vc, hpd	1801	HV	T iii, 13
		Loth to depart, see La partenza dal paese e dalli amici				
203	a:53	Love will find out the way, A	vn, bc	-1792	HV	N ii, 53; HW xxxii/1, 56
204	a:210	Low down in the broom, C	vn, vc, pf	1802/3	A (u)	W i, 11
		Lucky Nancy, see Dainty Davie				
205	a:182	Macpherson's farewell, A (with chorus, 2vv)	vn, vc, hpd	1801	HV	T iii, 44
		Madam Cossy, see Looking glass				
206	a:86	Maggie's tocher, e	vn, bc	-1792	HV	N ii, 86; HW xxxii/1, 90
207	a:35	Maggy Lauder, Bb	vn, bc	-1792	HV	N ii, 35; HW xxxii/1, 36
208	a:35bis	Maggy Lauder, A (cf H 24)	vn, vc, hpd	1800	HV	T iii, 25
209	a:35ter	Maggy Lauder, Bb	vn, vc, pf	?1804	HV	W ii, 64
		Maid in Bedlam, The, see Gramachree				
		Maid of Toro, The, see Captain O'Kain				
210	a:84	Maid's complaint, The, b	vn, bc	-1792	HV	N ii, 84; HW xxxii/1, 88
211	a:221	Maid that tends the goats, The, a	vn, vc, pf	?1802/3	HV	W i, 33

No.	hXXXI	Tune/Title, key	Accompaniment	Date	Authentication	Edition (no. = no. of piece except in HW)
212	a:221bis	Maid that tends the goats, The, a	vn, vc, pf	1801	HV	T iv, 166
213	b:36	Maltraeth, G	vn, vc, pf	1804	HV	TW ii, 58
214	b:5	Mantell Siani, G	vn, vc, pf	1803	HV	TW i, 8
215	a:65	Marg'ret's ghost, D	vn, bc	–1792	HV	N ii, 65; HW xxxii/1, 68
		Marg'ret's ghost, see William and Margaret				
216	b:49	Marsh of Rhuddlan, The, g	vn, vc, pf	1804	HV	—
217	a:1	Mary's dream, f♯	vn, bc	–1792	HV	N ii, 1; HW xxxii/1, 1
218	a:1bis	Mary's dream, f♯	vn, vc, hpd	1801	HV	T iii, 7
		McFarsence's testament, see Macpherson's farewell				
219	a:81	McGrigor of Rora's lament, C (Celtic air)	vn, bc	–1792	HV	N ii, 81; HW xxxii/1, 84
		McPherson's rant, see Macpherson's farewell				
220	b:6	Mentra Gwen, A (duet)	vn, vc, pf	1803	HV	TW i, 9
221	a:50	Merry may the maid be, d	vn, bc	–1792	HV	N ii, 50; HW xxxii/1, 53
222	a:50bis	Merry may the maid be, d (duet)	vn, vc, pf	?1804	HV	W ii, 56
		Miller, The, see Merry may the maid be				
		Miller's daughter, The, see If a body meet a body				
		Miller's wedding, The, see Auld lang syne				
223	a:92	Mill, mill O!, The, B♭	vn, bc	–1792	HV	N ii, 92; HW xxxii/1, 96
224	a:92bis	Mill, mill O!, The, B♭	vn, vc, pf	?1802/3	HV	W ii, 42
225	a:115	Minstrel, The, c	vn, bc	1795	HV	N iii, 15
226	a:115bis	Minstrel, The, b	vn, vc, hpd	1801	HV	T iv, 186
		Miss Admiral Gordon's strathspey, see Poet's ain Jean				
		Miss Farquharson's reel, see My love she's but a lassie yet				
		Miss Hamilton's delight, see My jo Janet				
227	a:143	Morag, d (Celtic air)	vn, bc	1795	HV	N iii, 43
228	a:143bis	Morag, c (Celtic air)	vn, vc, pf	1801	HV	—
		Moudiewart, The, see O, for ane-and-twenty Tam!				
229	a:42	Mount your baggage, C	vn, bc	–1792	HV	N ii, 42; HW xxxii/1, 45
230	a:51	Mucking of Geordie's byer, The, e	vn, bc	–1792	HV	N ii, 51; HW xxxii/1, 54
231	a:51bis	Mucking of Geordie's byer, The, e	vn, vc, pf	1801	—	T ii, 66
232	a:242	Muirland Willy, d (with chorus 2vv)	vn, vc, pf	1801	A (2nd version of introduction only, u), HV	T iv, 177
		Musket salute, The, see My heart's in the highlands				
233	b:31	Mwynen Cynwyd, E♭	vn, vc, pf	1804	HV	TW ii, 44
		My ain fireside, see Todlen hame				
		My ain kind deary, see Lea-rig				
234	a:189	My apron deary, G	vn, vc, pf	1801	A (u)	T i, 9
235	a:189bis	My apron deary, A	vn, vc, pf	?1802/3	HV	W i, 23

No.	HXXXI	Tune/Title, key	Accompaniment	Date	Authentication	Edition (no. = no. of piece except in HW')
		Oh, open the door, Lord Gregory, see Lass of Lochroyan				
263	a:248	Old highland laddie [lassie], The, D	vn, vc, pf	1801	HV	T iv, 189
		Old man, The, see My jo Janet				
		O let me in this ae night, see Let me in this ae night				
264	a:142	On a bank of flowers, c	vn, bc	1795	HV	N iii, 42
265	a:151	On Ettrick banks, D	vn, vc, hpd	1800	HV	T iii, 1
		On the death of Delia's linnet, see Death of the linnet				
266	a:249	Oonagh [Oonagh's waterfall], d (Irish air)	vn, vc, pf	1801	HV	T iv, 190
267	a:255	Open the door, Eb (?Irish air)	vn, vc, pf	?1804	HV	W ii, 41
		O poortith cauld, see I had a horse				
268	a:228	Oran gaoil, d (duet; Gallic air)	vn, vc, pf	1801	HV	T iv, 154
		O steer her up and had her gaun, see Steer her up				
		Palmer, The, see Open the door				
269	b:22	Pant corlant yr wyn: neu, Dafydd or Garreg-las, Bb (duet)	vn, vc, pf	1804	HV	TW ii, 33
270	a:241	Pat & Kate, Bb (duet; Irish air)	vn, vc, pf	1803	HV	T iv, 175
271	a:167	Peggy, I must love thee, G (duet)	vn, vc, hpd	1801	A (2nd version of coda only, u) HV	T iii, 24
272	a:96	Peggy in devotion, C	vn, bc	-1792	HV	N ii, 96; HW xxxii/1, 100
273	a:33	Pentland Hills, F	vn, bc	-1792	HV	N ii, 33; HW xxxii/1, 34
		Phely & Willy, see Jacobite air				
		Phoebe, see Yon wild mossy mountains				
274	a:183	Pinkie House, D	vn, vc, pf	1800	HV	T iii, 46
275	a:10	Ploughman, The, D	vn, bc	-1792	HV	N ii, 10; HW xxxii/1, 10
276	a:230	Poet's ain Jean, The, G	vn, vc, pf	1801	HV	T iv, 159
277	a:230bis	Poet's ain Jean, The, A (duet)	vn, vc, pf	?1804	HV	W ii, 66
278	a:265	Polwarth on the green, Bb (duet)	vn, vc, hpd	1801	HV	T v, 218
279	b:53	Poor pedlar, The, Bb	vn, vc, pf	1804	HV	—
280	a:113	Posie, The, c	vn, bc	1795	HV	N iii, 13
281	b:52	Pursuit of love, The, D	vn, vc, pf	1804	HV	—
282	a:161	Queen Mary's lamentation, Eb	vn, vc, pf	1800	HV	T iii, 18
		Ranting highlandman, The, see White cockade				
		Ranting, roving Willie, see Rattling roaring Willy				
283	a:227	Rattling roaring Willy, F	vn, vc, pf (hpd)	1801	A (u)	T iv, 153
		Raving winds, see McGrigor of Rora's lament				
284	b:38	Reged, G	vn, vc, pf	1804	HV	TW ii, 60
285	b:8	Rhyfelgyrch Cadpen Morgan, Bb	vn, vc, pf	1803	HV	TW i, 11
286	a:202	Robin Adair, C (duet; ?Irish air)	vn, vc, pf	1801	A (u)	T ii, 92

No.	HXXXI	Tune/Title, key	Accompaniment	Date	Authentication	Edition (no. = no. of piece except in HW')
		So for seven years, see Tho' for sev'n years				
318	a:60	Soger laddie, The, Eb	vn, bc	-1792	HV	N ii, 60; HW xxxii/1, 63
319	a:60bis	Soger laddie, The, Eb	vn, vc, pf	1801	HV	T iv, 172
		Soldier laddie, The, see Soger laddie				
		Soldier's dream, The, see Captain O'Kain				
		Soldier's return, The, see Mill, mill O!				
320	a:78	Steer her up, and had ger gawin, Bb	vn, bc	-1792	HV	N ii, 78; HW xxxii/1, 82
321	a:19	St Kilda song, F	vn, bc	-1792	HV	N ii, 19; HW xxxii/1, 19
322	a:145	Strathallan's lament, D	vn, bc	1795	HV	N iii, 45
323	a:145bis	Strathallan's lament, D	vn, vc, pf	1801	HV	T iv, 178
324	a:150	Strephon and Lydia, Eb	vn, bc	1795	HV	N iii, 50
		Sun had loos'd his weary team, The, see Looking glass				
325	a:198	Sutor's daughter, The, G (duet)	vn, vc, pf	1801	A (u)	T ii, 77
326	a:261	Sweet Annie, g	vn, vc, pf	?1802/3	HV	W ii, 62
327	b:44	Sweet melody of north Wales, The, Bb	vn, vc, pf	1803	HV	—
		Sweet's the lass that loves me, see Bess and her spinning wheel				
328	a:180	Tak' your auld cloak about ye, g	vn, vc, pf	1800	HV	T iii, 42
329	a:180bis	Tak' your auld cloak about ye, g	vn, vc, pf	?1804	HV	W ii, 57
		Tarry woo', see Lewie Gordon				
330	a:123	Tears I shed, The, e	vn, bc	1795	HV	N iii, 23
331	a:201	Tears of Caledonia, The, d	vn, vc, pf	1801	HV	T ii, 87
332	a:186	Tears that must ever fall, D	vn, vc, pf	1801	HV	T iii, 49
		Their groves o' sweet myrtle, see Humours o' glen				
333	a:14	This is no mine ain house, Bb	vn, bc	-1792	HV	N ii, 14; HW xxxii/1, 14
334	a:14bis	This is no mine ain house, Bb	vn, vc, pf	?1802/3	HV	W i, 38
335	a:146	Tho' for sev'n years and mair, F	vn, bc	1795	HV	N iii, 46
336	a:12	Thou'rt gane awa', A	vn, bc	-1792	HV	N ii, 12; HW xxxii/1, 12
337	a:12bis	Thou'rt gane awa', A	vn, vc, pf	?1802/3	HV	W i, 36
338	a:264	Three captains, The, Eb (Irish air)	vn, vc, pf	1803	HV	T iv (1817), 193
339	a:181	Thro' the wood, laddie, F	vn, vc, hpd	1800	HV	T iii, 43
340	a:52	Tibby Fowler, b	vn, bc	-1792	HV	N ii, 52; HW xxxii/1, 55
		'Tis woman, see Bonnie gray ey'd morn				
341	a:130	Tither morn, The, F	vn, bc	1795	HV	N iii, 30
342	a:98	To daunton me, d	vn, bc	-1792	HV	N ii, 98; HW xxxii/1, 102
343	a:6	Todlen hame, A	vn, bc	-1792	HV	N ii, 6; HW xxxii/1, 6
344	a:6bis	Todlen hame, A	vn, vc, pf	?1802/3	HV	W ii, 61
345	b:18	Ton y ceiliog du, Bb (duet)	vn, vc, pf	1804	HV	TW i, 24
346	b:3	Torriad y dydd, b	vn, vc, pf	1803	HV	TW i, 4
		To the rose bud, see Rose bud				

No.	Code	Title	Scoring	Date	Source	References
		Tranent Muir, see Killicrankie				
347	b:41	Troiad y droell, Bb (duet)	vn, vc, pf	1804	HV	TW iii, 75
348	b:17	Tros y garreg, g	vn, vc, pf	1804	HV	TW i, 23
349	a:206	Tweedside, G (duet)	vn, vc, pf	1802/3	A (u)	W i, 4
350	b:10	Twll yn ei boch, C	vn, vc, pf	1803	HV	TW i, 14
351	a:233	Up and war them a' Willy, F	vn, vc, pf	1801	HV	T iv, 163
352	a:28	Up in the morning early, g	vn, bc	-1792	HV	N ii, 28; HW xxxii/1, 29
353	a:28bis	Up in the morning early, g	vn, vc, pf	?1802/3	HV	W ii, 52
354	a:28ter	Up in the morning early, g	vn, vc, pf	1801	HV	—
355	a:133	Vain pursuit, The, C	vn, bc	1795	HV	N iii, 33
356	a:9·	Waefu' heart, The, F	vn, bc	-1792	HV	N ii, 9; HW xxxii/1, 9
357	a:9bis	Waefu' heart, The, F	vn, vc, pf	?1802/3	A (Sk), HV	W i, 10
358	a:214	Waly, waly, D	vn, vc, pf	1802/3	A (u)	W i, 18
359	a:214bis	Waly, waly, D (cf appx Z 30)	vn, vc, pf	1801	HV	—
		Wandering Willie, see Here awa'				
		Wap at the widow, my laddie, see Widow				
360	a:69	Wat ye wha I met yestreen?, Eb	vn, bc	-1792	HV	N ii, 69; HW xxxii/1, 73
361	a:69bis	Wat ye wha I met yestreen?, e	vn, vc, pf	1801	HV	T iv, 194a
362	a:40	Wawking of the fauld, The, D	vn, bc	-1792	HV	N ii, 40; HW xxxii/1, 42
363	a:129	Weary pund o' tow, The, G	vn, bc	1795	HV	N iii, 29
364	a:129bis	Weary pund o' tow, The, F	vn, vc, hpd	1801	HV	T iii, 4
365	a:124	Wee wee man, The, Eb	vn, bc	1795	HV	N iii, 24
366	a:124bis	Wee wee man, The, Eb	vn, vc, pf	1801	HV	T iii, 15
		Welcome home, old Rowley, see Thou'rt gane awa'				
367	a:244	What ails this heart of mine, g (duet)	vn, vc, pf	1804	SC, HV	T iv, 180
368	a:134	What can a young lassie do, b	vn, bc	1795	HV	N iii, 34
369	a:134bis	What can a young lassie do, b (with chorus 2vv)	vn, vc, pf	1801	HV	T iii, 45
		What shall I do with an auld man, see What can a young lassie do				
370	a:62	When she came ben she bobbit, e	vn, bc	-1792	HV	N ii, 62; HW xxxii/1, 65
		Where Helen lies, see Fair Helen of Kirkconnell				
371	a:104	While hopeless, e	vn, bc	1795	HV	N iii, 4
372	a:76	Whistle o'er the lave o't, F	vn, bc	-1792	HV	N ii, 76; HW xxxii/1, 80
373	a:76bis	Whistle o'er the lave o't, F	vn, vc, pf (hpd)	1801	A (u)	T iv, 169
374	a:22	White cockade, The, D	vn, bc	-1792	HV	N ii, 22; HW xxxii/1, 22
375	a:118	Widow, The, Eb	vn, bc	1795	HV	N iii, 18
376	a:75	Widow, are ye waking?, Eb	vn, bc	-1792	HV	N ii, 75; HW xxxii/1, 79
377	a:75bis	Widow, are ye waking?, Eb	vn, vc, pf	?1804	HV	W ii, 59
378	a:153	William and Margaret, g	vn, vc, hpd	1800	HV	T iii, 5
		Willie brew'd a peck o' maut, see Happy topers				
379	a:4	Willie was a wanton wag, C	vn, bc	-1792	HV	N ii, 4; HW xxxii/1, 4
380	a:4bis	Willie was a wanton wag, Bb	vn, vc, pf	1801	HV	T iv, 152
381	b:47	Willow hymn, The, d	vn, vc, pf	1803	HV	—
		Will ye go to Flanders, see Gramachree				

No.	hXXXI	Tune/Title, key	Accompaniment	Date	Authentication	Edition (no. = no. of piece except in HW)
382	a:82	Willy's rare, Bb	vn, bc	1792	HV	N ii, 82; HW xxxii/1, 86
		Wilt thou be my dearie, see Sutor's daughter				
383	b:46	Winifreda, Eb (duet)	vn, vc, pf	1803	HV	—
384	a:245	Wish, The, g	vn, vc, pf	1801	HV	T iv, 181
		Wo betyd thy wearie bodie, see Bonnie wee thing				
385	a:155	Woes my heart that we shou'd sunder, A (duet)	vn, vc, hpd	1800	HV	T iii, 9
		Women's work will never be done, see Black eagle				
386	a:38	Woo'd and married and a', d	vn, bc	−1792	HV	N ii, 38; HW xxxii/1, 40
387	a:38bis	Woo'd and married and a', d (with chorus, 2vv)	vn, vc, pf	1801	A (2nd version of coda only, u), HV	T iii, 50
388	b:19	Wyres Ned Puw, g	vn, vc, pf	1804	HV	TW i, 26
389	b:25	Y bardd yn ei awen, C	vn, vc, pf	1804	HV	TW ii, 36
390	b:32	Y Cymry dediwydd, Bb	vn, vc, pf	1804	HV	TW ii, 48
391	a:43	Ye Gods! was Strephon's picture blest, D	vn, bc	−1792	HV	N ii, 43; HW xxxii/1, 46
392	a:221	Yellow hair'd laddie, The, D (duet)	vn, vc, pf	1802/3	—	W i, 12
393	b:24	Y gadly's, c (duet)	vn, vc, pf	1803	HV	TW ii, 35
394	a:119	Yon wild mossy mountains, g	vn, bc	1795	HV	N iii, 19
395	a:71	Young Damon, Bb	vn, bc	−1792	HV	N ii, 71; HW xxxii/1, 75
		Young highland rover, The, see Morag				
396	a:64	Young Jockey was the blythest lad, a	vn, bc	1792	HV	N ii, 64; HW xxxii/1, 67
397	a:64bis	Young Jockey was the blythest lad, a	vn, vc, pf	1801	HV	TS suppl., 50
		Young laird and Edinburgh Katy, The, see Wat ye wha I met yestreen?				
		Young Peggy blooms, see Boatman				
398	b:37	Yr hen erddigan, c	vn, vc, pf	1803	HV	TW ii, 59

Note: 4 Scotch Songs, written in London, 1791–5 (Gr, Dies), lost or unidentified

Some settings of 1803 and later, doubtful: F. Kalkbrenner, during his stay with Haydn, 'was employed upon many of those popular Scottish airs, which are published by Mr. Thompson, of Edinburgh' (see 'Memoir of Mr. Frederick Kalkbrenner' in Walter (1982)

Appendix Z: Doubtful and spurious settings

No.	hXXXI	Tune/Title, key	Accompaniment	Date	Edition	Remarks
1	a:102quater	Bonnie wee thing, A	pf	?	TS vi, 22	arr. of Z 45 for 3vv ?by Haydn
2	a:232	Border widow's lament, The, A	vn, vc, pf	1803	T iv, 162	by Neukomm
3	a:226	Braes of Ballochmyle, The, Eb	vn, vc, pf	1803	T iv, 151	by Neukomm
4	a:224bis	Captain O'Kain, e (?Irish air)	vn, vc, pf	1803	—	by Neukomm
		Colin to Flora, see Rock and a wee pickle tow				
		Come under my plaidy, see Johny MacGill				
5	a:253A	Cro Challin, F	vn, vc, pf	1803	T iv, 198	by Neukomm
6	a:203	Erin-go-bragh, C	vn, vc, pf	1803	T ii, 98	by Neukomm
		Exile of Erin, The, see Erin-go-bragh				
		Get up and bar the door, see Rise up and bar the door				
		Good night, and God be with you, see Good night and joy be wi' ye a'				
7	a:254	Good night and joy be wi' ye a', G	vn, vc, pf	1803	T iv, 200	by Neukomm
8	a:63bis	Hallow ev'n, D	vn, vc, pf	1803	T v, 225	by Neukomm
9	a:247	Happy Dick Dawson, D	vn, vc, pf	1803	T iv, 185	by Neukomm
10	a:257bis	Here awa', there awa', d (duet)	vn, vc, pf	1803	—	?by Neukomm, see Angermüller (1974)
		I loe na a laddie but ane, see Happy Dick Dawson				
		Jenny beguil'd the webster, see Jenny dang the weaver				
11	a:240	Jenny dang the weaver, Bb	vn, vc, pf	1803	T iv, 174	by Neukomm
12	a:251	Johny Faw, Bb	vn, vc, pf	1804	T iv, 196	?by Neukomm, see Haydn's letter of 3 April 1804; altered version signed by Haydn
13	a:238	Johny MacGill, Eb (?Irish air)	vn, vc, pf	1803	T iv, 171	by Neukomm
14	a:269	Kelvin Grove, G	pf	?	TS vi, 30	doubtful
15	a:190	Lochaber, F	vn, vc, pf	1803	T i, 150	?by Neukomm, see Angermüller (1974)
16	a:81bis	McGrigor of Rora's lament, C	vn, vc, pf	1803	T iv, 176	by Neukomm
17	a:268	My love's a wanton wee thing, D	vn, vc, pf	1803	TS vi, p.44 (no vn, vc)	by Neukomm
		My silly auld man, see Johny MacGill				
		My wife's a wanton, wee thing, see My love's a wanton wee thing				
18	a:89bis	O bonny lass, Eb	vn, vc, pf	1803	T iv, 164	by Neukomm
19	a:122bis	O'er the moor amang the heather, Eb	vn, vc, pf	1803	T iv, 158	by Neukomm
20	a:273	O gin my love were yon red rose, a	vn, vc, pf	1804	—	?by Neukomm, see Haydn's letter of 3 April 1804
21	a:267	Over the water to Charlie, D	vn, vc, pf	1803	TS vi, p.36 (no vn, vc)	by Neukomm

208

No.	hXXXI	Tune/Title, key	Accompaniment	Date	Edition	Remarks
22	a:271	O were my love yon lilac fair, a	pf	?	TS vi, 32	doubtful
23	b:61	Parson boasts of mild ale, The, g (Irish air)	vn, vc, pf	1803	TI i, 30	by Neukomm
24	a:197	Rise up and bar the door, F	vn, vc, pf	1803	T i, 47	by Neukomm
25	a:253B	Rock and a wee pickle tow, The, F	vn, vc, pf	1803	T iv, 199	by Neukomm
26	a:266	Sailor's lady, The, A	pf	?	TS v, 37	doubtful
		Savourna deligh (Irish air), see Erin-go-bragh				
27	a:239	Sheiah O'Neal, F	vn, vc, pf	1803	T iv, 173	by Neukomm
		Tibbie Dunbar, see Johny MacGill				
28	a:52bis	Tibby Fowler, b	vn, vc, pf	1803	T iv, 192	by Neukomm
29	a:270	Tullochgorum, D	vn, vc, pf	1803	T v (suppl.), 246	by Neukomm
		Waes me for Prince Charlie, see Johny Faw				
30	a:214ter	Waly, waly, D	vn, vc, pf	?	T i (1822), 19	doubtful duet arr. of Z 359
31	a:62bis	When she came ben she bobbit, e	vn, vc, pf	1803	T v, 220	by Neukomm
32	a:22bis	White cockade, The, D	vn, vc, pf	1803	T iv, 188	by Neukomm

Bibliography

BASIC BIOGRAPHIES, COLLECTED LETTERS

G. A. Griesinger: 'Biographische Notizen über Joseph Haydn', *AMZ*, xi (Leipzig, 1809), 641, 657, 673, 689, 705, 721, 737, 776; also pubd separately (Leipzig, 1810/*R*1981, 2/1819; Eng. trans. in Gotwals, 1963); ed. F. Grasberger (Vienna, 1954); ed. P. Krause (Leipzig, 1979)

A. C. Dies: *Biographische Nachrichten von Joseph Haydn: nach mündlichen Erzählungen desselben entworfen und herausgegeben von Albert Christoph Dies, Landschaftmahler* (Vienna, 1810; Eng. trans. in Gotwals, 1963); ed. H. Seeger (Berlin, 1959, 4/1976)

C. F. Pohl: *Joseph Haydn*, i (Berlin, 1875, 2/1878), ii (Leipzig, 1882), iii (Leipzig, 1927) [completed by H. Botstiber]; all *R*1970–71

H. C. R. Landon, ed.. *The Collected Correspondence and London Notebooks of Joseph Haydn* (London, 1959)

V. Gotwals, ed.: *Joseph Haydn: Eighteenth-century Gentleman and Genius* (Madison, 1963, 2/1968 as *Haydn: Two Contemporary Portraits*) [trans. of Griesinger (1809) and Dies (1810)]

D. Bartha, ed.: *Joseph Haydn: Gesammelte Briefe und Aufzeichnungen: unter Benützung der Quellensammlung von H. C. Robbins Landon* (Kassel, 1965), 599

H. C. R. Landon: *Haydn: Chronicle and Works*, i–v (London, 1976–80)

CATALOGUES, BIBLIOGRAPHIES, SOURCES, RESEARCH

A. Fuchs: *Thematisches Verzeichniss der sämmtlichen Compositionen von Joseph Haydn zusammengestellt . . . 1839*, ed. R. Schaal (Wilhelmshaven, 1968)

La Mara [M. Lipsius]: 'Verzeichniss der Werke Haydn's', *Joseph Haydn: Musikalische Studienköpfe*, iv: *Classiker* (Leipzig, ?1880)

A. Artaria: *Verzeichnis von musikalischen Autographen, revidierten Abschriften und einigen seltenen gedruckten Original-Ausgaben* (Vienna, 1893)

A. Csatkai: *Joseph Haydn: Katalog der Gedächtnisausstellung in Eisenstadt 1932* (Eisenstadt, 1932)

R. Lachmann: 'Die Haydn-Autographen der Staatsbibliothek zu Berlin', *ZMw*, xiv (1932), 289

A. Orel: *Katalog der Haydn-Gedächtnisausstellung Wien 1932* (Vienna, 1932)

G. de Saint-Foix: 'Les manuscrits et les copies d'oeuvres de Joseph Haydn à la Bibliothèque du Conservatoire (Fonds Malherbe)', *RdM*, xiii (1932), 206; suppl. by Y. Rokseth in *RdM*, xiv (1933), 40

J. P. Larsen: *Die Haydn-Überlieferung* (Copenhagen, 1939)

J. P. Larsen, ed.: *Drei Haydn Kataloge in Faksimile mit Einleitung und ergänzenden Themenverzeichnissen* (Copenhagen, 1941, rev. New York, 1979)

A. van Hoboken: *Joseph Haydn: Thematisch-bibliographisches Werkverzeichnis*, i: *Instrumentalwerke*; ii: *Vokalwerke*; iii: *Register, Addenda und Corrigenda* (Mainz, 1957–78)

R. Feuchtmüller, F. Hadamowsky and L. Nowak: *Joseph Haydn und seine Zeit: Ausstellung Schloss Petronell (N.Ö.) Mai bis Oktober 1959* (Vienna, 1959)

H. C. R. Landon: 'Survey of the Haydn Sources in Czechoslovakia', *Internationale Konferenz zum Andenken Joseph Haydns: Budapest 1959*, 69

L. Nowak, ed.: *Joseph Haydn: Ausstellung zum 150. Todestag: vom 29. Mai bis 30. September 1959* (Vienna, 1959)

J. Vécsey and others, eds.: *Haydn művei az Országos Széchényi Könyvtár zenei gyűjteményében: kiadásra került az 1809–1959 évforduló alkalmából* [Haydn compositions in the National Széchényi Library, Budapest: published on the 150th anniversary of Haydn's death] (Budapest, 1959; Ger. trans., 1959; Eng. trans., 1960)

D. Bartha and L. Somfai: *Haydn als Opernkapellmeister: die Haydn-Dokumente der Esterházy-Opernsammlung* (Budapest, 1960) [correction and updating in *New Looks at Italian Opera: Essays in Honor of Donald J. Grout* (Ithaca, 1968), 172–219]

G. Feder: 'Zur Datierung Haydnscher Werke', *Anthony van Hoboken: Festschrift zum 75. Geburtstag* (Mainz, 1962), 50

——: 'Die Überlieferung und Verbreitung der handschriftlichen Quellen zu Haydns Werken (Erste Folge)', *Haydn-Studien*, i (1965), 3–42; Eng. trans., *Haydn Yearbook*, iv (1968), 102–39

J. Sehnal: 'Die Kapelle des Olmützer Bischofs Leopold Egk (1758–1760) und ihr Repertoire', *Acta musei moraviae*, l (1965), 203

G. Feder: 'Lo stato attuale degli studi su Haydn', *NRMI*, ii (1968), 625–54

I. Becker-Glauch: 'Haydn, Franz Joseph', *RISM*, A/i/4 (1974), 140–279

A. P. Brown, J. T. Berkenstock and C. V. Brown: 'Joseph Haydn in Literature: a Bibliography', *Haydn-Studien*, iii/3–4 (1974)

——: 'Joseph Haydn in Literature: a Survey', *Notes*, xxxi (1974–5), 530

G. Feder: 'The Collected Works of Joseph Haydn', *Haydn Studies: Washington 1975*, 26

J. P. Larsen: 'A Survey of the Development of Haydn Research: Solved and Unsolved Problems', *Haydn Studies: Washington 1975*, 14

S. C. Fisher: 'A Group of Haydn Copies for the Court of Spain', *Haydn-Studien*, iv (1978), 65

A. Hahn and H. Schmid: Haydn-Museum Eisenstadt, Katalog Neue Folge, 13 (Eisenstadt, 1980)

SPECIALIST PUBLICATIONS, COMMEMORATIVE ISSUES
Die Musik, viii/16 (1908–9)

IMusSCR, iii *Vienna 1909*
Musikalisches Wochenblatt, xl/9 (1909)
Neue Musik-Zeitung, xxx/17 (1909)
The Musician, xiv/10 (1909)
Die Musik, xxiv/6 (1931–2)
Burgenländische Heimatblätter, i/1 (Eisenstadt, 1932)
MQ, xviii/2 (1932)
MT, lxxiii/3 (1932)
Österreichische Kunst, ii/3–4 (1932)
Zeitschrift für Schulmusik, v/3 (1932)
ZfM, xcix/4 (1932)
Burgenländische Heimatblätter, xxi/2 (Eisenstadt, 1959)
Internationale Konferenz zum Andenken Joseph Haydns: Budapest 1959
Musica, xiii/5 (1959)
Musikerziehung, xii/3 (Vienna, 1959)
ÖMz, xiv/5–6 (1959)
SovM (1959), no.6
Approdo musicale (1960), no.11
Zenetudományi tanulmányok, viii (1960) [Haydn Emlékere] [with Ger. summaries]
Haydn Yearbook, i– (1962–)
Haydn-Studien, i– (1965–)
Der junge Haydn: Internationale Arbeitstagung des Instituts für Aufführungspraxis: Graz 1970
Jb für österreichische Kulturgeschichte, ii: *Joseph Haydn und seine Zeit* (1972)
Haydn Studies: Proceedings of the International Haydn Conference: Washington 1975
MT, cxxiii/3 (1982)

BIOGRAPHIES

GerberNL
Framery: *Notice sur Joseph Haydn* (Paris, 1810)
J. LeBreton: *Notice historique sur la vie et les ouvrages de Joseph Haydn* (Paris, 1810); repr. in *Bibliographie musicale de la France et de l'étranger*, ed. C. Gardeton (Paris, 1822), 350
G. Carpani: *Le Haydine, ovvero Lettere su la vita e le opere del celebre maestro Giuseppe Haydn* (Milan, 1812, 2/1823/R1969; Eng. trans., 1839 as *The Life of Haydn in Letters*)
M. H. Beyle [L. A. C. Bombet, Stendhal]: *Lettres écrites de Vienne en Autriche, sur le célèbre compositeur Joseph Haydn, suivies d'une vie de Mozart, et de considérations sur Métastase et l'état présent de la musique en France et en Italie* (Paris, 1814, 3/1872, rev: H. Martineau as *Vies de Haydn, de Mozart et de Métastase*, 1928; Eng. trans. R. Brewin, 1817, 2/1818, rev. R. N. Coe as *Lives of Haydn, Mozart and Metastasio*, 1972) [plagiarism of Carpani (1812)]

C. von Wurzbach: *Joseph Haydn und sein Bruder Michael: zwei bio-bibliographische Künstler-Skizzen* (Vienna, 1861)

J. C. Hadden: *Haydn* (London and New York, 1902, rev. 2/1934)

M. Brenet: *Haydn* (Paris, 1909, 2/1910; Eng. trans., 1926/*R*1972)

A. Schnerich: *Joseph Haydn und seine Sendung* (Zurich, 1922, 2/1926 with suppl. by W. Fischer)

K. Geiringer: *Joseph Haydn* (Potsdam, 1932)

——: *Haydn: a Creative Life in Music* (New York, 1946, enlarged 2/1963/*R*1968)

R. Hughes: *Haydn* (London, 1950, 5/1975)

L. Nowak: *Joseph Haydn: Leben, Bedeutung und Werk* (Zurich, 1951, 3/1966)

B. Redfern: *Haydn: a Biography, with a Survey of Books, Editions and Recordings* (London, 1970)

H. C. R. Landon: *Haydn* (London, 1972)

LIFE: PARTICULAR ASPECTS

Ancestry, character, death, acquaintances

F. Menčik: 'Haydn-Testamente', *Die Kultur*, ix (1908). 82

F. Scherber: 'Joseph Haydns Tod', *Neue Musik-Zeitung*, xxx (1909), 365

I. Schwarz: 'Wie der handschriftliche Nachlass Josef Haydns nach Ungarn kam', *Österreichische Rundschau*, xix (1909), 239

J. Tandler: 'Über den Schädel Haydns', *Mitteilungen der Anthropologischen Gesellschaft*, xxxix (1909), 260

R. Bernhardt: 'Aus der Umwelt der Wiener Klassiker: Freiherr Gottfried van Swieten (1734–1803)', *Der Bär: Jb von Breitkopf & Härtel 1929–30*, 74–164

R. F. Müller: 'Heiratsbrief, Testament und Hinterlassenschaft der Gattin Joseph Haydns', *Die Musik*, xxii (1929–30), 93

——: 'Joseph Haydns letztes Testament: nach der Urschrift veröffentlicht', *Die Musik*, xxiv (1931–2), 440

O. E. Deutsch: 'Haydn und Nelson', *Die Musik*, xxiv (1931–2), 436; repr. in *ÖMz*, xxiii (1968), 13

H. Botstiber: 'Haydn and Luigia Polzelli', *MQ*, xviii (1932), 208

G. de Saint-Foix: 'Haydn and Clementi', *MQ*, xviii (1932), 252

E. F. Schmid: *Joseph Haydn: ein Buch von Vorfahren und Heimat des Meisters* (Kassel, 1934)

D. Bartha: 'Zur Abstammung Joseph Haydns', *AcM*, vii (1935), 152

W. Schmieder: 'Joseph Haydns Kopist und Bediensteter schreibt einen Brief', *AMz*, lxiv (1937), 425

R. S. M. Hughes: 'Dr. Burney's Championship of Haydn', *MQ*, xxvii (1941), 90

P. A. Scholes: 'Burney and Haydn', *MMR*, lxxi (1941), 155, 172

E. F. Schmid: 'Josef Haydns Jugendliebe', *Festschrift Wilhelm Fischer* (Innsbruck, 1956), 109

O. E. Deutsch: 'Haydn als Sammler', *ÖMz*, xiv (1959), 188

J. P. Larsen: 'Haydn und Mozart', *ÖMz*, xiv (1959), 32 [special Haydn issue]

E. H. Müller von Asow: 'Joseph Haydns Tod in zeitgenössischen Berichten', *Musikerziehung*, xii (1959), 141

E. Schenk: 'Das Weltbild Joseph Haydns', *Österreichische Akademie der Wissenschaften: Almanach*, cix (1959), 245; repr. in *Ausgewählte Aufsätze, Reden und Vorträge* (Graz, Vienna and Cologne, 1967), 86

E. Schultheiss: 'Ärztliches über Haydn', *Musica*, xiii (1959), 291

V. Gotwals: 'Joseph Haydn's Last Will and Testament', *MQ*, xlvii (1961), 331

E. Olleson: 'Gottfried van Swieten, Patron of Haydn and Mozart', *PRMA*, lxxxix (1962–3), 63

F. Blume: 'Haydn als Briefschreiber', *Syntagma musicologicum: gesammelte Reden und Schriften* (Kassel, 1963), 564

L. Somfai: 'Haydns Tribut an seinen Vorgänger Werner', *Haydn Yearbook*, ii (1963–4), 75

R. Elvers: 'Ein nicht abgesandter Brief Zelters an Haydn', *Musik und Verlag: Karl Vötterle zum 65. Geburtstag* (Kassel, 1968), 243

A. van Hoboken: 'Joseph Haydns Schwager', *Festschrift Josef Stummvoll* (Vienna, 1970), 788

G. Feder: 'Joseph Haydn als Mensch und Musiker', *Jb für österreichische Kulturgeschichte*, ii: *Joseph Haydn und seine Zeit* (1972), 43; also in *ÖMz*, xxvii (1972), 57

N. Platz and H. Walter: 'Neukomms Bemerkungen über Haydns Grab', *Haydn-Studien*, iii (1974), 154

F. H. Franken: 'Joseph Haydns Leben aus medizinischer Sicht', *Wiener klinische Wochenschrift* (1976), no.88, p.429

Eisenstadt, Eszterháza, England, travels

T. G. von Karajan: *Joseph Haydn in London, 1791 und 1792* (Vienna, 1861/R1975); also in *Jb für Vaterländische Geschichte* (1861)

C. F. Pohl: *Mozart und Haydn in London*, ii: *Haydn in London* (Vienna, 1867/R1971)

O. A. Mansfield: 'Haydn at Bath', *MMR*, lviii (1928), 201

E. Csatkai: 'Die Beziehungen Gregor Josef Werners, Joseph Haydns und der fürstlichen Musiker zur Eisenstädter Pfarrkirche', *Burgenländische Heimatblätter*, i (Eisenstadt, 1932), 13

E. F. Schmid: 'Joseph Haydn in Eisenstadt: ein Beitrag zur Biographie des Meisters', *Burgenländische Heimatblätter*, i (Eisenstadt, 1932), 2

M. M. Scott: 'Haydn in England', *MQ*, xviii (1932), 260

——: 'Haydn: Relics and Reminiscences in England', *ML*, xiii (1932), 126

R. Hughes: 'Haydn at Oxford: 1773–1791', *ML*, xx (1939), 242

O. E. Deutsch: 'Haydn in Cambridge', *Cambridge Review*, lxii (1940–41), 312

214   *Haydn*

M. M. Scott: 'Haydn Stayed Here', *ML*, xxxii (1951), 38
——: 'The Opera Concerts of 1795', *MR*, xii (1951), 24
A. Valkó: 'Haydn magyarországi működése a levéltári akták tükrében'
  [Haydn's activities in Hungary, as revealed in the archives],
  Zenetudományi tanulmányok, vi (1957), 627–67; viii (1960), 527–
  668 [with Ger. summaries]; see also Harich (1963–71)
J. Harich: *Esterházy-Musikgeschichte im Spiegel der zeitgenössischen
  Textbücher: Festgabe anlässlich der 150. Wiederkehr des Todestages
  von Joseph Haydn* (Eisenstadt, 1959) [orig. in *H-Bn*]
M. Horányi: *Esterházi vigasságok* (Budapest, 1959; Ger. trans., 1959;
  Eng. trans., 1962 as *The Magnificence of Eszterháza*)
D. Bartha and L. Somfai: *Haydn als Opernkapellmeister: die Haydn-
  Dokumente der Esterházy-Opernsammlung* (Budapest, 1960) [cor-
  rection and updating in *New Looks at Italian Opera: Essays in Honor
  of Donald J. Grout* (Ithaca, 1968), 172–219]
E. Csatkai: 'Haydnra és zenekarára vonatkozó adatok a Süttöri any-
  akönyvekböl' [Data from the municipal archives of Süttör concerning
  Haydn and his orchestra], *Zenetudományi tanulmányok*, viii (1960),
  669 [with Ger. summary]
J. Harich: 'Das Repertoire des Opernkapellmeisters Joseph Haydn in
  Eszterháza (1780–1790)', *Haydn Yearbook*, i (1962), 9–110
C. Stadtlaender: *Joseph Haydns Sinfonia domestica: von Joseph Haydns
  häuslichem Leben . . .: eine Dokumentation* (Munich, 1963; Eng.
  trans., rev. and enlarged P. M. Young, 1968 as *Joseph Haydn of
  Eisenstadt*)
J. Harich: 'Haydn Documenta', *Haydn Yearbook*, ii (1963–4), 2–44; iii
  (1965), 122–52; iv (1968), 39–101; vii (1970), 47–168; viii (1971),
  70–163 [corrections and addns. to Valkó, 1957 and 1960]
B. Matthews: 'Haydn's Visit to Hampshire and the Isle of Wight,
  Described from Contemporary Sources', *Haydn Yearbook*, iii
  (1965), 111
J. Harich: 'Das fürstlich Esterházy'sche Fideikommiss', *Haydn
  Yearbook*, iv (1968), 5–38
G. Feder: 'Haydn und Eisenstadt', *ÖMz*, xxv (1970), 213
J. Harich: 'Das Opernensemble zu Eszterháza im Jahr 1780', *Haydn
  Yearbook*, vii (1970), 5–46
——: 'Das Haydn-Orchester im Jahr 1780', *Haydn Yearbook*, viii
  (1971), 5–69
H. C. R. Landon: 'Haydns erste Erfahrungen in England: von der
  Ankunft in London bis zum ersten Salomon-Konzert', *Jb für
  österreichische Kulturgeschichte*, i/2: *Beiträge zur Musikgeschichte
  des 18. Jahrhunderts* (1971), 154
P. Bryan: 'Haydn's Hornists', *Haydn-Studien*, iii (1973), 52
J. Harich: 'Inventare der Esterházy-Hofmusikkapelle in Eisenstadt',
  Haydn Yearbook, ix (1975), 5–126

S. Gerlach: 'Haydns Orchester-Musiker von 1761 bis 1774', *Haydn-Studien*, iv (1976), 35

U. Tank: 'Die Dokumente der Esterházy-Archive zur fürstlichen Hofkapelle in der Zeit von 1761 bis 1770', *Haydn-Studien*, iv (1980), 129–333

———: *Studien zur Esterházyschen Hofmusik von etwa 1620 bis 1790* (Regensburg, 1981)

Miscellaneous

G. Nottebohm: *Beethoven's Studien*, i: *Beethoven's Unterricht bei J. Haydn, Albrechtsberger und Salieri: nach den Original-Manuskripten dargestellt* (Leipzig and Winterthur, 1873/*R*1971)

F. Menčik: 'Einige Beiträge zu Haydns Biographie', *Musikbuch aus Österreich*, vi (1909), 26

M. Unger: 'Haydn-Studien', *Musikalisches Wochenblatt*, xl (1909), 317, 333; xli (1910), 297, 413, 440

A. Diemand: 'Josef Haydn und der Wallersteiner Hof', *Zeitschrift des Historischen Vereins für Schwaben und Neuburg*, xlv (1920–22), 1–40

F. von Reinöhl: 'Neues zu Beethovens Lehrjahr bei Haydn', *NBJb*, vi (1935), 36

F. Pfohl: 'Joseph Haydn, der Leopoldsorden und die sancta simplicitas', *ZfM*, civ (1937), 66, 212

A. Boschot: 'Haydn et l'Institut ou l'immédiate célébrité du compositeur viennois', *Maîtres d'hier et de jadis* (Paris, 1944), 54

N. A. Solar-Quintes: 'Las relaciones de Haydn con la casa de Benavente', *AnM*, ii (1947), 81

C.-G. Stellan Mörner: *Johan Wikmanson und die Brüder Silverstolpe: einige Stockholmer Persönlichkeiten im Musikleben des Gustavianischen Zeitalters* (Uppsala, 1952)

O. E. Deutsch: 'Haydn bleibt Lehrling: nach den Freimaurer-Akten des Österreichischen Staatsarchivs', *Musica*, xiii (1959), 289

F. Högler: 'Haydn als Schüler, Lehrer und Musikerzieher', *Musikerziehung*, xii (1959), 131

H. Seeger: 'Zur musikhistorischen Bedeutung der Haydn-Biographie von Albert Christoph Dies (1810)', *BMw*, i/3 (1959), 24 [incl. Neukomm's remarks about Dies (1810)]

A. van Hoboken: *Discrepancies in Haydn Biographies* (Washington, DC, 1962) [lecture at the Library of Congress, 18 May 1962]

E. Olleson: 'Haydn in the Diaries of Count Karl von Zinzendorf', *Haydn Yearbook*, ii (1963–4), 45

M. Vignal: 'A Side-aspect of Sigismund Neukomm's Journey to France in 1809', *Haydn Yearbook*, ii (1963–4), 81

E. Olleson: 'Georg August Griesinger's Correspondence with Breitkopf & Härtel', *Haydn Yearbook*, iii (1965), 5–53

H. Unverricht: 'Unveröffentlichte und wenig bekannte Briefe Joseph

Haydns', *Mf*, xviii (1965), 40

G. Feder: 'Ein vergessener Haydn-Brief', *Haydn-Studien*, i (1966), 114

G. Thomas: 'Griesingers Briefe über Haydn: aus seiner Korrespondenz mit Breitkopf & Härtel', *Haydn-Studien*, i (1966), 49–114

H. C. R. Landon: 'Haydniana', *Haydn Yearbook*, iv (1968), 199; vii (1970), 307 [letters]

C. B. Oldman: 'Haydn's Quarrel with the "Professionals" in 1788', *Musik und Verlag: Karl Vötterle zum 65. Geburtstag* (Kassel, 1968), 459

E. Radant, ed.: 'Die Tagebücher von Joseph Carl Rosenbaum 1770–1829', *Haydn Yearbook*, v (1968), 7–159

C. Roscoe: 'Haydn and London in the 1780's', *ML*, xlix (1968), 203

C.-G. Stellan Mörner: 'Haydniana aus Schweden um 1800', *Haydn-Studien*, ii (1969), 1–33

J. Chailley: 'Joseph Haydn and the Freemasons', *Studies in Eighteenth-century Music: a Tribute to Karl Geiringer* (New York, 1970), 117

A. Mann: 'Beethoven's Contrapuntal Studies with Haydn', *MQ*, lvi (1970), 711; another version in *GfMKB, Bonn 1970*, 70

——: 'Haydn as Student and Critic of Fux', *Studies in Eighteenth-century Music: a Tribute to Karl Geiringer* (New York, 1970), 323; another version in *Musik und Verlag: Karl Vötterle zum 65. Geburtstag* (Kassel, 1968), 433

H. Walter: 'Die biographischen Beziehungen zwischen Haydn und Beethoven', *GfMKB, Bonn 1970*, 79

M. Pandt and H. Schmidt: 'Musik zur Zeit Haydns und Beethovens in der Pressburger Zeitung', *Haydn Yearbook*, viii (1971), 165–293

T. Antonicek: *Musik im Festsaal der Österreichischen Akademie der Wissenschaften* (Vienna, 1972)

R. Angermüller: 'Sigismund Ritter von Neukomm (1778–1858) und seine Lehrer Michael und Joseph Haydn: eine Dokumentation', *Haydn-Studien*, iii (1973), 29

A. Mann: 'Haydn's Elementarbuch: a Document of Classic Counterpoint Instruction', *Music Forum*, iii (1973), 197

H. Walter: 'Ein Billett Haydns vom 6. November 1805', *Haydn-Studien*, iii (1973), 43

A. Weinmann: 'Neues über Joseph Haydn und das Grazer Musikleben', *Mitteilungen des Steierischen Tonkünstlerbundes*, lvii (1973), 1

G. Feder and S. Gerlach: 'Haydn-Dokumente aus dem Esterházy-Archiv in Forchtenstein', *Haydn-Studien*, iii (1974), 92

G. Thomas: 'Contradictions in Haydn Biography', *Haydn Studies: Washington 1975*, 67

H. Walter: 'On Haydn's Pupils', *Haydn Studies: Washington 1975*, 60

Katalog Nr.192: Musikerautographen, Musikantiquariat Hans Schneider (Tutzing, 1975), 43 [letter to Pleyel]

G. Feder: 'Zwei unbekannte Haydn-Briefe', *Haydn-Studien*, iv (1976), 49

H. Zeman, ed.: *Joseph Haydn und die Literatur seiner Zeit* (Eisenstadt, 1976)

H. R. Hollis: 'The Musical Instruments of Joseph Haydn: an Introduction', *Smithsonian Studies in History and Technology* (Washington, 1977), 38

Katalog 617: Autographen aus allen Gebieten, J. A. Stargardt, Antiquariat (Marburg, 1979), 217 [letter from Haydn of 11 Jan 1794, with facs.]

Katalog Nr.241: Bedeutende Musikerautographen, Musikantiquaritat Hans Schneider (Tutzing, 1980), 26f [letters from Haydn of 6 June 1801 and 6 March 1806]

G. Thomas: 'Haydn-Anekdoten', *Ars musica–Musica scientia, Festschrift Heinrich Hüschen zum 65. Geburtstag* (Cologne, 1980), 435

H. Walter: 'Haydns Schüler am Esterházyschen Hof', *Ars musica–Musica scientia, Festschrift Heinrich Hüschen zum 65. Geburtstag* (Cologne, 1980), 449

G. Feder and F. H. Franken: 'Ein wiedergefundener Brief Haydns an Artaria & Co.', *Haydn-Studien*, v (1982)

H. Walter: 'Kalkbrenners Lehrjahre und sein Unterricht bei Haydn', *Haydn-Studien*, v (1982)

PUBLISHERS

W. Sandys and S. A. Forster: *The History of the Violin, and Other Instruments* (London; 1864) [correspondence of Haydn and Forster]

F. Artaria and H. Botstiber: *Joseph Haydn und das Verlagshaus Artaria: nach den Briefen des Meisters an das Haus Artaria & Compagnie dargestellt* (Vienna, 1909)

H. von Hase: *Joseph Haydn und Breitkopf & Härtel* (Leipzig, 1909)

J. C. Hadden: 'George Thomson and Haydn', *MMR*, xl (1910), 76

W. Matthäus: 'Das Werk Joseph Haydns im Spiegel der Geschichte des Verlages Jean André', *Haydn Yearbook*, iii (1965), 54–110

H. Unverricht: 'Haydn und Bossler', *Festskrift Jens Peter Larsen* (Copenhagen, 1972), 285

G. Feder: 'Die Eingriffe des Musikverlegers Hummel in Haydns Werken', *Musicae scientiae collectanea: Festschrift Karl Gustav Fellerer* (Cologne, 1973), 88

J. P. Larsen: 'A Haydn Contract', *MT*, cxvii (1976), 737

ICONOGRAPHY

A. Fuchs: 'Verzeichniss aller Abbildungen Joseph Haydn's', *Wiener Allgemeine Musik-Zeitung*, vi (1846), 237

E. Vogel: 'Joseph Haydn: Portraits', *JbMP 1898*, 11

H. Marcel: 'L'iconographie d'Haydn', *BSIM*, vi (1910), 17

J. Muller: 'Haydn Portraits', *MQ*, xviii (1932), 282

L. Somfai: *Joseph Haydn: sein Leben in zeitgenössischen Bildern* (Budapest and Kassel, 1966; Eng. trans., 1969)

H. Unverricht: 'Ein unbeachteter authentischer Schattenriss Joseph

Haydns von 1785', *ÖMz*, xxvii (1972), 68

H. C. R. Landon: 'A New Haydn Portrait', *Soundings*, ix (1979–80), 2

AUTHENTICITY

H. Reimann: 'Eine "klassische" Liedfälschung', *Musikalische Rückblicke*, i (Berlin, 1900), 105

R. Steglich: 'Eine Klaviersonate Johann Gottfried Schwanbergs (Schwanenberg[er]s) in der Joseph Haydn Gesamtausgabe', *ZMw*, xv (1932–3), 77

J. P. Larsen: 'Haydn und das "kleine Quartbuch" ', *AcM*, vii (1935), 111 [beginning of Larsen–Sandberger controversy; see Brown, Berkenstock and Brown (1974), no.1134]

E. F. Schmid: 'Franz Anton Hoffmeister und die "Göttweiger Sonaten" ', *ZfM*, civ (1937), 760, 889, 992, 1109

——: 'Leopold Mozart und die Kindersinfonie', *MJb 1951*, 69; see also *MJb 1952*, 117

H. C. R. Landon: 'Haydn and Authenticity: some New Facts', *MR*, xvi (1955), 138

——: 'Doubtful and Spurious Quartets and Quintets Attributed to Haydn', *MR*, xviii (1957), 213

——: 'Problems of Authenticity in Eighteenth-century Music', *Instrumental Music: Isham Memorial Library 1957*, 31

E. Schenk: 'Ist die Göttweiger Rorate-Messe ein Werk Joseph Haydns?', *SMw*, xxiv (1960), 87

T. Straková: 'J. A. Štěpán und Haydns Divertimento in Es dur', *Acta musei moraviae*, xlvi (1961), 132

A. Tyson: 'Haydn and Two Stolen Trios', *MR*, xxii (1961), 21

P. Mies: 'Anfrage zu einem Joseph Haydn unterschobenen Werk', *Haydn Yearbook*, i (1962), 200

J. LaRue: 'A Haydn (?) Première at Yale', *MR*, xxiv (1963), 333

P. Mies: 'Joseph Haydns "Abschiedslied" – von Adalbert Gyrowetz', *Haydn Yearbook*, ii (1963–4), 88

A. Tyson and H. C. R. Landon: 'Who Composed Haydn's Op.3?', *MT*, cv (1964), 506

H. Schwarting: 'Über die Echtheit dreier Haydn-Trios', *AMw*, xxii (1965), 169

L. Somfai: 'Zur Echtheitsfrage des Haydn'schen "Opus 3" ', *Haydn Yearbook*, iii (1965), 153

H. C. R. Landon: 'Haydniana (i)', *Haydn Yearbook*, iv (1968), 199

H. Unverricht, A. Gottron and A. Tyson: *Die beiden Hoffstetter: zwei Komponisten-Porträts mit Werkverzeichnissen* (Mainz, 1968)

R. Münster: 'Wer ist der Komponist der "Kindersinfonie"?', *Acta Mozartiana*, xvi (1969), 76

E. Badura-Skoda: 'An Unknown Singspiel by Joseph Haydn?', *IMSCR, xi Copenhagen 1972*, i, 236

A. P. Brown: 'Problems of Authenticity in Two Haydn Keyboard Works (Hoboken XVI:47 and XIV:7)', *JAMS*, xxv (1972), 85

G. Feder: 'Die Bedeutung der Assoziation und des Wertvergleichs für das Urteil in Echtheitsfragen', *IMSCR, xi Copenhagen 1972*, i, 365

C. E. Hatting: 'Haydn oder Kayser? – eine Echtheitsfrage', *Mf*, xxv (1972), 182

W. T. Marrocco: 'The String Quartet attributed to Benjamin Franklin', *Proceedings of the American Philosophical Society*, cxvi (1972), 477

G. Thomas: ' "Gioco filarmonico" – Würfelmusik und Joseph Haydn', *Musicae scientiae collectanea: Festschrift Karl Gustav Fellerer* (Cologne, 1973), 598

G. Feder: 'Apokryphe "Haydn"-Streichquartette', *Haydn-Studien*, iii (1974), 125

G. Thomas: 'Die zwölf Deutschen Tänze Hob. IX:13 – echt oder gefälscht?', *Haydn-Studien*, iv (1978), 117

G. Croll: 'Musik mit Kinderinstrumenten aus dem Salzburger und Berchtesgadener Land', *Denkmäler der Musik in Salzburg*, ii (1981) [preface and critical commentary]

S. Gerlach: 'Haydn's Works for Musical Clock (Flötenuhr): Problems of Authenticity, Grouping and Chronology', *Haydn Studies: Washington 1981*, 126

WORKS: GENERAL

F. S. Kuhač: 'Josip Haydn i hrvatske narodne popievke' [Joseph Haydn and national folk music], *Vienac: zabavi i pouci*, xii (Zagreb, 1880), 202, 217, 241, 254, 272, 301, 317, 356, 387, 403, 418, 433, 452, 466; also pubd separately (Zagreb, 1880)

W. H. Hadow: *A Croatian Composer: Notes toward the Study of Joseph Haydn* (London, 1897); repr. in *Collected Essays* (London, 1928) [based on Kuhač, 1880]

T. de Wyzewa: 'A propos du centenaire de la mort de Joseph Haydn', *Revue des deux mondes*, lxxix (1909), 935

H. Jalowetz: 'Beethovens Jugendwerke in ihren melodischen Beziehungen zu Mozart, Haydn und Ph. E. Bach', *SIMG*, xii (1910–11), 417–74

W. Fischer: 'Zur Entwicklungsgeschichte des Wiener klassischen Stils', *SMw*, iii (1915), 24–84

H. Kretzschmar: *Führer durch den Konzertsaal* (Leipzig, 5/1919–21)

G. Becking: *Studien zu Beethovens Personalstil: das Scherzothema: mit einem bisher unveröffentlichten Scherzo Beethovens* (Leipzig, 1921) [chap.2, Haydn's minuets]

F. Blume: 'Fortspinnung und Entwicklung: ein Beitrag zur musikalischen Begriffsbildung', *JbMP 1929*, 51; repr. in *Syntagma musicologicum: gesammelte Reden und Schriften* (Kassel, 1963), 504

E. F. Schmid: 'Joseph Haydn und Carl Philipp Emanuel Bach', *ZMw*, xiv (1931–2), 299

G. Adler: 'Haydn and the Viennese Classical School', *MQ*, xviii (1932), 191

R. von Tobel: *Die Formenwelt der klassischen Instrumentalmusik* (diss., U. of Berne, 1935)

D. F. Tovey: *Essays in Musical Analysis* (London, 1935–44/*R*)

K. Dale: 'Schubert's Indebtedness to Haydn', *ML*, xxi (1940), 23

J. A. Westrup: 'Haydn the Romantic', *Sharps and Flats* (London, 1940/*R*1970)

M. M. Scott: 'Haydn: Fresh Facts and Old Fancies', *PRMA*, lxviii (1941–2), 87

J. P. Larsen: 'Haydn, Joseph', *Sohlmans Musiklexicon* (1948–50)

I. M. Bruce: 'An Act of Homage?', *MR*, xi (1950), 277 [Mozart's ᴋ551 and Haydn's ʜ I:100]

T. Georgiades: 'Zur Musiksprache der Wiener Klassiker', *MJb 1951*, 50

J. P. Larsen: 'Zu Haydns künstlerischer Entwicklung', *Festschrift Wilhelm Fischer* (Innsbruck, 1956), 123

E. E. Lowinsky: 'On Mozart's Rhythm', *MQ*, xlii (1956), 162

E. F. Schmid: 'Mozart and Haydn', *MQ*, xlii (1956), 145

D. Arnold: 'Haydn's Counterpoint and Fux's *Gradus*', *MMR*, lxxxvii (1957), 52

F. Noske: 'Le principe structural génétique dans l'oeuvre instrumental de Joseph Haydn', *RBM*, xii (1958), 35

H. Besseler: 'Einflüsse der Contratanzmusik auf Joseph Haydn', *Internationale Konferenz zum Andenken Joseph Haydns: Budapest 1959*, 25

H. Engel: 'Haydn, Mozart und die Klassik', *MJb 1959*, 46–79; another version in *IMSCR*, viii *New York 1961*, i, 285

B. Szabolcsi: 'Joseph Haydn und die ungarische Musik', *BMw*, i/2 (1959), 62; repr. in *Internationale Konferenz zum Andenken Joseph Haydns: Budapest 1959*, 159

H. Schwarting: 'Ungewöhnliche Repriseneintritte in Haydns späterer Instrumentalmusik', *AMw*, xvii (1960), 168

G. Feder: 'Bemerkungen über die Ausbildung der klassischen Tonsprache in der Instrumentalmusik Haydns', *IMSCR*, viii *New York 1961*, i, 305

K. Geiringer: 'Gluck und Haydn', *Festschrift Otto Erich Deutsch* (Kassel, 1963), 75

G. Feder: 'Eine Methode der Stiluntersuchung, demonstriert an Haydns Werken', *GfMKB, Leipzig 1966*, 275

D. Bartha: 'Volkstanz–Stilisierung in Joseph Haydns Finale-Themen', *Festschrift für Walter Wiora* (Kassel, 1967), 375

L. Schrade: 'Joseph Haydn als Schöpfer der klassischen Musik', *De scientia musicae studia atque orationes* (Stuttgart, 1967), 506

M. S. Cole: 'The Rondo Finale: Evidence for the Mozart–Haydn Exchange?', *MJb 1968–70*, 242

B. S. Brook: 'Sturm und Drang and the Romantic Period in Music', *Studies in Romanticism*, ix (1970), 269

G. Feder: 'Similarities in the Works of Haydn', *Studies in Eighteenth-century Music: a Tribute to Karl Geiringer* (New York, 1970), 186

——: 'Die beiden Pole im Instrumentalschaffen des jungen Haydn', *Der junge Haydn: Internationale Arbeitstagung des Instituts für Aufführungspraxis: Graz 1970*, 192

——: 'Stilelemente Haydns in Beethovens Werken', *GfMKB, Bonn 1970*, 65

G. Gruber: 'Musikalische Rhetorik und barocke Bildlichkeit in Kompositionen des jungen Haydn', *Der junge Haydn: Internationale Arbeitstagung des Instituts für Aufführungspraxis: Graz 1970*, 168

R. Leavis: 'Die "Beethovenianismen" der Jenaer Symphonie', *Mf*, xxiii (1970), 297

C. Rosen: *The Classical Style: Haydn, Mozart, Beethoven* (New York, 1971, rev. 2/1972)

D. S. Cushman: *Joseph Haydn's Melodic Materials: an Exploratory Introduction to the Primary and Secondary Sources together with an Analytical Catalogue and Tables of Proposed Melodic Correspondence and/or Variance* (diss., Boston U., 1972)

L. Somfai: 'Vom Barock zur Klassik: Umgestaltung der Proportionen und des Gleichgewichts in zyklischen Werken Joseph Haydns', *Jb für österreichische Kulturgeschichte*, ii: *Joseph Haydn und seine Zeit* (1972), 64

W. Steinbeck: *Das Menuett in der Instrumentalmusik Joseph Haydns* (Munich, 1973)

E. Wellesz and F. Sternfeld, eds.: *The Age of Enlightenment 1745–1790*, NOHM, vii (1973)

S. Wollenberg: 'Haydn's Baryton Trios and the "Gradus" ', *ML*, liv (1973), 170

E. Badura-Skoda: 'The Influence of the Viennese Popular Comedy on Haydn and Mozart', *PRMA*, c (1973–4), 185

L. Somfai: 'The London Revision of Haydn's Instrumental Style', *PRMA*, c (1973–4), 159

G. Feder: 'Bemerkungen zu Haydns Skizzen', *Beethoven Jahrbuch 1973–7*, 69

G. Chew: 'The Night-watchman's Song quoted by Haydn and its Implications', *Haydn-Studien*, iii (1974), 106

A. P. Brown: 'Joseph Haydn and C. P. E. Bach: The Question of Influence', *Haydn Studies: Washington 1975*, 158

G. Feder: 'A Special Feature of Neapolitan Opera Tradition in Haydn's Vocal Works', *Haydn Studies: Washington 1975*, 367

L. Finscher: 'Mozart's Indebtedness to Haydn: Some Remarks on K. 168–173', *Haydn Studies: Washington 1975*, 407

S. Gerlach: 'On the Chronological Correlation of Haydn's Scoring and the Esterházy Musicians', *Haydn Studies: Washington 1975*, 93

E. Helm: 'To Haydn from C. P. E. Bach: Non-tunes', *Haydn Studies: Washington 1975*, 382

J. M. Levy: 'Gesture, Form, and Syntax in Haydn's Music', *Haydn Studies: Washington 1975*, 355

S. E. Paul: 'Comedy, Wit, and Humor in Haydn's Instrumental Music', *Haydn Studies: Washington 1975*, 450

L. G. Ratner: 'Theories of Form: Some Changing Perspectives', *Haydn Studies: Washington 1975*, 347

E. R. Sisman: 'Haydn's Hybrid Variations', *Haydn Studies: Washington 1975*, 509

A. P. Brown: 'Critical Years for Haydn's Instrumental Music: 1787–90', *MQ*, lxii (1976), 374

H. Walter: 'Das Posthornsignal bei Haydn und anderen Komponisten des 18. Jahrhunderts', *Haydn-Studien*, iv (1976), 21

G. Feder: 'Joseph Haydns Skizzen und Entwürfe: Übersicht der Manuskripte, Werkregister, Literatur- und Ausgabenverzeichnis', *FAM*, xxvi (1979), 172

——: 'Über Haydns Skizzen zu nicht identifizierten Werken' *Ars musica – Musica scientia, Festschrift Heinrich Hüschen zum 65. Geburtstag* (Cologne, 1980), 100

SACRED WORKS, ORATORIOS

A. Schnerich: *Der Messen-Typus von Haydn bis Schubert* (Vienna, 1892)

A. Sandberger: 'Zur Entstehungsgeschichte von Haydns "Sieben Worten des Erlösers am Kreuze" ', *JbMP 1903*, 47; repr. in *Ausgewählte Aufsätze zur Musikgeschichte*, i (Munich, 1921), 266

G. Schünemann: 'Ein Skizzenblatt Joseph Haydns', *Die Musik*, viii (1908–9), 211 [The Seasons]

M. Friedlaender: 'Van Swieten und das Textbuch zu Haydns "Jahreszeiten" ', *JbMP 1909*, 47

J. Tiersot: 'Le Lied "Ein Mädchen, das auf Ehre hielt" et ses prototypes français', *ZIMG*, xii (1910–11), 222

E. Mandyczewski: Preface and critical commentary to *Die Jahreszeiten*, Joseph Haydns Werke, xvi/6–7 (1922)

H. Schenker: 'Haydn: Die Schöpfung: die Vorstellung des Chaos', *Das Meisterwerk in der Musik*, ii (1926), 159

K. Geiringer: 'Haydn's Sketches for "The Creation" ', *MQ*, xviii (1932), 299

C. M. Brand: *Die Messen von Joseph Haydn* (Würzburg, 1941)

——: Critical commentary to *Masses 1–4*, Joseph Haydn Gesamtausgabe, xxiii/1 (1951)

H. C. R. Landon: 'Eine aufgefundene Haydn-Messe', *ÖMz*, xii (1957), 183 [allegedly the Missa Rorate coeli desuper]

K. Geiringer: 'The Small Sacred Works by Haydn in the Esterházy Archives at Eisenstadt', *MQ*, xlv (1959), 460; see also *KJb*, xliv (1960), 54, and *Internationale Konferenz zum Andenken Joseph Haydns: Budapest 1959*, 49

E. F. Schmid: 'Haydns Oratorium "Il ritorno di Tobia": seine

Entstehung und seine Schicksale', *AMw*, xvi (1959), 292; see also Preface to Werke, xxviii (1963)

D. Bartha: 'A "Sieben Worte" változatainak keletkezése az Esterházy-gyüjte-mény kéziratainak tükrében' [The origin of the 'Seven last Words' as revealed by the Haydn collection in Budapest], *Zenetudományi tanulmányok*, viii (1960), 107–86 [with Ger. summary]

H. Unverricht: Preface to *Die Sieben letzten Worte . . . Vokalfassung*, Werke, xxviii/2 (1961)

G. Thomas: Preface and critical commentary to *Messen Nr.9–10*, Werke, xxiii/3 (1965–71)

M. Stern: 'Haydns "Schöpfung": Geist und Herkunft des van Swietenschen Librettos: ein Beitrag zum Thema "Säkularisation" im Zeitalter der Aufklärung', *Haydn-Studien*, i (1966), 121–98

F. Lippmann: Preface and critical commentary to *Messe Nr.12*, Werke, xxiii/5 (1966–7)

I. Becker-Glauch: 'Haydns Cantilena pro adventu in D', *Haydn-Studien*, i (1967), 277

——: 'Joseph Haydns "Te Deum" für die Kaiserin: eine Quellenstudie', *Colloquium amicorum: Joseph Schmidt-Görg* (Bonn, 1967), 1

D. McCaldin: 'Haydn's First and Last Work: the "Missa Brevis" in F major', *MR*, xxviii (1967), 165

A. Riedel-Martiny: 'Das Verhältnis von Text und Musik in Haydns Oratorien', *Haydn-Studien*, i (1967), 205–40

H. Walter: 'Gottfried van Swietens handschriftliche Textbücher zu "Schöpfung" und "Jahreszeiten" ', *Haydn-Studien*, i (1967), 241–77

I. Becker-Glauch: 'Haydns Cantilena pro adventu in D', *Haydn-Joseph Haydn Gesamtausgabe*, xxiii/4 (1967–9)

H. C. R. Landon: 'Haydn's Newly Discovered "Responsorium ad absolutionem: Libera me, Domine" ', *Haydn Yearbook*, iv (1968), 140, 228 [with facs. and modern edn.]

E. Olleson: 'The Origin and Libretto of Haydn's "Creation" ', *Haydn Yearbook*, iv (1968), 148

I. Becker-Glauch: 'Joseph Haydn's "Ave Regina" in A', *Studies in Eighteenth-century Music: a Tribute to Karl Geiringer* (New York, 1970), 68

——: 'Neue Forschungen zu Haydns Kirchenmusik', *Haydn-Studien*, ii (1970), 167–241 [with thematic catalogue of small sacred works]

M. Chusid: 'Some Observations on Liturgy, Text and Structure in Haydn's Late Masses', *Studies in Eighteenth-century Music: a Tribute to Karl Geiringer* (New York, 1970), 125

G. Croll: 'Mitteilungen über die "Schöpfung" und die "Jahreszeiten" aus dem Schwarzenberg-Archiv', *Haydn-Studien*, iii (1974), 85

H.-J. Horn: 'FIAT LVX: zum kunsttheoretischen Hintergrund der "Erschaffung" des Lichtes in Haydns Schöpfung', *Haydn-Studien*, iii (1974), 65

J. D. Drury: *Haydn's Seven last Words: an Historical and Critical Study* (diss., U. of Illinois, 1975)

H. C. R. Landon: 'The Newly Discovered Autograph to Haydn's Missa Cellensis of 1766 (formerly known as the "Missa sanctae Caeciliae")', *Haydn Yearbook*, ix (1975), 306

D. Heartz: 'The Hunting Chorus in Haydn's Jahreszeiten and the "Airs de chasse" in the Encyclopédie', *Eighteenth-century Studies*, ix (1976), 523

O. Biba: 'Beispiele für die Besetzungsverhältnisse bei Aufführungen von Haydns Oratorien in Wien zwischen 1784 und 1808', *Haydn-Studien*, iv (1978), 94

G. Feder: 'Haydns Korrekturen zum Klavierauszug der "Jahreszeiten"', *Festschrift Georg von Dadelsen zum 60. Geburtstag* (Neuhausen-Stuttgart, 1978), 101

H. Zeman: 'Das Textbuch Gottfried van Swietens zu Joseph Haydns "Die Schöpfung"', *Die österreichische Literatur. Ihr Profil an der Wende vom 18. zum 19. Jahrhundert* (Graz, 1979), 403

B. MacIntyre: 'Haydn's Doubtful and Spurious Masses: An Attribution Update', *Haydn-Studien*, v (1982)

(for *Seven last Words*, see also 'Orchestral')

OPERAS

L. Wendschuh: *Über Joseph Haydn's Opern* (Halle, 1896)

R. Haas: 'Teutsche Comedie Arien', *ZMw*, iii (1921), 405

H. Wirth: *Joseph Haydn als Dramatiker: sein Bühnenschaffen als Beitrag zur Geschichte der deutschen Oper* (Wolfenbüttel and Berlin, 1940)

——: *Joseph Haydn: Orfeo ed Euridice: Analytical Notes* (Boston, Mass., 1951) [disc notes, incl. essay on operas before *Orfeo*]

D. Bartha: Preface and critical commentary to *La canterina*, Werke, xxv/2 (1959–61)

H. Wirth: Preface and critical commentary to *Lo speziale*, Werke, xxv/3 (1959–62)

H. C. R. Landon: 'Some Notes on Haydn's Opera "L'infedeltà delusa" ', *MT*, cii (1961), 356; Ger. version in *ÖMz*, xvi (1961), 481

——: 'Haydn's Marionette Operas and the Repertoire of the Marionette Theatre at Esterház Castle', *Haydn Yearbook*, i (1962), 111–97

H. Wirth: Preface and critical commentary to *L'incontro improvviso*, Werke, xxv/6 (1962–72)

D. Bartha and J. Vécsey: Preface and critical commentary to *L'infedeltà delusa*, Werke, xxv/5 (1964–5)

W. Pfannkuch: Preface to *Armida*, Werke, xxv/12 (1965)

A. Porter: 'L'incontro improvviso', *MT*, cvii (1966), 202

G. Thomas: Preface and critical commentary to *La fedeltà premiata*, Werke, xxv/10 (1968–70)

G. Feder: 'Einige Thesen zu dem Thema: Haydn als Dramatiker',

Haydn-Studien, ii (1969), 126

——: 'Ein Kolloquium über Haydns Opern', *Haydn-Studien*, ii (1969), 113 [incl. catalogue of roles in Haydn's operas]

J. Müller-Blattau: 'Zu Haydns Philemon und Baucis', *Haydn-Studien*, ii (1969), 66

G. Thomas: 'Zu "Il mondo della luna" und "La fedeltà premiata": Fassungen und Pasticcios', *Haydn-Studien*, ii (1969), 122

E. Badura-Skoda: ' "Teutsche Comoedie-Arien" und Joseph Haydn', *Der junge Haydn: Internationale Arbeitstagung des Instituts für Aufführungspraxis: Graz 1970*, 59

J. Braun: Preface and critical commentary to *Philemon und Baucis*, Werke, xxiv/1 (1971)

A. Porter: 'Haydn and "La fedeltà premiata"', *MT*, cxii (1971), 331

A. van Hoboken: 'Nunziato Porta und der Text von Joseph Haydns Oper "Orlando Paladino" ', *Symbolae historiae musicae: Hellmut Federhofer zum 60. Geburtstag* (Mainz, 1971), 170

H. C. R. Landon: 'A New Authentic Source for La Fedeltà Premiata by Haydn', *Soundings*, ii (1971–2), 6; Ger. version in *Beiträge zur Musikdokumentation: Franz Grasberger zum 60. Geburtstag* (Tutzing, 1975), 213

D. Bartha and I. Becker-Glauch: Preface and critical commentary to *Le pescatrici*, Werke, xxv/4 (1972)

K. Geiringer: 'From Guglielmi to Haydn: the Transformation of an Opera', *IMSCR, xi Copenhagen 1972*, i, 391

——: Preface and critical commentary to *Orlando Paladino*, Werke, xxv/11 (1972–3)

H. C. R. Landon: 'The Operas of Haydn', *NOHM*, vii (1973), 172

H. Wirth: Preface and critical commentary to *L'anima del filosofo ossia Orfeo ed Euridice*, Werke, xxv/13 (1974)

G. Allroggen: 'Piccinnis "Origille"', *AnMc*, no.15 (1975), 258–97 [incl. remarks on libretto of *La canterina*]

G. Feder: 'Opera seria, opera buffa und opera semiseria bei Haydn', *Opernstudien: Anna Amalie Abert zum 65. Geburtstag* (Tutzing, 1975), 37

J. Kolk: '"Sturm und Drang" and Haydn's Opera', *Haydn Studies: Washington 1975*, 440

G. Thomas: 'Observations on *Il mondo della luna*', *Haydn Studies: Washington 1975*, 144

H. Walter: 'On the History of the Composition and the Performance of *La vera costanza*', *Haydn Studies: Washington 1975*, 154

——: Preface and critical commentary to *La vera costanza*, Werke, xxv/8 (1976–8)

G. Thomas: Preface and critical commentary to *Il Mondo Della Luna, Dramma Giocoso*, Werke, xxv/7 (1979–82)

G. Feder: 'Haydns Opern und ihre Ausgaben', *Musik – Edition –*

Interpretation, Gedenkschrift Günter Henle (Munich, 1980), 165

——: *Joseph Haydn, L'anima del filosofo ossia Orfeo ed Euridice. Rekonstruktion der Versform und wortgetreue deutsche Übersetzung* (Kassel, 1980)

F. Lippmann: 'Haydns "La fedeltà premiata" und Cimarosas "L'infedeltà fedele"', *Haydn-Studien*, v (1982)

G. Thomas: 'Kostüme und Requisiten für die Uraufführung von Haydns "Le pescatrici"', *Haydn-Studien*, v (1982)

SECULAR VOCAL

A. Schnerich: 'Zur Vorgeschichte von Haydn's Kaiserhymne', *ZMw*, i (1918–19), 295

L. Landshoff: Introduction to *J. Haydn: Englische Canzonetten* (Munich, 1924)

R. Tenschert: 'Unbekanntes Autograph eines Kanons von Joseph Haydn', *Die Musik*, xxi (1928–9), 253 [with facs.]

M. Friedlaender: Preface and critical commentary to *Einstimmige Lieder und Gesänge*, Joseph Haydns Werke, xx/1 (1932)

O. E. Deutsch: 'Haydns Kanons', *ZMw*, xv (1932–3), 112, 172

C. Hopkinson and C. B. Oldman: 'Thomson's Collections of National Song with Special Reference to the Contributions of Haydn and Beethoven', *Edinburgh Bibliographical Society Transactions*, ii (1938–9), 1–64 [with thematic catalogue]; pubd separately (Edinburgh, 1940); see also *Edinburgh Bibliographical Society Transactions*, iii (1949–51), 121; suppl. in 'Haydn's Settings of Scottish Songs in the Collections of Napier and Whyte', *Edinburgh Bibliographical Society Transactions*, iii (1949–51), 85–120; pubd separately (Edinburgh, 1954)

A. Sandberger: 'Ein Lied-Autograf von Josef Haydn', *ZfM*, cix (1942), 535 [incl. facs. of 'Ein kleines Haus']

M. M. Scott: 'Some English Affinities and Associations of Haydn's Songs', *ML*, xxv (1944), 1

K. Geiringer: 'Haydn and the Folk Song of the British Isles', *MQ*, xxxv (1949), 179–208; repr. as introduction to Geiringer (1953)

——: *A Thematic Catalogue of Haydn's Settings of Folksongs from the British Isles* (Superior, Wisc., 1953) [microfilm]

P. Mies: Preface and critical commentary to *Mehrstimmige Gesänge*, Werke, xxx (1958)

O. E. Deutsch: Preface and critical commentary to *Kanons*, Werke, xxxi (1959–65)

P. Mies: 'Textdichter zu J. Haydns "Mehrstimmigen Gesängen"', *Haydn Yearbook*, i (1962), 201

J. Reindl: 'Zur Entstehung des Refrains der Kaiserhymne Joseph Haydns', *SMw*, xxv (1962), 417

G. Feder: 'Zu Haydns schottischen Liedern', *Haydn-Studien*, i (1965), 43

F. Grasberger: *Die Hymnen Österreichs* (Tutzing, 1968)

J. Lunn: 'The Quest of the Missing Poet', *Haydn Yearbook*, iv (1968), 195

I. Becker-Glauch and H. Wiens: Preface and critical commentary to *Applausus*, Werke, xxvii/2 (1969–71)

R. Angermüller: 'Neukomms schottische Liedbearbeitungen für Joseph Haydn', *Haydn-Studien*, iii (1974), 151

I. Becker-Glauch: 'Some Remarks about the Dating of Haydn's Settings of Scottish Songs', *Haydn Studies: Washington 1975*, 88

H. C. R. Landon: 'Auf den Spuren Joseph Haydns', *ÖMz*, xxxi (1976), 579

A. P. Brown: 'Joseph Haydn and Leopold Hofmann's "Street Songs"', *JAMS*, xxxii (1980), 356

ORCHESTRAL

H. Kretzschmar: 'Die Jugendsinfonien Joseph Haydns', *JbMP 1908*, 69

A. Heuss: 'Der Humor im letzten Satz von Haydns Oxford-Symphonie', *Die Musik*, xii (1912–13), 271

B. Rywosch: *Beiträge zur Entwicklung in Joseph Haydns Symphonik, 1759–1780* (Turbenthal, 1934)

A. Schering: 'Bemerkungen zu J. Haydns Programmsinfonien', *JbMP 1939*, 9; repr. in *Vom musikalischen Kunstwerk*, ed. F. Blume (Leipzig, 1949, 2/1951)

H. J. Therstappen: *Joseph Haydns sinfonisches Vermächtnis* (Wolfenbüttel, 1941)

K. Haas: 'Haydn's English Military Marches', *The Score* (1950), no.2, p.50

L. Nowak: 'Das Autograph von Joseph Haydns Cello-Konzert in D-Dur, Op.101', *ÖMz*, ix (1954), 274

H. C. R. Landon: *The Symphonies of Joseph Haydn* (London, 1955) [incl. thematic catalogues of authentic, spurious and doubtful syms., pp.605–823]; suppl. (London, 1961)

J. P. Larsen: 'The Symphonies', *The Mozart Companion*, ed. H. C. R. Landon and D. Mitchell (London and New York, 1956), 156–99

H. Unverricht: Preface and critical commentary to *Die Sieben letzten Worte . . . Orchesterfassung*, Werke, iv (1959–63)

A. Tyson: 'One of Haydn's Lost "Countrydances"?', *MT*, cii (1961), 693; also in *Haydn Yearbook*, i (1962), 202

J. P. Larsen: 'Probleme der chronologischen Ordnung von Haydns Sinfonien', *Festschrift Otto Erich Deutsch* (Kassel, 1963), 90

H. Walter: Preface and critical commentary to *Sinfonien: 1764 und 1765*, Werke, i/4 (1964)

H. C. R. Landon: Prefaces and remarks to each vol. of *Kritische Ausgabe sämtlicher Symphonien* (1965–8)

——: *Haydn Symphonies* (London, 1966)

E. K. Wolf: 'The Recapitulations in Haydn's London Symphonies', *MQ*, lii (1966), 71

W. Stockmeier: Preface and critical commentary to *Sinfonien: 1773 und 1774*, Werke, i/7 (1966–7)

C.-G. Stellan Mörner: Preface and critical commentary to *Sinfonien: 1767–1772*, Werke, i/6 (1966–9)

H. Walter: Preface and critical commentary to *Londoner Sinfonien: 3. Folge*, Werke, i/17 (1966–72)

W. Matthäus and H. Unverricht: 'Zur Abhängigkeit der Frühdrucke von Joseph Haydns Londoner Sinfonien', *AMw*, xxiv (1967), 145; see also xxi (1964), 243, and xxiii (1966), 61

S. Gerlach: 'Die chronologische Ordnung von Haydns Sinfonien zwischen 1774 und 1782', *Haydn-Studien*, ii (1969), 34–66

G. Thomas and H. Lohmann: Preface and critical commentary to *Konzerte für Violine und Orchester*, Werke, iii/1 (1969)

S. Gerlach and W. Stockmeier: Preface and critical commentary to *Sinfonien: um 1775/76*, Werke, i/8 (1970)

L. Nowak: 'Die Skizzen zum Finale der Es-dur-Symphonie GA 99 von Joseph Haydn', *Haydn-Studien*, ii (1970), 137–66

J. H. van der Meer: 'Die Verwendung der Blasinstrumente im Orchester bei Haydn und seinen Zeitgenossen', *Der junge Haydn: Internationale Arbeitstagung des Instituts für Aufführungspraxis: Graz 1970*, 202

H. Nakano: Preface and critical commentary to *Pariser Sinfonien: 1. Folge*, Werke, i/12 (1971–9)

S. Gerlach: 'Ein Fund zu Haydns verschollener Sinfonie', *Haydn-Studien*, iii (1973), 44 [H I:106]

G. Thomas: 'Studien zu Haydns Tanzmusik', *Haydn-Studien*, iii (1973), 5; see also *Jb für österreichische Kulturgeschichte*, ii: *Joseph Haydn und seine Zeit* (1972), 73

P. R. Bryan: 'The Horn in the Works of Mozart and Haydn', *Haydn Yearbook*, ix (1975), 189–256

B. Churgin: 'The Italian Symphonic Background to Haydn's Early Symphonies and Opera Overtures', *Haydn Studies: Washington 1975*, 347

S. C. Fisher: 'Sonata Procedures in Haydn's Symphonic Rondo Finales of the 1770s', *Haydn Studies: Washington 1975*, 481

J. L. Schwartz: 'Thematic Asymmetry in First Movements of Haydn's Early Symphonies', *Haydn Studies: Washington 1975*, 501

K. Marx: 'Über thematische Beziehungen in Haydns Londoner Symphonien', *Haydn-Studien*, iv (1976), 1

R. Angermüller: 'Haydns "Der Zerstreute" in Salzburg (1776)', *Haydn-Studien*, iv (1978), 85

K. W. Niemöller: 'Aufführungspraxis und Edition von Haydns Cellokonzert D-dur', *Musik – Edition – Interpretation, Gedenkschrift Günter Henle* (Munich, 1980), 394

S. Gerlach: Preface and critical commentary to *Konzerte für Violoncello und Orchester*, Werke, iii/2 (1981)

——: Preface and critical commentary to *Concertante,* Werke, ii (1982) (for *Seven last Words,* see also 'Sacred Works, Oratorios')

CHAMBER

A. Sandberger: 'Zur Geschichte des Haydnschen Streichquartetts', *Altbayerische Monatshefte* (1900), 1; rev. in *Ausgewählte Aufsätze zur Musikgeschichte,* i (Munich, 1921), 224

D. F. Tovey: 'Franz Joseph Haydn', *Cobbett's Cyclopedic Survey of Chamber Music,* i (London, 1929, 2/1963), 514–48; repr. as 'Haydn's Chamber Music', *Essays and Lectures on Music* (London, 1943), 1–64

M. M. Scott: 'Haydn's "83": a Study of the Complete Editions', *ML,* xi (1930), 207

F. Blume: 'Josef Haydns künstlerische Persönlichkeit in seinen Streichquartetten', *JbMP 1931,* 24; repr. in *Syntagma musicologicum: gesammelte Reden und Schriften* (Kassel, 1963), 526

G. de Saint-Foix: 'Les sonates pour violon et alto de Haydn', *ReM* (1932), no.128, p.81

W. O. Strunk: 'Haydn's Divertimenti for Baryton, Viola, and Bass', *MQ,* xviii (1932), 216–51

C. S. Smith: 'Haydn's Chamber Music and the Flute', *MQ,* xix (1933), 341, 434

R. Sondheimer: *Haydn: a Historical and Psychological Study based on his Quartets* (London, 1951)

H. C. R. Landon: 'On Haydn's Quartets of Opera 1 and 2: Notes and Comments on Sondheimer's Historical and Psychological Study', *MR,* xiii (1952), 181

R. Hughes: 'Joseph Haydn (1732–1809)', *Chamber Music,* ed. A. Robertson (Harmondsworth, 1957), 13–55

H. Keller: 'The Interpretation of the Haydn Quartets', *The Score* (1958), no.23, p.14

H. Unverricht: Preface and critical commentary to *Barytontrios Nr.25–48, 49–72, 73–96,* Werke, xiv/2–4 (1958–64)

H. R. Edwall: 'Ferdinand IV and Haydn's Concertos for the "Lira Organizzata" ', *MQ,* xlviii (1962), 190

G. Feder: Preface to *Streichquartette: 'Opus 9' und 'Opus 17',* Werke, xii/2 (1963)

R. Hughes: *Haydn String Quartets* (London, 1966)

W. Kirkendale: *Fuge und Fugato in der Kammermusik des Rokoko und der Klassik* (Tutzing, 1966), 179ff

L. Finscher: 'Joseph Haydn und das italienische Streichquartett', *AnM,* iv (1967), 13

H. Walter and M. Härting: Preface and critical commentary to *Baryton Trios Nr.97–126,* Werke, xiv/5 (1968–9)

D. Bartha: 'Thematic Profile and Character in the Quartet-finales of Joseph Haydn (a Contribution to the Micro-analysis of Thematic Structure)', *SM,* xi (1969), 35

I. Saslav: *Tempos in the String Quartets of Joseph Haydn* (diss., Indiana U., 1969)

H. Unverricht: *Geschichte des Streichtrios* (Tutzing, 1969)

S. Gerlach: Preface and critical commentary to *Werke mit Baryton*, Werke, xiii (1969–70)

H. Unverricht: 'Zur Chronologie der Barytontrios von Joseph Haydn', *Symbolae historiae musicae: Hellmut Federhofer zum 60. Geburtstag* (Mainz, 1971), 180

M. Ohmiya: Preface and critical commentary to *Notturni mit Orgelleiern*, Werke, vii (1971–2)

L. Somfai: ' "Ich war nie ein Geschwindschreiber . . .": Joseph Haydns Skizzen zum langsamen Satz des Streichquartetts Hoboken III:33', *Festskrift Jens Peter Larsen* (Copenhagen, 1972), 275

G. Feder and G. Greiner: Preface and critical commentary to *Frühe Streichquartette*, Werke, xii/1 (1973)

J. Webster: *The Bass Part in Haydn's Early String Quartets and in Austrian Chamber Music 1756–1780* (diss., Princeton U., 1973)

R. Barrett-Ayres: *Joseph Haydn and the String Quartet* (London, 1974)

G. Feder and S. Gerlach: Preface and critical commentary to *Streichquartette 'opus 20' und 'opus 33'*, Werke, xii/3 (1974)

L. Finscher: *Studien zur Geschichte des Streichquartetts*, i: *Die Entstehung des klassischen Streichquartetts: von den Vorformen zur Grundlegung durch Joseph Haydn* (Kassel, 1974)

O. Moe: 'Texture in Haydn's Early Quartets', *MR*, xxv (1974), 4

J. Webster: 'Towards a History of Viennese Chamber Music in the Early Classical Period', *JAMS*, xxvii (1974), 212–47

S. Gerlach: 'The Reconstructed Original Version of Haydn's Baryton Trio Hob. XI:2', *Haydn Studies: Washington 1975*, 88

I. Saslav: 'The alla breve "March": Its Evolution and Meaning in Haydn's String Quartets', *Haydn Studies: Washington 1975*, 308

J. Webster: 'Freedom of Form in Haydn's Early String Quartets', *Haydn Studies: Washington 1975*, 522

——: 'The Chronology of Haydn's String Quartets', *MQ*, lxi (1975), 17

M. Ohmiya: Preface and critical commentary to *Concerti mit Orgelleiern*, Werke, vi (1976)

F. Salzer: 'Haydn's Fantasia from the String Quartet, Opus 76, No.6', *Music Forum*, iv (1976), 161–94

J. Webster: 'The Bass Part in Haydn's Early String Quartets', *MQ*, lxiii (1977) 390–424

G. Feder: Preface to *Streichquartette 'Opus 64' und 'Opus 71/74'*, Werke, xii/5 (1978)

K. Fischer: 'Einflüsse Haydns in Kammermusikwerken Boccherinis', *Studi Musicali*, iv (1978), 169

L. Somfai: 'An Introduction to the Study of Haydn's Quartet Autographs (with special attention to Opus 77/G)', *The String Quartets of Haydn, Mozart and Beethoven: Studies of the Autograph*

Manuscripts: Cambridge, Mass. 1979, 5

G. Feder: 'Haydn's Corrections in the Autographs of the Quartets Opus 64 and Opus 71/74', *The String Quartets of Haydn, Mozart and Beethoven: Studies of the Autograph Manuscripts: Cambridge, Mass. 1979*, 99

J. Webster: 'The Significance of Haydn's Quartet Autographs for Performance Practice', *The String Quartets of Haydn, Mozart and Beethoven: Studies of the Autograph Manuscripts: Cambridge, Mass. 1979*, 62

J. Braun and S. Gerlach: Preface and critical commentary to *Barytontrios 1–24*, Werke xiv/1 (1980)

M. Fillion: Eine bisher unbekannte Quelle für Haydns frühes Klaviertrio Hob. XV:C1, *Haydn-Studien*, v (1982)

(for *Seven last Words*, see 'Orchestral', and 'Sacred Works, Oratorios')

KEYBOARD (SOLO, ENSEMBLE, CONCERTO) ETC

K. Päsler: Preface and critical commentary to *Klavierwerke*, Joseph Haydns Werke, xiv/1–3 (1918)

H. Abert: 'Joseph Haydns Klavierwerke', *ZMw*, ii (1919–20), 553; iii (1920–21), 535

H. Schenker: 'Haydn: Sonate Es Dur' [H XVI:52], *Der Tonwille*, i (1922), 3

——: 'Haydn: Sonate C Dur' [H XVI:50], *Der Tonwille*, ii (1923), 15

P. James: 'Haydn's Clavichord and a Sonata Manuscript', *MT*, lxxi (1930), 314

E. F. Schmid: 'Joseph Haydn und die Flötenuhr', *ZMw*, xiv (1931–2), 193

E. J. Dent: 'Haydn's Pianoforte Works', *MMR*, lxii/733 (1932), 1; see also *Australian Musical News*, xxii/3 (1932), 21

H. Schenker: *Fünf Urlinie-Tafeln* (New York, 1933; repr. 1969 with new introduction and glossary by F. Salzer as *Five Graphic Music Analyses*) [Piano Sonata H XVI:49]

W. O. Strunk: 'Notes on a Haydn Autograph', *MQ*, xx (1934), 192

P. Radcliffe: 'The Piano Sonatas of Joseph Haydn', *MR*, vii (1946), 139

J. P. Larsen: 'Eine bisher unbeachtete Quelle zu Haydns frühen Klavierwerken', *Festschrift Joseph Schmidt-Görg zum 60. Geburtstag* (Bonn, 1957), 188

H. Heussner: 'Zwei neue Haydn-Funde', *Mf*, xiii (1960), 451 [H XV:40, XVIII:5]

A. Tyson: 'New Light on a Haydn Trio (XV:32)', *Haydn Yearbook*, i (1962), 203

G. Feder: 'Probleme einer Neuordnung der Klaviersonaten Haydns', *Festschrift Friedrich Blume* (Kassel, 1963), 92

C. Landon: Foreword to *Haydn: Sämtliche Klaviersonaten* (Vienna, 1963)

W. S. Newman: *The Sonata in the Classic Era* (Chapel Hill, 1963, rev. 2/1972), 454ff

G. Feder: Preface to *Klaviersonaten: 1.–3. Folge*, Werke, xviii/1–3 (1966–70)

A. P. Brown: *The Solo and Ensemble Keyboard Sonatas of Joseph Haydn: a Study of Structure and Style* (diss., Northwestern U., 1970)

F. Eibner: 'Die authentische Klavierfassung von Haydns Variationen über "Gott erhalte" ', *Haydn Yearbook*, vii (1970), 281

G. Feder: 'Haydns frühe Klaviertrios: eine Untersuchung zur Echtheit und Chronologie', *Haydn-Studien*, ii (1970), 289

——: 'Wieviel Orgelkonzerte hat Haydn geschrieben?', *Mf*, xxiii (1970), 440

H. C. R. Landon: Preface to *Die Klaviertrios von Joseph Haydn* (Vienna, 1970)

E. F. Schmid: 'Neue Funde zu Haydns Flötenuhrstücken', *Haydn-Studien*, ii (1970), 249

H. Walter: 'Das Tasteninstrument beim jungen Haydn', *Der junge Haydn: Internationale Arbeitstagung des Instituts für Aufführungspraxis: Graz 1970*, 237

——: 'Haydns Klaviere', *Haydn-Studien*, ii (1970), 256–88

W. Stockmeier: Preface and critical commentary to *Klaviertrios: 1. Folge*, Werke, xvii/1 (1970–71)

E. Badura-Skoda: 'Haydn, Mozart and their Contemporaries', *Keyboard Music*, ed. D. Matthews (Harmondsworth, 1972), 108–65

G. Feder: 'Eine Haydn-Skizze in Ostiglia', *AnMc*, no.12 (1973), 224

W. Stockmeier: Preface and critical commentary to *Klaviertrios*, Werke, xvii/2 (1974–5)

A. P. Brown: 'The Structure of the Exposition in Haydn's Keyboard Sonatas', *MR*, xxxvi (1975), 102

——: 'Haydn's Keyboard Idiom and the Raigern Sonatas', *Haydn Studies: Washington 1975*, 111

G. Feder: 'The Sources of the Two Disputed Raigern Sonatas', *Haydn Studies: Washington 1975*, 107

M. Fillion: 'Sonata-Exposition Procedures in Haydn's Keyboard Sonatas', *Haydn Studies: Washington 1975*, 475

J. C. Graue: Haydn and the London Pianoforte School, *Haydn Studies: Washington 1975*, 422

E. M. Ripin: 'Haydn and the Keyboard Instruments of His Time', *Haydn Studies: Washington 1975*, 302

B. Wackernagel: *Joseph Haydns frühe Klaviersonaten: ihre Beziehungen zur Klaviermusik um die Mitte des 18. Jahrhunderts* (Tutzing, 1975)

H. Walter: 'Haydn's Keyboard Instruments', *Haydn Studies: Washington 1975*, 213

REPUTATION

L. de La Laurencie: 'L'apparition des oeuvres d'Haydn à Paris', *RdM*, xiii (1932), 191

M. D. H. Norton: 'Haydn in America (before 1820)', *MQ*, xviii (1932), 309

L. Schrade: 'Das Haydn-Bild in den ältesten Biographien', *Die Musikerziehung*, ix (1932), 163, 200, 244

A. Sandberger: 'Zur Einbürgerung der Kunst Josef Haydns in Deutschland', *NBJb*, vi (1935), 5

F. Lesure: 'Haydn en France', *Internationale Konferenz zum Andenken Joseph Haydns: Budapest 1959*, 79

K. G. Fellerer: 'Zum Joseph-Haydn-Bild im frühen 19. Jahrhundert', *Anthony van Hoboken: Festschrift zum 75. Geburtstag* (Mainz, 1962), 73

A. Palm: 'Unbekannte Haydn-Analysen', *Haydn Yearbook*, iv (1968), 169 [analyses by Momigny]

M. S. Cole: 'Momigny's Analysis of Haydn's Symphony no.103', *MR*, xxx (1969), 261

B. Steinpress: 'Haydns Oratorien in Russland zu Lebzeiten des Komponisten', *Haydn-Studien*, ii (1969), 77–112

C. Höslinger: 'Der überwundene Standpunkt: Joseph Haydn in der Wiener Musikkritik des 19. Jahrhunderts', *Jb für österreichische Kulturgeschichte*, i/2: *Beiträge zur Musikgeschichte des 18. Jahrhunderts* (1971), 116

A. Basso: 'La rappresentazione a Torino (1804) dell' "Armida" di Haydn', *Quadrivium*, xiv (1973), 235

A. P. Brown: 'The Earliest English Biography of Haydn', *MQ*, lix (1973), 339

I. Lowens: 'Haydn in America', [with Otto E. Albrecht: 'Haydn Autographs in the United States'], *Bibliographies in American Music*, 5 (Detroit, 1979)

J. P. Larsen: 'Haydn im 20. Jahrhundert', *Musik – Edition – Interpretation, Gedenkschrift Günter Henle* (Munich, 1980), 319

Index